Resurrec

Resurrection

Essays in Honour of Leslie Houlden

edited by

Stephen Barton
and
Graham Stanton

First published in Great Britain 1994

Society for Promoting Christian Knowledge
Holy Trinity Church
Marylebone Road
London NW1 4DU

British Library Cataloguing-in-Publication Data

A catalogue record for this book is available from the British Library

ISBN   0-281-04775-8

Typesetting by David Mackinder, using *Nota Bene* software
Printed in Great Britain by Redwood Books, Trowbridge, Wiltshire

CONTENTS

FRONTISPIECE: Leslie Houlden   ii

PREFACE • *Stephen Barton and Graham Stanton*   vii

FOREWORD • *The Rt Revd David Jenkins, Bishop of Durham*   ix

CONTRIBUTORS   xi

1   The Ending of Mark's Gospel • *John Fenton*   1

2   Flesh is Precious: The Significance of
Luke 24.36–43 • *Robert Morgan*   8

3   The Emmaus Story and its Sequel • *Colin Hickling*   21

4   The Women's Resurrection Testimony • *Judith Lieu*   34

5   The Hermeneutics of the Gospel Resurrection
Narratives • *Stephen Barton*   45

6   Did Jesus of Nazareth Rise from the Dead? • *Michael
Goulder*   58

7   'They discussed among themselves what
this "rising from the dead" could
mean' (Mark 9.10) • *Anthony Harvey*   69

8   Early Objections to the Resurrection of
Jesus • *Graham Stanton*   79

9   'He is not here': Towards a Theology of
the Empty Tomb • *Francis Watson*   95

10   Why Does the Resurrection of Christ Matter? • *John
Barton*   108

11 A Naked Pillar of Rock • *Maurice Wiles*   116

12 'I Believe in the Resurrection of
    the Body' • *John Muddiman*   128

13 The Mark of the Nails • *Frances Young*   139

14 The Descent into Hell: Hans Urs von Balthasar
    and Pastoral Theology • *Gordon Mursell*   154

15 'The Body of Christ has AIDS': Resurrection
    and Pastoral Theology • *Anthony Dyson*   165

16 Global Threats and Global Hope in
    Multi-religious Perspective • *Alan Race*   177

17 Resurrection in Music • *John Bowden*   188

18 According to Poetry • *John Drury*   198

19 Tolstoy's *Resurrection* Revisited • *Dennis Nineham* 213

    Leslie Houlden: Curriculum Vitae   223

    Leslie Houlden: Publications   225

    Suggestions for Further Reading   231

Preface

The claim that God raised Jesus from the dead unites the diverse forms that Christianity has taken in the past and still takes today. On the other hand, the New Testament writings already bear witness to the very different ways the first followers of Jesus understood the significance of what happened 'on the third day'. 'Resurrection' is not simply a theme that has always been at the centre of distinctively Christian convictions: it continues to provoke Christians to reflect on the nature of their faith and its implications for discipleship today.

Like the New Testament writers themselves, the essayists in this volume approach 'resurrection' from a number of different perspectives. Since it is often helpful to consider the final form of the New Testament writings before exploring the historical issues 'behind' the text, the first three essays discuss some of the emphases of the evangelists. They precede several essays that examine central historical issues. Essays that consider hermeneutical questions then pave the way for discussions of broader theological and doctrinal themes. As is to be expected, most of the essays focus on the resurrection of Jesus. However, several essays range more widely, exploring both the pastoral implications of 'resurrection', and some of the ways this theme has stirred the imaginations of writers and musicians.

Discussion of 'resurrection' does not often embrace such a wide range of issues. But there is good reason for breaking the mould. In the past, biblical and doctrinal specialists have often failed to listen to one another sufficiently carefully. And the insights of those who work outside the traditional theological disciplines have rarely been appropriated.

The essays in this volume reflect the biblical and theological interests of Leslie Houlden, and are written to mark his sixty-fifth birthday and retirement from his Chair at King's College London. As the list of his publications at the back of this book confirms, in recent years Leslie has frequently sought to make connections between biblical and doctrinal studies. Indeed, he has made the borderlands between these two disciplines his own special territory, but always in the hope that others will join him. Several essayists in this volume have taken up his invitation. How many other theologians subscribe and contribute regularly to the *Times Literary Supplement* and use its reviews to point them to the best contemporary writing in numerous fields? This is why we are confident that Leslie will welcome also the final essays in this volume.

The lists of Leslie Houlden's publications and of the posts he has held reflect, but only imperfectly, the considerable contribution he has made to the life of the Church. Above all else, as former colleagues and students readily confirm, Leslie is a wise and gracious pastor. He has always generously supported and encouraged younger scholars of all persuasions. We know that he will read with appreciation the essays that do not reflect his own views just as avidly as he will read those that do.

We are grateful to the contributors for heeding our request that their essays should be accessible to a wide range of readers, just as many of Leslie's own writings are. The contributors have all been Leslie's colleagues, close associates, or students at some stage in his varied career. Constraints of space have not allowed us to invite a number of distinguished friends who would willingly have contributed to this volume.

It is a pleasure to record our thanks to many who have assisted us. Philip Law, editor of SPCK, has been enthusiastic about this project from the very beginning. Noreen Norton of SPCK has taken good care of numerous details, as has David Mackinder, our copy-editor and typesetter. Lavinia Harvey (King's College London) has given outstanding secretarial assistance. Dr Andrew Walker (King's College London) readily provided computing expertise. The Revd Alan Le Grys and Philip Hesketh (Ripon College Cuddesdon) helped to prepare the list of publications.

Stephen Barton

Graham Stanton

Foreword

This volume of essays discussing the resurrection from a variety of perspectives, ranging from critical New Testament studies through doctrinal and philosophical issues to matters of faith, devotion, and practice, constitutes a very appropriate offering from friends and colleagues to Leslie Houlden as he reaches his sixty-fifth birthday and formal retirement.

For Leslie has exercised a notable ministry by the way in which he has been quietly, persistently, and searchingly teaching and researching in the writings and faith of the New Testament ever since he first moved into the sphere of theological teaching as Chaplain of Chichester Theological College in 1958. Publications began to appear only from the end of his ten years as Fellow and Chaplain at Trinity College, Oxford – but then that was the time of innocence and non-cost-effective non-accountability when we were allowed to believe that teaching students was of first importance and publication of second importance for at least some staff in a university.

Characteristically, as the publications and articles did appear – as they continue to do – they blended scholarly and critical study with a concern to expound what the faith reflected in the New Testament documents might have meant as a living possibility to the original writers. This concern for the living possibilities of faith was then extended into a consideration for possibilities and understandings of faith today. This teaching and pastoral concern for present-day possibilities was never allowed to obscure radical questions and difficult issues. Hence Leslie's particular contribution of integrity and insight as a critical scholar within the ministry of the Church.

He has backed up his church commitment by careful service on such bodies as the Liturgical Commission and the Doctrine Commission of the Church of England, and in many other ways. It is much to be hoped that formal retirement leaves more opportunities for continued critical searching and gently provocative probings.

David Dunelm

Contributors

Canon John Fenton is Honorary Canon Emeritus, Christ Church Cathedral, Oxford. Recent publications include: *Sunday Readings* (Norwich: Canterbury Press, 1991); *Affirmations* (Norwich: Canterbury Press, 1993).

The Revd Robert Morgan is Priest-in-charge, Sandford-on-Thames, and University Lecturer in Theology, Oxford. Recent publications include: *Biblical Interpretation* (with John Barton) (Oxford: Oxford University Press, 1988); as editor: *The Religion of the Incarnation* (Bristol: Bristol Classical Press, 1991).

The Revd Canon Colin Hickling is Vicar of Arksey, Honorary Lecturer in the University of Sheffield, and Canon Theologian of Leicester. Recent publications include: 'Baptism in the First Century Churches: A Case for Caution', in D. J. A. Clines, S. E. Fowl, and S. E. Porter (eds), *The Bible in Three Dimensions* (Sheffield: Sheffield Academic Press, 1990).

Dr Judith M. Lieu is Lecturer in Christian Origins and Early Judaism at King's College London. Recent publications include: *The Theology of the Johannine Epistles* (Cambridge: Cambridge University Press, 1991); as editor: J. Lieu, J. North, and T. Rajak (eds), *The Jews Among Pagans and Christians in the Roman Empire* (London: Routledge, 1992).

The Revd Dr Stephen Barton is Lecturer in New Testament in the Department of Theology, University of Durham. Recent publications include: *The Spirituality of the Gospels* (London: SPCK, 1992); *People of the Passion* (London: SPCK/Triangle, 1994).

Professor Michael Goulder is Professor of Biblical Studies at the University of Birmingham. Recent publications include: *Luke: A New Paradigm* (Sheffield: JSOT Press, 1989); *The Prayers of David* (Sheffield: JSOT, 1990); *A Tale of Two Missions* (London: SCM Press, 1994).

The Revd Dr Anthony Harvey is Sub-Dean of Westminster. Recent publications include: *Strenuous Commands: The Ethic of Jesus* (London: SCM Press, 1990).

Professor Graham Stanton is Professor of New Testament Studies, King's College London. Recent publications include: *The Gospels and Jesus* (Oxford: Oxford University Press, 1989); *A Gospel for a New People: Studies in Matthew* (Edinburgh: T. & T. Clark, 1992).

Dr Francis Watson is Lecturer in New Testament Studies, King's College London. Recent publications include: *Paul, Judaism and the Gentiles: A Sociological Approach* (Cambridge: Cambridge University Press, 1986); *Text, Church and World: Towards a Theological Hermeneutic for Biblical Studies* (Edinburgh: T. & T. Clark, 1994).

Professor John Barton is Oriel and Laing Professor of the Interpretation of Holy Scripture, University of Oxford. Recent publications include: *People of the Book? The Authority of the Bible in Christianity* (London: SPCK, 1988; new edition, 1993); *Love Unknown: Meditations on the Death and Resurrection of Jesus* (London: SPCK, 1989).

The Revd Professor Maurice Wiles is The Regius Professor of Divinity (Emeritus) at the University of Oxford. Recent publications include: *Faith and the Mystery of God* (London: SCM Press, 1982); *God's Action in the World* (London: SCM Press, 1986); *Christian Theology and Inter-religious Dialogue* (London: SCM Press, 1992).

The Revd Dr John Muddiman is Fellow of Mansfield College, and Lecturer in the Faculty of Theology, Oxford. Recent publications include several articles in R. J. Coggins and J. L. Houlden (eds), *A Dictionary of Biblical Interpretation* (London: SCM Press, 1990); 'The Holy Spirit and Inspiration', in Robert Morgan (ed.), *The Religion of the Incarnation* (Bristol: Bristol Classical Press, 1989).

The Revd Professor Frances Young is Edward Cadbury Professor of Theology, and Head of the Department of Theology, University of Birmingham. Recent publications include: *The Art of Performance* (London: Darton, Longman & Todd, 1990); *The Making of the Creeds* (London: SCM Press, 1991).

The Revd Gordon Mursell is Team Rector of Stafford. Recent publications include: 'The Psalms', in *The Way*, Supplement 72,

'Spirituality and Scripture' (1991); 'The Spirituality of St Peter Damian', in Judith Loades (ed.), *Monastic Studies II, The Continuity of Tradition* (Bangor: Headstart History, 1991).

Professor Anthony Dyson is Samuel Fergusson Professor of Social and Pastoral Theology in the Victoria University of Manchester. Recent publications include: editor (with J. Harris) and contributor to *Experiments on Embryos* (London: Routledge, 1989); *Ethics and the New Reproductive Technologies: On Listening to Feminism* (Contact Pastoral Monograph, no. 1, 1991); *Ethics and the New Reproductive Technologies* (University of Kent at Canterbury: Centre for the Study of Religion and Society, 1993); editor (with J. Harris) and contributor to *Ethics and Biotechnology* (London: Routledge, 1994).

The Revd Alan Race is Director of Studies, Southwark Ordination Course. Recent publications include: *Christians and Religious Pluralism*, 2nd edn (London: SCM Press, 1993); as contributor: 'Truth is Many-Eyed', in J. Bowden (ed.), *Thirty Years of Honesty* (London: SCM Press, 1993).

The Revd Dr John Bowden is Managing Director, SCM Press Ltd. Recent publications include: *Jesus – The Unanswered Questions* (London: SCM Press, 1988).

The Very Revd John Drury is Dean of Christ Church, Oxford. Recent publications include: *The Burning Bush* (London: Collins, 1990); *Critics of the Bible 1724–1873* (Cambridge: Cambridge University Press, 1989).

Dr Dennis Nineham is retired. He was formerly Regius Professor of Divinity at Cambridge, and then Warden of Keble College, Oxford. Recent publications include: *Christianity Medieval and Modern* (London: SCM Press, 1993).

1
The Ending of Mark's Gospel

John Fenton

Professor C. F. Evans said to me once that a good way to teach Mark's Gospel was to begin with the end of the book, at 16.8. (It is a method used to great effect by Professor Houlden in *Backward into Light*.[1]) When it can be demonstrated that the evangelist does not tell his readers what happened next, but leaves them to make up their own minds whether they will believe what the young man has said, or not, it will then be easier to show what sort of book we are dealing with when we read Mark: a Gospel (whatever that is), not a collection of an apostle's reminiscences.

In point of fact, it was the question of the ending of Mark's Gospel that, historically speaking, opened up new ways of reading it. When R. H. Lightfoot[2] was arguing that the evangelist meant to stop at 16.8, and that there never had been a lost ending or any intention of continuing the narrative further, the first objection that was always raised was: Surely he must have meant to include at least one account of an appearance of Jesus after the resurrection; this was the most important event in the life of Peter; Mark could not have missed it out.[3] And the answer that was given was: Mark is not that sort of a book; you are reading it with inappropriate expectations; you are repeating the mistake of the person who is told a joke and then asks, 'What happened next?' What used to be called 'The Marcan Hypothesis', the theory that in Mark's 'presentation of the life of Christ the facts of history are set down with a minimum of disarrangement, interpretation, and embellishment',[4] fell to pieces as a result of the study of the ending of the Gospel: if it were that kind of book, it would not end in this way; since it did end at 16.8, it cannot be that kind of book.

But is there any need to take up the question of the ending of Mark again, after so much has been written on the subject in the last fifty years? That the Gospel is complete cannot be regarded as one of the generally accepted results of biblical criticism. Three examples must suffice, arranged in chronological order.

First, in 1971 the United Bible Societies published *A Textual Commentary on the Greek New Testament*, subtitled 'A Companion Volume to the United Bible Societies' Greek New Testament (third edition)', by Bruce M. Metzger 'on behalf of and in cooperation with the Editorial Committee of the United Bible Societies' Greek New Testament': Kurt Aland, Matthew Black, Carlo M. Martini, Bruce M. Metzger, and Allen Wikgren. The two volumes, the *Greek New Testament* and the *Textual Commentary*, are published in the same material and in the same colour, and the unwary reader might think the second had the same authority as the first. After discussing the textual evidence for the various endings of Mark, Metzger and his colleagues continue in a footnote:

> Three possibilities are open: (*a*) the evangelist intended to close his Gospel at this place; or (*b*) the Gospel was never finished; or, as seems most probable, (*c*) the Gospel accidentally lost its last leaf before it was multiplied by transcription.[5]

One might dismiss this reference to the hypothesis of a lost ending of Mark as a suggestion made in a footnote twenty years ago; but as recently as 1992 it was still being said of Mark's Gospel that it is 'quite possibly truncated at both ends'.[6]

Second, in 1989 the University Presses of Oxford and Cambridge published *The Revised English Bible*. After their translation of Mark 16.1–8, as if it were another paragraph but still part of verse 8, they printed what is known as the Shorter Ending, without any sign in the text to indicate that this was not in all manuscripts, etc. After a double space, there follows their translation of the Longer Ending, verses 9–20; and there are notes at the foot of the page that explain the problem. Anyone asked to read Mark 16.1–8, who had not studied the footnotes, would assume that the passage ended immediately before the beginning of verse 9, and would therefore include the Shorter Ending in the reading. Was this, however, simply a printer's error that escaped the eye of the proof-reader? There was a reprint of the book in the year of publication, but there was no correction of the text at this point. (A similar problem arises when the *Alternative Service Book 1980* describes a reading as 'Mark 16'.[7] Has no one told the General Synod of the Church of England that there are matters here that make this expression ambiguous?)

Third, a major commentary on Mark was published in 1993, by Robert H. Gundry;[8] his view is that Mark 16.8 is not the last verse of the paragraph that began at 16.1, but the first verse of another paragraph that is incomplete. In this now mutilated paragraph the evangelist described how the disciples saw Jesus in Galilee in fulfilment of the prediction in Mark 14.28. Gundry provides twelve reasons for thinking that this is how Mark's Gospel originally ended, together with further notes. He does not, however, explain how the disciples received the message to go to Galilee, which 16.7 implies they needed; or provide a satisfactory account of why Mark has told his readers about the visit of the women to the tomb, if it was to have no connection with the continuation of the narrative of the disciples.

The suggestion that Mark intended to end his Gospel at 16.8 was first made by Wellhausen in 1903, and in taking up the topic again, over ninety years later, I want to draw attention to an English writer, the first English writer, I suppose, to support Wellhausen on this matter.[9] J. M. Creed's article, 'The Conclusion of the Gospel according to Saint Mark', was published in 1930,[10] eight years before R. H. Lightfoot's *Locality and Doctrine in the Gospels*, and as it has never been republished and is only available to those who have access to back numbers of the *Journal of Theological Studies*, I shall attempt to give a selective summary of the argument; but the reader should be warned that this is only a summary, and that the argument in the article is concise and, in some parts, obscure.

Creed begins by stating the problem of the variant readings: (i) the ending at 16.8 in אB, the old Syriac, codex *a*;[11] (ii) the Shorter Ending, in codex *k*; (iii) the last twelve verses of the received text. Neither (ii) nor (iii) is thought to be by Mark, but to end at 16.8 as in (i) would be very abrupt; hence 'many scholars are inclined to conjecture that a further paragraph recounting at the least the appearance of the risen Jesus to the disciples in Galilee, which the angel predicts in v. 7, has disappeared'. (Throughout the article, Creed refers to the young man in Mark 16.5–7 as an angel, though Mark himself does not describe him in this way.) Creed's intention, he says, is to argue that 'it is very improbable that the genuine Gospel was ever longer than it now is'; he refers to Wellhausen and E. Meyer, who both held the same view as Creed, but he believes that he is stating the argument in a different way from them.

He then notices briefly the hypotheses that have been framed to account for the supposed incompleteness of the Gospel, namely: (i) that the author died before finishing it; (ii) that the text was deliberately mutilated; and (iii) that it was mutilated by accident, and he finds them all inadequate as explanations of the conjecture that the text is incomplete, 'unless we are compelled to do so by the document itself'. This is the main purpose of the article, and what makes it so significant: Creed is attending to Mark's text, and enquiring whether there is anything in it that suggests incompleteness.

He then draws our attention to what he calls 'a strange incoherence' in the Marcan text; namely, the contradiction between what the women are commanded to do, in verse 7, and what they fail to do, in verse 8: they are charged to tell the disciples, but they remain silent. He says that this is 'a very startling phenomenon', which is not always remarked.

> There is incoherence in the Marcan narrative – significant incoherence – but it is latent. So long as we stop at v. 8 it does not really matter. But, on the theory of the lost conclusion, how are we to proceed? The latent incoherence will at once become intolerable. For we must suppose one of two things: either the lost conclusion was continuous with the story of the women, or else it made a fresh start with the disciples and their vision of the Lord in Galilee. It is hard to combine either supposition with verses 7 and 8 of chapter xvi. For v. 8 has effectively dismissed the women from further immediate participation in events, while v. 7 urgently demands their intervention.

He then considers the suggestion that had been made a few years earlier by C. H. Turner, that the lost ending related how Jesus appeared to the women and quieted their fears, so that they were able to tell the disciples; but he criticizes this, on the ground that 'they said nothing to anybody' must mean 'they did not deliver the message'. 'If the narrative of the women at the tomb is to be linked up with narratives of the appearances, it is essential that the women should deliver the message.' Creed then draws our attention to the way in which Matthew and Luke have achieved this result: 'by suppressing the tell-tale words, "they said nothing to anybody"'; that was the only way in which they could make the story of the women lead on to the story of the disciples.

He then takes up the alternative hypothesis, that Mark made a fresh start with the journey of the disciples to Galilee, and refers to Kirsopp Lake's suggestion that the disciples had already left Jerusalem; that was why the women were unable to tell them what the 'angel' had said. But Creed points out that there is a decisive objection to this: 'The angel, on this theory, gives a message to the women which it was impossible for them to deliver. This ought not to be, and we may securely assume that it was not so.'

Creed then explains that what he is doing is asking how Mark could have proceeded, if he did; he must, Creed says, either have left 'the angel's message hanging in the air', or else he must have explained why it was not delivered to the disciples. Neither of these two courses seems probable. 'Internal evidence, therefore, as well as external probability, seems to point to the conclusion that the Marcan narrative never went beyond the words, "for they were afraid".'

Creed makes one further point: he suggests an explanation of how it was that the 'incoherence' arose. Mark, he thinks, was working on traditions that were already in existence; one of them was the story of the women at the tomb, which might have 'but recently come into circulation'. He follows E. Meyer in thinking that Mark inserted verse 7 into this traditional unit, without noticing that the silence of the women would make it impossible for the narrative to continue – but, in any case, he had no intention of continuing. The problem only arose when Matthew and Luke wanted to link the story of the women at the tomb to the account of appearances to disciples. 'The absence of that link in Mark is an indication that in his Gospel no narrative followed.'

The strength of Creed's argument that 16.8 was the intended conclusion to the Gospel lies in the method that he used: he paid attention to what Mark actually wrote; and he asks, Having written this, in these words, could he have written more? Creed challenges anyone who upholds the hypothesis of a lost ending to the Gospel to say how that ending could have followed on from verses 1–8, without hiatus, contradiction or redundancy. He observes the distinction, which is not always made, between what happened (to the women and the disciples, on Easter day) and what Mark wrote (when he composed his book); it is a method of studying a Gospel that has yielded rich results, but in 1930 it was novel, and Creed should be honoured as one of the earliest writers in England to approach a problem in the Gospels in this way.

I do not intend to go further and offer an explanation as to why Mark ended his Gospel thus. There has been no shortage of interpretations. Was it that the evangelist had an anti-Jerusalem bias – the apostles themselves ('his disciples and Peter') never received the message from the young man, therefore they did not believe in the resurrection, but were still in sin? Or was it that the evangelist was engaged in a controversy between followers of Paul and the sort of people he described as super-apostles (2 Cor. 12.11) – he describes the disciples in Mark as failures, because he is attacking people who do not understand the cross or the resurrection? Or is the ending a literary device, whereby the audience is addressed over the shoulders of the women, and the question is left in the air, Was the young man right? Is Christ risen? One could compare the way in which the book of Jonah ends with a question.

I do not intend to comment on these or on any other interpretations of the end of Mark, because it seems to me that it is important to separate, as far as we possibly can, two kinds of question: What is the text? and, Why was it written? There were terms that described the distinction, but they are seldom used now: lower criticism and higher criticism.[12] The end of Mark belongs more to the former than to the latter.

I suspect that the reason why there is still opposition to the view that 16.8 was the intended ending of the Gospel is because people do not want to buy any of the explanations that have been offered with it as a package deal. There is no need to attach the question of the ending to any particular explanation; it is a question on its own.

Nor, of course, is there any need to think that, if Mark meant to end there, it was because he did not believe in the resurrection. It would not follow that if he did not include resurrection appearances, he did not believe that Christ was risen. He refers to the resurrection directly or indirectly at the following points in his book: 8.31, 38; 9.9, 31; 10.34; 12.10-11, 18-27, 35-7; 13.26-7; 14.28, 58, 62; 16.6. Did he need to say more?

Notes

[1] J. L. Houlden, *Backward into Light* (London: SCM Press, 1987).

[2] R. H. Lightfoot, *Locality and Doctrine in the Gospels* (London: Hodder & Stoughton, 1938); *The Gospel Message of St Mark* (Oxford: Clarendon Press, 1950).

3 See, for example, C. E. B. Cranfield, *The Gospel according to Saint Mark* (Cambridge: Cambridge University Press, 1959), pp. 470f.

4 F. L. Cross (ed.), *The Oxford Dictionary of the Christian Church*, 2nd edn (Oxford: Oxford University Press, 1974), *sub* 'Marcan Hypothesis'.

5 Bruce Metzger (ed.), *A Textual Commentary on the Greek New Testament*, corrected edn (London: United Bible Societies, 1975), p. 126, n. 7.

6 N. T. Wright, *Who was Jesus?* (London: SPCK, 1992), p. 85.

7 *The Alternative Service Book 1980* (London: Hodder & Stoughton, 1980), pp. 1028, 1040.

8 R. H. Gundry, *Mark: A Commentary on His Apology for the Cross* (Grand Rapids, MI: Wm B. Eerdmans, 1993).

9 There had, however, been an article in the *Journal of Theological Studies* 27 (July 1926), pp. 407ff., by R. R. Ottley on the use of *gar* as the last word in a sentence.

10 J. M. Creed, 'The Conclusion of the Gospel according to Saint Mark', *Journal of Theological Studies* 31 (1930), pp. 175ff.

11 I take it that by 'codex *a*' Creed meant to refer to the Old Latin codex Vercellensis; as far as I can see, no other writer includes *a* as a witness to the ending at 16.8, and Nestle-Aland, *Novum Testamentum Graece* 26th edn, p. 712, says that it includes Mark 15.15–16.20.

12 See Cross (ed.), *Oxford Dictionary of the Christian Church*, *sub* 'Higher Criticism'.

2
Flesh is Precious:
The Significance of Luke 24.36-43

Robert Morgan

How should Christians read the New Testament? That simple question to which New Testament theology proposes answers is close to the surface in many of Leslie Houlden's writings. Their aim can be summed up in the subtitle of *Connections*: 'the integration of theology and faith'.[1] And theology for him requires a hard nose and a sensitive heart – not to be confused with the hard heart and sensitive nose sometimes encountered in discussions of resurrection (cf. Luke 24.25; John 11.39). In one of his many contributions to this theme he observes that 'Here more than anywhere else in the programme of Christian beliefs, history and doctrine, texts and ideas intertwine', and that there are probably many who cannot 'give any meaning to the resurrection unless the gospel stories are, at least broadly, true'.[2] Since the 'many' take 'true' to mean historically reliable, and since most New Testament scholars since Peter Annet and Reimarus have known that this part of the gospel tradition is most vulnerable to historical criticism, it is here above all that New Testament theologians have been accused of a *trahison des clercs*.

The generally positive reaction to Archbishop Peter Carnley's *The Structure of Resurrection Belief*[3] is indicative of a more mature (or resigned?) attitude to biblical scholarship among Christians than existed when C. F. Evans' admirable *Resurrection and the New Testament*[4] perplexed some clergy of his generation. That change speaks well for the biblical teaching in England of theologians now retired such as Evans and Houlden, Moule and Nineham, Barrett and Fenton (to match a senior Cambridge trio with the younger Oxford men). But their pupils still have questions, and one who has learned, but failed to learn enough, from all six is glad of an opportunity to continue the conversation with a friend and former colleague.

Most theologians have long since learned to distinguish between the reality of God's Yes to Jesus articulated in the metaphors of exaltation and resurrection, and the historicity of particular Easter traditions. The former does not depend on the latter, though these traditions presumably stand in some relation to how the disciples first became convinced of the mysterious divine event, and this is hard to imagine without its historical effects.

¨ Our sense that there must be some relationship between these stories and the way the disciples first became convinced of Jesus' resurrection, not to mention the relationship between these stories and contemporary resurrection faith, still accounts for some reluctance to deny their historicity. We identify some traditions as secondary and some narratives as apologetic, but it is a bold step actually to deny their historicity. Non-believers may be sceptical, but Christians cannot deny that God could have worked in this way, and some think it presumptuous to deny that he would. A reverent agnosticism seems the safe policy.

But that smacks of diplomatic evasion. To refuse to make a historical judgement that one certainly would make were it not for the imperatives of faith looks to some like intellectual dishonesty. Besides, fear of causing little ones to stumble is not only paternalistic, but also cuts two ways. Theologians owe it to the person in the pew as well as to themselves to be frank about their scepticism and to make it clear that doubts on certain matters are compatible with Christian faith and may cohabit with reverent agnosticism. If some of these stories are so poorly attested as to be scarcely credible at the historical level, it seems sensible for theologians and preachers to direct attention to such content of their religious message as is independent of their historical veracity.

A clear example of a historically dubious story, whose apologetic aims are as transparent as they are in Matthew's legend of the guard at the tomb (which gave Reimarus his cue) is St Luke's account at 24.41–3 of the risen Lord eating a morsel of baked fish. Yet even here traces of the old eighteenth-century apologetic represented by Bishop Thomas Sherlock's *The Tryal of the Witnesses of the Resurrection of Jesus*[5] can still be found in scholarly literature.

J. M. Creed remarked in his commentary on Luke 24.41–3, 'If the original scene of this appearance was by the lake-side in Galilee, it would be very natural that fish should be at hand.'[6] That may not seem very profound, but Creed's valid point was the comparison with the similar wording of John 21.5, and the possibility that a common source or tradition stood behind these two narratives. He thought it was Galilean and probably 'true to fact', and that Luke represents a later modification, in conflict with Mark 16.7. He does not consider the possibility, now advocated by Barbara Shellard,[7] that Luke knew John and composed his story on the basis of John 20.19–29 and 21.2–14 ('third' appearance), but his literary observations are good as far as they go, and his hunch that the fish belong in Galilee at the literary as well as any historical level is a reasonable even if unprovable suggestion.

It is, however, surely the old historical apologetic which leads Howard Marshall to respond that 'the evidence that fish was readily available in Jerusalem is indisputable (cf. Ne. 3.3; 13.16; Jeremias, *Jerusalem*, 20; for the use of salted fish, which could be readily transported, see SB I, 683f.)'.[8] The historical availability of fish (fresh or salted) in Jerusalem does not weaken Creed's literary suggestion, which does not depend on the fish shops being empty. J. A. Fitzmyer is rightly dismissive, but his impatience over the historical question should not have led him to dismiss even the literary issue as 'the kind of question which should not be asked of the Lucan gospel'.[9]

In fact, of course, it is neither lack of fish in Jerusalem nor the probable history of the tradition that explains the widespread scepticism about the Lucan story. Those who reject it do so because they do not think of the resurrection in such 'crudely' physical terms. If they are Christians, they no doubt accept the point of the story – which Luke makes very clear: to insist that the resurrection of Jesus was real, that it was really Jesus who was raised, and that the disciples were not suffering from hallucinations. But they find Luke guilty of a rather tactless (or rather tactile) way of preserving these essential Christian truths. Fitzmyer offers little defence: 'Only Luke among the evangelists indulges (*sic*) in this sort of realism about the existence of the risen Christ; and for this he is castigated by twentieth-century readers!'[10]

Fitzmyer's defence, if such it be, consists in the lapidary sentence that follows: 'In 20.27–29 John as an evangelist has his own way of stressing the reality, yet he is rarely castigated in the same way.'[11] Rightly not, one might respond. John does not have Thomas actually bring his finger or cast his hand into the stricken side, and it is possible to read the invitation as ironic. Such behaviour would surely be as inappropriate as Thomas' unbelief. The Johannine Christ is not said to eat the fish he apparently cooks for them at 21.9–13 either.

There is no symposiac indication here that the chosen witnesses 'ate and drank with him after he rose from the dead', as Luke supposes (Acts 10.42). Not even the secondary Marcan endings pursue this apologetic line.

On the other hand, none of the gospel stories can accurately be described as visions, unlike Paul's list in 1 Corinthians 15.3–8. The risen Lord can pass through locked doors (John 20.26), and appears and disappears at will (Luke 24.36), but a figure who can be mistaken for the gardener (John 20.15), or whose feet can be clasped (Matt. 28.9; cf. John 20.17), or who can walk along the road with people (Luke 24.15), or meet them in the path (Matt. 28.9) or by the seaside (John 21), and who can converse with them at length (Luke 24.27, 45; Acts 1.3), is quite corporeally imagined. Luke's alleged indelicacy lies only in his brutal consistency.

One may well (like Bishop David Jenkins) prefer St Paul. The appearances in 1 Corinthians 15.3–8 are easily construed as visions, and if the distinction between visions and hallucinations reflects faith's judgement about the trans-subjective reference of the event rather than an observable difference, that is appropriate too. Paul did not doubt the divine reality of the event, but seems not to have conceived the appearances as realistically as the evangelists. His listing his own appearance as comparable with the others is clearly at odds with Luke, and historians will surely prefer his testimony even if his metaphor alluding to his own situation as one who had not known Jesus beforehand is admitted to understate the differences.

Theologians who follow the preference of historians for Paul's witness over Luke's can offer a historical defence even if their choice is guided by scientific or philosophical objections to a physical resurrection. It is reasonable to want to imagine the first Easter as it was, rather than as Luke imagined it. That preference for our own rational judgement about how it was, over the actual text of Scripture, reflects the modern ordeal of biblical authority in the fires of a rational criticism fuelled by the contradictions between the biblical witnesses. Paul's statements that the last Adam became a life-giving Spirit (1 Cor. 15.45) and that flesh and blood cannot inherit the kingdom of God (v. 50) stand in some tension with Luke 24. That fluctuation allows believers a certain freedom in how they think about the central mystery of their faith. But if the preference for a historical judgement based on Paul over the more realistic gospel narratives totally undermines the latter, some reconsideration is surely needed. Both

Paul and the Gospels are central scriptural witnesses, and playing one off against another is a dangerous game in which Christian belief is eroded. Both ways of speaking of the mystery may contain some truth, and their contradictions warn against supposing that any single image is adequate.

Historians are naturally more likely to explain the disciples' convictions in terms of visions than of physical appearances because these do not require a belief in miracle. Theologians also have reasons for disliking this category when speaking of the resurrection. By inviting comparison with Lazarus, Jairus' daughter, and the widow's son at Nain, it neglects the cosmic and universal scope of Jesus' resurrection, and also misleadingly confuses the eschatological event itself with its alleged effects in history and nature. It seems better to call God's vindication of Jesus a mystery, like God's identification with Jesus in the incarnation, and to insist that how the disciples became convinced of it is a secondary question that cannot be answered for sure. Christian belief in the resurrection of Jesus does not depend on the historicity of these gospel reports. Something must have happened, but we cannot say what.

There is no reason for theologians to court a clash between faith and historical reason at this (or any other) point. Belief in God's vindication of Jesus should not turn on anyone's ability to believe that here the processes of nature were reversed or suspended or accelerated. Even if they were, the point is transfiguration, not reversal or suspension or acceleration, and in any case it looks like a category mistake to invoke religious faith to overcome a deficit in the historical evidence and establish a historical argument. If we finally come back to appreciate Luke's narrative, it will not be to make a historical case for Christianity.

In matters of historical judgement, we believe what we believe, and there is little point in being told to do otherwise. Where the gospel record makes a historical claim, we may accept it, be sceptical, or remain agnostic. Our judgements may be influenced by our metaphysical beliefs, but these are unlikely to be reshaped by such weak historical evidence as the Gospels provide. It is therefore liberating to learn that God's raising Jesus is not a historical event, whatever its historical effects, and that the grounds for our believing it are not the evidence of Easter Sunday (or thereabouts), even if those now obscure historical events played a role in establishing the faith of the first disciples.[12]

Christians who do not believe in the physicality of Jesus' resurrection can adduce further considerations. The Gospels do not intend to relate a resuscitation. There is no question of Jesus dying again. A physical resurrection looks dangerously like resuscitation, and invites the rationalist explanation that Jesus did not really die on the cross. It is better avoided.

The more serious objection, that the Gospels isolate the resurrection of Jesus from the eschatological context which determines its meaning, is only partly valid. Mark provides a hint of this link in the ambiguity of his 'you will see him',[13] and Matthew's proleptic general resurrection (27.51b-3) and proleptic parousia (28.16-20) overcome the constraints of his narrative mode and make the connection. John has dispensed with the eschatological framework anyway. But Luke seems guilty as charged. He makes the resurrection of Jesus central, and rightly relates it to both the past history of the ministry and the present experience of believers who know Jesus in the breaking of the bread. But his deferral of the eschatological hope has separated what Paul could still hold together: the resurrection of Jesus (the first-fruits, first-begotten of the dead, first-born of many brethren), and that of believers at his coming.

Such a separation, reflected also in the thoroughly Lucan Old Roman and later Apostles' Creed, is hard to avoid in a narrative presentation of salvation-history, and this structural flaw in Luke's double work is evident in the speeches of Acts. They present the resurrection of Jesus as more the reversal of the tragic events of Good Friday than the inauguration of the new age by an event that anticipates God's final victory. The problem is not that Luke is without eschatology, but that his salvation-historical presentation obscures the eschatological character of Jesus' death and resurrection.

However, the strengths of Luke's narrative theology surely outweigh its weaknesses. Its clarity and simplicity commended it to subsequent Catholicism, and it has provided much of the basis for the Christian liturgical year. The subtleties of Matthew and John have been understood as rarely as Paul's theology. It is Luke who still does most to establish Christian identity by his picture of Christian origins, and it was above all Luke to whom Irenaeus turned for a conceptual framework by which to overcome the gnostic divorce of creation and redemption.

Orthodox second-century writers followed Luke in most things, but went further along the line of his flesh-and-bones resurrection of

Jesus. They spoke of the future resurrection for judgement in similar terms. Their doctrine of the future resurrection of the flesh provides a possible line of defence for Luke's physical view of Jesus' resurrection. Instead of arguing about the historical accuracy of Luke's presentation, we need to ask about its theological appropriateness, especially in view of 1 Corinthians 15.50. That is quite different from noting its apologetic intention, which has already been acknowledged. The question now before us is not merely the reality of the resurrection and the identity of the risen Jesus, but his flesh and bones in all their Lucan realism. Despite the historical incredibility of this story, reflection on their own futures may lead Christian readers into a willing suspension of disbelief.

That second-century language about the future resurrection of the flesh both supplements Luke's theology and justifies his narrative. The latter is more important to Christians than the former. Luke's so-called theology is a scholarly reconstruction. Arguing about it and criticizing it is one of the ways biblical theologians maintain their historical and theological conversation about the Bible. The narrative itself, by contrast, is a valuable part of the Christian tradition, and not to be lightly dismissed. It is sometimes necessary to criticize human, all too human, elements in Scripture where these are inadequate, immoral, or otherwise damaging to faith. But such *Sachkritik* or theological criticism in the light of the gospel is, like matrimony, to be undertaken reverently, responsibly, and after serious thought. A careless criticism of Scripture cuts off the branch on which Christian faith depends. We should hesitate to dismiss the gospel narratives just because our modern beliefs about nature prevent us from passing a favourable historical judgement on them.

It matters only to literalists whether the risen Jesus actually ate the fish. However, Christians who do not believe Luke's story at the historical level (and guess he composed it on the basis of John 20.27, and 21.9–14, as hinted above), may value the narrative for other than historical reasons. Christians are expected to hear, read, mark, learn and inwardly digest their scriptural traditions, not necessarily to accept their historicity. That would be important if how exactly the first disciples came to their convictions were essential for Christian faith. If it had been, the first Christians would have preserved their memories more carefully. As it was not important for them, it need not be so for us.

Setting aside the historical question of what exactly the first disciples saw, and how they came to believe that Jesus was vindicated by God and alive with God, we are free to consider what else the narrative may have to say, and how it makes its impact on the reader. The force of its claim to disclose truth and reality has generally resided in the reader's assumption that it records accurately what actually happened (cf. Luke 1.4). What remains if that assumption is abandoned?

The choice between Paul and the later evangelists' ways of imagining the risen Christ does not affect the shared conviction of them all that God vindicated Jesus. But it may have some bearing on other matters, notably the value of the material world, especially human bodies, and the way we imagine the still future judgement and salvation. Some Christians follow the Johannine path, insisting that life or judgement takes place now in the present decision of faith or unbelief, but even John speaks of a future with Christ (14.3), and the creeds speak of a future judgement. Because that lies beyond all experience, imaginative representations are needed, but the images chosen imply the personal identity of all those to be judged, with the men and women whose moral responsibility is affirmed in this way. It is surely essential that it is I myself and not another (cf. Job 19.27) who shall appear before the judgement-seat of Christ, I myself who hope by God's mercy to praise and glorify God for ever (whatever that involves).

Continuing personal identity is quite incredible to a materialist, and 'we are all materialists now', at least to the point that we cannot believe these images literally. But it still might be more truthful to tell some incredible stories than to make them more believable. In restating Christian faith for one's own generation, it is often necessary to do just that. 'Christianity is always adapting itself into something that can be believed.'[14] But critical theological judgement consists in deciding what to let go and what to retain, whether restated or not, and however differently understood. Some historical claims have to be relinquished in the light of present knowledge, but the last judgement is not a historical claim. There is a difference between avoiding collisions with historical judgement and adjusting our mythological stories to make them believable in a different way. In the case of general resurrection and judgement, unlike the resurrection appearances of Jesus, we are necessarily in the realm of fantastic images and stories. The priority here is not to make those stories rational, but to see that they articulate a truth to which Christians are committed.

Nevertheless, stories that sound as though they are intended to be taken literally are better avoided. The Church was wise to abandon its second-century talk of a resurrection of the flesh. It is the incompatibility of the image with what we know of nature that makes it sound ridiculous to modern ears, rather than what offended the gnostics against whom it was directed, and who believed that matter was inherently evil. On the other hand, we should not yield to the old literalist protest against this fantastic image without ensuring that its original point is preserved. If the goodness of the created order, including human flesh and blood, could be asserted in no other way than this, it would be necessary to retain the image and add that it cannot be taken literally. But Christian belief about the material world is surely sufficiently protected by orthodox understandings of the creation and the incarnation; there was and is therefore no need to cling to this image. Paul's language of the *body* that shall be (1 Cor. 15.37) is echoed in the Apostles' Creed's 'resurrection of the body'. The Old Roman creed's resurrection of the flesh was rightly abandoned.

Paul's body language asserts the continuing personal identity that is essential to Christian belief, but also employs a strategy familiar in religious language and described by I. T. Ramsey as 'model and qualifier'.[15] The anthropological concept 'body' (*soma*) is qualified by the adjective 'spiritual'. Even without the qualifier, Paul's elusive anthropological concept could almost have sustained the necessary ambiguity. If Käsemann is roughly right to interpret 'body' in Paul as 'humanity as a bit of the *world*', and to insist (on appeal to 1 Cor. 6) on the physical connotations of the word,[16] the value of materiality is preserved by it. But *soma* in Paul is multivalent; the celestial bodies of 1 Corinthians 15.40 are scarcely physical. At the very least, Paul's language is open to gnostic interpretations. Even Bultmann's suspiciously Heideggerian interpretation[17] evades the physical connotations of *soma*. It seems that early catholicism's resolute, even crude, insistence on the flesh can be defended as a necessary bulwark against the ever-present tendency towards gnostic depreciation of human bodies.

Flesh in all its sensuality signifies human life as we know and enjoy it. Physical intimacy and food and drink belong to human life in its fullness. We retain the language of messianic banquet because a bloodless existence in Sheol or Hades sounds less than the life more abundant promised in the gospel (John 10.10). We know that food and drink and sex, unlike diamonds, are not for ever, but we hope that the endless sabbaths to which we look forward (*O quanta qualia*) will be more like continental than puritan Sundays. We know we are not talking literally when we anticipate parties and even (against Mark 12.25) physical intimacy (cf. John 20.17?), but the Christian hope sounds flat and boring unless it is spoken of in fully human terms, and that includes flesh.

Contemporary Western society is not in danger of devaluing the physical, and surely needs to recover the opposite emphasis. A stronger reason for keeping flesh on the agenda of Christian eschatology is to keep alive the horror of physical mutilation in a culture saturated by images and the reality of violence. The value of the human body and the consequent evil of physical brutality, the absolute exclusion of torture that has been scandalously betrayed in Christian history, can be underlined by the image of a resurrection of the flesh. John 19.37 quotes the torn flesh of Zechariah 12.10 ('They shall look upon him whom they pierced') with reference to the crucifixion, and Revelation 1.7 quotes it with reference to the last judgement. It scarcely needs a link such as Matthew 25.31–46 to justify the suggestion that the last judgement may include the horror of facing those we have hurt.

Despite the fruitfulness of this idea, the image of a general resurrection of the flesh, and judgement in the flesh, remains an absurdity, and we are glad that the Church has relieved us of it. The question then is how to preserve the truths it enshrined. A solution is provided by the conceptual link between Jesus' resurrection and our own, which is provided by the background of the eschatological idea in Jewish apocalyptic. We are encouraged by this association to see in our images of Jesus' resurrection body a hint about our own. The image of Christ's resurrection in the flesh, with wounds that can be seen and handled, is unlikely to be historical, but it is less obviously open to criticism than the idea of a general resurrection of the flesh, and in view of their conceptual relationship it can serve as a pointer to what that has to say to us.

If we want to entertain the image of a general resurrection of the flesh for the theological reasons given above, but cannot without sounding ridiculous, Luke offers a way out of the dilemma by speaking of the risen Christ's body as flesh. Even that is incredible, and it runs the risk of being misunderstood as a resuscitation. Every image carries some risk, and has to be balanced by alternatives that contain other dangers. Here the dangers are outweighed by the benefits of 'flesh' talk, both in affirming the reality of Jesus' resurrection, and in providing a pointer to some implications of the Christian hope. Luke's image is a vivid reminder of the validity and joy of food and physical intimacy, and of God's judgement on sin against the image of God. Possibly indebted to John 20.27, Luke, followed by Ignatius (*Smyrnaeans* 3), extends the reference to flesh that can be tenderly handled, from the incarnation (John 1.14; 1 John 1.1; 4.2) into the realm where it is strictly inappropriate (1 Cor. 15.50). John or his editor at 6.51–6 used similarly inappropriate language to make a strong point, and his shocking language has like Luke's been retained in the liturgy but not in the creeds. Provided that complementary models are available, misplaced flesh can stand and point to truths about the material world that second-century catholic writers expressed in a now unacceptable way.

Imagining *Christ's* risen body in physical terms is less problematic than a *general* resurrection of the flesh. However unhistorical, it expresses Christian claims that God really vindicated Jesus, and that it really was Jesus that God vindicated. It also underlines that it is in our personal identities that we hope to see God, and trust in God's mercy to be judged. It further symbolizes the Christian belief that human flesh and bones are precious, and that the violence we have done to others will accuse us in the last judgement, and yet says that in a resurrection context which affirms God's final victory over evil. We have been able to draw these last points from Luke's story on account of the relationship in Christian belief between the resurrection of Jesus, the first-fruits of those who have fallen asleep, and that of those who belong to him, at his parousia. This connection, asserted by Paul in 1 Corinthians 15, has frequently been obscured, not least by Luke. But whether deliberately or not, Luke's talk of Jesus' flesh and bones has left us a useful pointer to aspects of Christian belief that could not be sustained in their second-century form, but that remain essential and have to be asserted in other ways. Human bodies, flesh and bones, flesh and blood, remain valuable whether or not they can inherit the kingdom of God untransfigured. We need to envision things beyond the scope of historical verification or even rational reflection in order to keep hope alive and give substance to things unseen. Luke's legendary portrayal of Christ's risen body provides a lively image of the new age that the mysterious event of Jesus' resurrection by God is said by Christians to have inaugurated.

In doing so, it also confronts and challenges life in a present evil age in which human flesh is abused and tortured. 'Realism about the existence of the risen Christ' (above, p. 10) need not be 'castigated'. David's prophecy (Ps. 16) that God would not give his Holy One to see corruption (Acts 2.27) provided Luke with testimony in support of a gospel tradition that can reinforce our sense of the permanent value of human flesh and bones.

Notes

[1] Leslie Houlden, *Connections* (London: SCM Press, 1986).

[2] ibid., p. 139.

[3] Peter Carnley, *The Structure of Resurrection Belief* (Oxford: Oxford University Press, 1987).

[4] C. F. Evans, *Resurrection and the New Testament* (London: SCM Press, 1970).

[5] Thomas Sherlock, *The Tryal of the Witnesses of the Resurrection of Jesus* (1729, [13]1755).

[6] J. M. Creed, *The Gospel According to St. Luke* (London: Macmillan, 1930), p. 299.

[7] In a forthcoming long article in *Journal of Theological Studies*, 'The relationship of Luke and John: A fresh look at an old problem', and work in progress for an Oxford D.Phil.

[8] I. H. Marshall, *The Gospel of Luke* (Exeter: Paternoster Press, 1978), p. 903.

[9] J. A. Fitzmyer, *The Gospel According to Luke X–XXIV* (Garden City, NY: Doubleday, 1985), p. 1577.

[10] ibid.

[11] ibid.

[12] Rather than the reverse, as suggested by E. Schillebeeckx, *Jesus: An Experiment in Christology* (London: Collins, 1979), pp. 380–97.

[13] Mark 14.28 and 16.7 were taken by Lohmeyer, Marxsen and others to refer to the parousia rather than the resurrection partly on account of the 'you will see' found also at 13.26; 14.62. Mark might possibly have even intended the ambiguity.

[14] T. S. Eliot's remark is adopted as a motto by Leslie Houlden's teacher Dennis Nineham in *The Use and Abuse of the Bible* (London: Macmillan, 1976).

[15] I. T. Ramsey, *Religious Language* (London: SCM Press, 1957).

[16] On Käsemann's Pauline interpretation, see D. Way, *The Lordship of Christ* (Oxford: Oxford University Press, 1989).

[17] Cf. J. Macquarrie, *An Existentialist Theology* (Harmondsworth: Penguin, 1970).

3

The Emmaus Story and its Sequel

Colin Hickling

In the last chapter of his Gospel, Luke gives us an account of the twenty-four hours[1] during which, following his resurrection, Jesus made three recorded appearances to disciples (Peter, v. 34; Cleopas and his companion, v. 15 – we have no information about the chronological order of these two; and the Eleven 'and those who were with them', v. 36). He does so in a narrative of which the greater part (vv. 13–53) falls into two matching yet contrasting components.[2] Luke first gives us his long, leisured, and relatively circumstantial narrative, presented with great artistry, of the two disciples walking to Emmaus and of what happened there. This is followed without a break by an account, only five verses shorter, of the appearance of the risen Jesus to the Eleven and others. For the attentive reader of this second episode (vv. 36–53), there are some interesting correspondences between it and its predecessor (vv. 13–35). Closer inspection reveals further features indicating both match and contrast between the two leaves of what we may think of as a diptych. This is an intriguing characteristic of the narrative, and may throw light on Luke's purposes in presenting the risen Jesus as he does. We should begin by considering the features that constitute first the match and then the contrast between verses 13–35 and 36–53.

There is a general similarity between the openings of the two stories. In both cases Jesus arrives from somewhere else so as to join disciples who have been together, with Jesus absent, for an appreciable length of time. His first action, in each case, is to interrupt a conversation (vv. 15, 36) in order to interrogate them. It was very unusual for the Jesus of earlier pages in this Gospel to put questions to his disciples, though there are instances at 9.18, when it was not Jesus who joined his disciples, but they who came to him, and just before his arrest, at 22.35 (and one might add v. 46). Both interrogations, moreover, concern debates or discussions, on the one hand between the two walkers to Emmaus, on the other hand within the minds of the Eleven and their companions. We can go even further. It would appear that there was an element of dissension in each case. Cleopas and his companion had been in conversation about 'everything that had happened', presumably including the reports of the women. These had failed to carry conviction in the minds of those who heard them (v. 11). There was, accordingly, plenty to keep an argument going on the Emmaus road.[3] Set beside this the words of the risen Lord at verse 38b. Jesus asks, 'Why do questionings rise in your hearts?' (RSV). The enquiry attracts attention through being a slightly odd one to follow the entirely natural 'Why are you troubled?' But, further, the noun (διαλογισμός) which the RSV renders as 'questioning' often suggests sharp controversy.[4] Doubtful or discussible matters, then, have arisen in the disciples' minds, the kind of subject that the disciples would soon be arguing about, given opportunity: the parallel to verses 14f. is fairly close. Further, yet again, just as the question put by Jesus to the two travellers about their conversation had left them σκυθρωποί, 'sad' or 'gloomy', so the Eleven and their companions in Jerusalem were frightened as Jesus questioned them. In each case the interrogation is closely associated with an unhappy frame of mind.

The beginnings of the two stories, then, are linked by some related narrative features. Their endings have only one feature in common, but it is striking enough. The 'becoming invisible' of Jesus at verse 31 (ἄφαντος ἐγένετο) has a parallel – in sense, at least – at verse 51: 'taken up into Heaven' obviously implies disappearance as far as terrestrial observers are concerned, and the author of an important study of this chapter is 'sure that διέστη . . . ἀπ' αὐτῶν ("he was separated from them") has the same meaning as . . . ἄφαντος ἐγένετο ("he became invisible")'.[5]

What intervenes between the opening and closing verses of the two stories also shows clear points of correspondence. Both presentations of the teaching of Jesus about his own suffering and resurrection include reference to Moses and the prophets, the statement that Jesus interpreted these Scriptures, and, most tellingly of all, the phrase παθεῖν τὸν Χριστόν ('that the Christ should suffer'). Further, similar wording is used in each story to describe the second of these. At verse 32 the two disciples remember how Jesus had 'opened' (διήνοιγεν) the Scriptures to them; at verse 45 he 'opened (διήνοιξεν) their minds to understand the Scriptures'.

In all, then, quite a number of features link the two stories. The reader – whether in the first century or the twentieth – may by now be asking whether there may not be something behind all this. Is he being covertly invited to compare the one with the other?[6] Reflective rereading would bring to his notice some sharply pointed contrasts, which we may list as follows.

First, in the narrative of verse 15, Jesus' arrival on the scene is unobtrusive: he could hardly present a lower profile as he 'approached them and began to walk along with them'. At verse 36, on the other hand, Jesus 'appeared',[7] suddenly, even dramatically, as the aorist tense of the verb ($\dot{\epsilon}\sigma\tau\dot{\alpha}\theta\eta$) suggests. There is a strong suggestion of supernatural majesty. This contrast is reflected and extended in a further one. We have already seen that the disciples' state of mind associated with their respective encounters with Jesus was in a broad sense unhappy. The travellers to Emmaus were $\sigma\kappa\upsilon\theta\rho\omega\pi o\acute{\iota}$, 'sullen' or 'sad'. In the same way, the Eleven and their companions in Jerusalem were shaken and afraid. Yet Luke's choice of words – if it is his[8] – also suggests a marked difference. $\Pi\tau o\eta\theta\dot{\epsilon}\nu\tau\epsilon\varsigma$ and $\ddot{\epsilon}\mu\phi o\beta o\iota$ (v. 37) suggest a terror that is the very opposite of aggressiveness. $\Sigma\kappa\upsilon\theta\rho\omega\pi\acute{o}\varsigma$, on the other hand, has a semantic range that includes 'angry-looking'.[9] Dramatically, the contrast between the two reactions to Jesus – servile terror and a kind of hostility – is considerable. The former is the response appropriate to a divinity. The latter – whether the travellers' hostility is directed towards the stranger or towards one another – is one of the features underlining the everyday, normal nature of the human experience depicted.

More combinations of likeness and contrast must be noted. The two disciples (who are of course included in the plural subject of $\dot{\epsilon}\delta\acute{o}\kappa o\upsilon\nu$) twice make a mistake as to who Jesus is. On the road to Emmaus, they thought he was simply a stranger. In Jerusalem, where they had rejoined the Eleven, they thought he was a ghost. Yet this second misidentification is of a different and contrasting kind. A travelling companion, presumably unarmed, can be accepted, even a little condescended to, for what he appears to be. One who manifests himself as a supernatural being might bring at least a hint of danger.

Misidentification is of course in each story the prelude to recognition. This is crucially important in both cases, but how differently! In the Emmaus narrative we are impressed by the ironies arising from the long period of *non*-recognition, adding as they do so much to the pathos of the moment of recognition itself. The first part of the second story is exclusively devoted to establishing beyond further doubt not so much Jesus' identity in the strict sense, as his still being fully, tangibly corporeal and hence human.

The evidence we have been considering suggests that Luke intended these stories to be read synoptically.[10] Such a reading may throw into relief both motifs and wording in both stories. We should expect to find that statements implied by each story sometimes complement what is said in the other and are sometimes in some degree of opposition to it. These implied statements may now be considered, to see whether they throw light on two related questions, one major, the other a little less so. How does Luke view the purpose of the resurrection? And what is the real importance of the Lord's Supper, the embryonic Eucharist, now that Jesus is absent in heaven? To the first question an answer can be given with much confidence. With the second, we remain in the sphere of the enigmatic.

For the Luke of the Gospel, at any rate, Jesus' having risen from the dead meant that the supreme, archetypal Evangelist of God's fulfilment of his promises – 4.16ff. states a role for Jesus that is taken up more than once in what follows – was now able to train others to be themselves evangelists of the same gospel of fulfilment. Those others include both the surviving apostles, who receive their instruction at 24.44–6, and non-apostles such as Cleopas and, we are probably to assume, his travelling companion; their preparation for bearing testimony was given on the road (vv. 25–7). Jesus fulfilled the prophecies of the Scriptures by being raised from the dead. At the same time, this resurrection enabled him to ensure that the supreme fulfilment of Scripture would be adequately preached.

In this respect both the stories we are considering speak with the same voice. Both present the risen Jesus as the dedicated and urgent Teacher that we had encountered in the rest of this Gospel. Further, the content of his teaching is, as we have seen, the same in both stories, and continues what he had already been accustomed to expound before his arrest. So Luke 24.25–7 and 44–6 repeat what Jesus had said earlier[11] about the divinely ordained necessity of his destiny of death and resurrection, and about this destiny having been prophesied in the Scriptures.

Jesus gave this instruction all over again; he had to. The Emmaus road travellers, for all we know, had never heard it: nothing indicates whether 'the rest' who were with the apostles at 24.9 had been travelling with them in Galilee. In any case, their fault lay in their inadequate insight into the true meaning of the Scriptures (v. 25). With the Eleven the matter is more complex. Earlier that very day they had received and rejected the women's report. This had (presumably) included the two men's command to remember what Jesus had announced 'while still in Galilee' (v. 6) about his own destiny of suffering and resurrection. Jesus had then encountered a degree of incomprehension on his disciples' part that Luke describes in strong terms (9.45; 18.34). So all concerned fail to understand what Scripture meant. The Twelve (as they then were) had done so despite the guidance of the wisest of tutors. Now, at verses 44–6, with the truth of the resurrection at last made fully plain, the risen Lord gave this teaching again.

He did so in order that those at last able to master it should pass it on with authority to the audiences who would so soon be hearing their preaching. For that reason, we may note in passing, the verses we have been considering form a substantial part of the bridge Luke has constructed between his two volumes. This bridge can reasonably be taken as reaching as far as Acts 2.14–40. For here Peter begins to fulfil the prophecy interpreted at Luke 24.47. Like the others, he was a witness (cf. v. 48). He was able to bear testimony, first to Jesus' deeds and words, including the prophecies just mentioned, and then to the fact that Jesus had been raised. From the moment of 24.44–6 onwards, he was in possession of the interpretation of Scripture by which all this was to be related to God's plan.

Thus in his sermon after the miracle of Pentecost (Acts 2.14–40), he offers the first example of the apostolic testimony and proclamation desiderated in Luke 24.47. At a key point, after Jesus has been brought into the discourse, he asserts (v. 23) the divinely ordered necessity of Jesus' being handed over to death. He announces Jesus' resurrection (v. 24), and at once proceeds to give (vv. 25–8), by an extended citation of Psalm 16 (LXX 15), scriptural proof of the impossibility of Jesus' being retained in death's grasp. After this he adduces, at 3.22f. and 4.11, further citations from Scripture (all, in fact, from the Pentateuch and the Psalter, the only biblical books specifically named in Luke 24), though these are less directly applied to the death and resurrection of Jesus.

Luke surely wishes us to note the implication. Peter had learned well the lesson taught on Luke's Easter Day. Acts 10.43 shows him again offering proof from Scripture – the prophets – though this time only in general terms, as was appropriate for a Gentile audience. At 13.33–41 Paul takes over the same apologetic technique.

Luke 24.26f. and 44–6, then, make clear what is for this evangelist the outstanding significance of the resurrection. It is partly a matter of continuity. Just as the risen Jesus is one and the same person as the teacher of the Galilee days, so those who preach his gospel after his ascension proclaim the same message that had been a principal part of his own teaching, reinforced on the day of his resurrection. More specifically, 'proof-from-prophecy theology is', if not quite 'Luke's central theological idea throughout the two-volume work',[12] then at least firmly embedded in his conception of what it means to preach the gospel. So it is fitting that 'proof-from-prophecy theology is the heart of his concern in chapter 24'.[13] Reflection on the 'two leaves' of the diptych at verses 13–53 has enabled us to see how this centrality of the idea of Scripture-fulfilment is nuanced a little in relation to its communicators being, or not being, apostles (a distinction that hovers intriguingly in the background of this whole chapter, cf. vv. 9, 24, 33). But in general this reflection has enabled us to endorse Schubert's assessment.

What can we say, in the light of these verses, about the Lord's Supper? It is impossible to do more than sketch possibilities, under the compulsion of the sense that Luke is saying *something* by placing in such clear relation the mysterious passages verses 30f. and 35, and verses 41–3. We do not usually judge Luke to be an enigmatic writer, but here – intentionally or otherwise – he makes it hard for us to grasp his thrust. The correspondence between the two passages is obvious. Both are concerned with food and with recognition in close association. Beyond that, little is clear.

The uncertainties are compounded by the fact that verses 30f. and 34 are ambiguous. In verses 30f., Jesus takes the loaf, recites the blessing, breaks it, and distributes it. Thereby he prompts, as it were, the bringing about in the two travellers of a second miracle to undo the first: they now recognize who it is that has just broken the loaf. Most readers probably identify this sequence as in some way eucharistic, with that term including 'communion'. The whole ritual with the bread has taken place, including its consumption. But Luke does not, in fact, tell us whether the bread was eaten or not (perhaps the NEB translators recognized this when they rendered ἐπεδίδου, literally 'gave', 'handed over', by 'offered', leaving it open whether the offer was accepted). Recognition seems to occur between the preliminaries to eating and what would have been the eating itself. For it appears that after the recognition and Jesus' disappearance there was no leisure to complete the meal. Cleopas and his friend hurried back to Jerusalem with all possible haste (literally 'at the same hour'; NEB is, again, surely right in paraphrasing 'without a moment's delay').

So Luke leaves us with a puzzle. Perhaps, despite what has just been said, he means us to think that a prototypical Lord's Supper was completed, if with somewhat unseemly dispatch. But perhaps the reverse was his real purpose, and the narrative should be read without tacit interpolations as the story of a 'Lord's Supper that never was' – not least since the host disappeared, apparently without consuming his own portion of the bread.

Verses 41-3, by contrast, read clearly enough. It is their implications that are less easy to detect. The disciples are bidden to watch while Jesus eats in front of them (it being assumed that a 'spirit' would not be able to consume food). Nothing is said about a meal taking place. If it were, one would hardly need to ask whether there were anything edible there (v. 41)! The Eleven produce a scrap of broiled fish; Jesus takes it, and eats it while they watch (ἐνώπιον αὐτῶν). The slightly curious incident is as far removed from being a meal as could well be imagined, and eucharistic overtones can be heard only by the very imaginative.[14]

We should remember that these ambiguities would have registered with first-century readers more sharply than they do with us, who attach so much less importance to meals. They would have seemed particularly strange to the attentive reader of Luke's Gospel as a whole. Meals had a special importance for Luke, figuring some seven or eight times in his Gospel from 5.27-32 onwards[15] (so that the scene at Emmaus, and to a lesser extent the episode at 24.41-3, have, like Jesus' teaching about Scripture-fulfilment, resonances in the whole Gospel. Significantly, however, the strong links that anchor 24.30 and 43 backward into the text of Luke have no counterpart in the second volume beyond 2.42-7 and the somewhat adventitious mentions at 20.7 and 27.35).

Luke gives us, then, what looks like the interrupted first part of a Lord's Supper, in which Jesus bestows and then immediately withdraws his recognized presence. And he gives us, as counterpart to this, Jesus guaranteeing that same presence by eating fish, as his hosts had done with him in a deserted place near Bethsaida (9.16). We have the beginning of a Eucharist such as Luke may have known, but a Eucharist in which (if the above suggestion is right) neither host nor guests receives the bread; and we have Jesus, now acting like a guest, receiving food not associated with the Eucharist. Is it possible that Luke is making an oblique comment on the inadequacy of all eucharistic rites – they bestow something, but can never replace table-fellowship with the visible, 'real' Jesus? May he even have been critical of the Eucharist as it was coming to be observed in the churches he knew? The Eucharist of Justin Martyr's *First Apology* may have seemed – to Luke as to us – somewhat remote from the meals in Galilee (so that, over this matter, Luke may prove to have been – in sharp contradiction to a more usual designation – an early Protestant!).

We turn back finally to what is surely the main focus of both the stories we have had in mind, namely the renewing of relationship with One who – recognized or not – is the same person that had been killed two days previously. What did it mean to be met, to be joined in conversation, by Jesus as he was between his resurrection and his being taken up into heaven? An answer may be sought in the components in each story that show least aptitude for either comparison or pointed contrast with anything in the other.

In 24.19–24 – roughly a quarter of the whole narrative – the two disciples first recapitulate in extremely compressed form (vv. 19f.) the contents of the Gospel as a whole up to the crucifixion, and then, after their confession of faith (if such it may be called) at verse 21,[16] a much more detailed reproduction (with interesting changes) of verses 1–12 of this chapter, narrating the women's experience at the tomb and its verification by 'certain of those who are with us'.[17] It is as though the disciples on the Emmaus road stand for the past events concerning Jesus, with all the pathos they hold for those who think that they have now come to a close. The recital is imbued with powerful irony: the Lord whom the visitors to the tomb failed to see forms the audience for this narration, and does so as the man he had been throughout. The two travellers had been miraculously prevented from recognizing him. But this very statement implies that in himself, as to physical appearance, dress and so on, he was the Jesus of the Galilee days and of the passion. Were their vision not supernaturally occluded, the disciples would have noticed, if they had looked closely, the scars on his hands and feet.

In the slightly shorter narrative of verses 36–53, on the other hand, the emphasis lies on the present and the future. Verses 39f. show Jesus inviting his disciples (as he invites Thomas at John 20.27[18]) to inspect and even palpate his hands and feet. There could hardly be a more effective way of focusing on the concrete factuality of the present moment of Jesus' restored companionship with his disciples. The last seven verses of the chapter (vv. 47–53) then forecast the future in terms taken up almost at once in the second volume.

The difference in emphasis highlights and makes some comment on two aspects of the resurrection. Jesus risen as the Living One (24.5) remains what he had always been as teacher, friend, and so much else. But he, the Preacher, is now also – above all, through his having fulfilled Scripture – the content of the preaching that must soon begin, and that is to bring repentance and forgiveness to all nations (v. 47). The two stories give elements of specificity to the faith of Luke as it is expressed in his decision to write a second volume to continue the story of what had begun with the prophecies of his first two chapters. God did not end his activity in Jesus when the ascension had taken place. On the contrary, that activity goes on until the final consummation.[19]

Notes

[1] The notes of time at 24.1, 13, 29, 33 and 36 imply that, in contrast to Acts 1.3, everything between the discovery of the empty tomb and the ascension occupied one full day. There is a 'unity of time' in the chapter which is one of the 'unities of composition' (Evans 1990, p. 888), suggesting (cf. Aristotle's rules about tragedy) a good deal of artistry in Luke's mind. This impression is strengthened by the central role, in the double narrative we are to consider here, of recognition of One initially misidentified. Recognition (or 'discovery', Aristotle's ἀναγνώρισις) played an important part in classical tragedy and other fiction, much of which will have been familiar to some of Luke's readership.

[2] It has long been established that Luke thinks in terms of paired personalities or stories: see, e.g., Cadbury 1958, pp. 233f., and Flender 1967, p. 20. J. A. Fitzmyer (1985, pp. 1559f.) sees that vv. 36–53 contains a 'similar sequence' to that in the preceding section, but

limits the parallels to 'an appearance that is not comprehended, a revelation through exposition of Scripture and a meal, and the departure of the risen Christ'.

[3] Various lexical data might suggest that the conversation is accompanied by an element of acrimony. Συ$ητεῖν (v. 15) often has the sense of discussion between parties who disagree. The rare word ἀντιβάλλω (v. 17) strengthens this impression. The LXX, it is true, in its only use of this term, shows the neutral sense 'consider'. But Thucydides illustrates a literal sense, 'throw against . . . , return the shots'. Associations of words may convey an undertone in addition to the sense actually being used. And the two walkers' state of mind when they halt (they were σκυθρωποί, 'sullen' or 'sad') slightly reinforces a sense that the conversation had not been smooth.

[4] Διαλογισμός has, alongside a neutral sense ('consideration, reasoning'), a more aggressive one, 'arguing' (so H. G. Liddell and R. Scott, *A Greek-English Lexicon*, new edn rev. H. S. Jones (Oxford: Clarendon Press, 1925–40) [LSJ]) or 'hostile thoughts' (Evans), which prevails in New Testament usage: see Evans 1990, p. 220.

[5] Schubert 1954, p. 168, n. 13. It is assumed here that the majority reading at v. 51b is correct.

[6] It is worth noting that 'comparison (*sunkrisis*) is a common critical tool in this period [late antiquity], learned as an exercise in grammar schools' (Russell 1989, p. 300). Although in principle one compared one historical figure, or narrative about one, with another, it is possible that Luke's reader would have been alert to an invitation to compare these stories. (Normally this was done with a view to seeing which of two comparable figures or stories was the better, which hardly obtains here.)

[7] This rendering is warranted by the translators of the LXX, who 'employ this idiom [the use of the intransitive ἱστάναι] in reference to the advent of heavenly messengers' (Dillon 1978, p. 185).

[8] Many writers on this chapter agree that it is virtually impossible to separate Luke's composition from *Vorlagen* of some sort. In the present essay it is assumed that for all intents and purposes it can be read as Luke's creation.

[9] So LSJ.

[10] It tells a little in favour of this suggestion that the two stories exhibit the two sides of a simple chiasmus: 24.25-7 anticipates 44-6; between them come the two scenes of *anagnorisis* at vv. 31 and 39, giving a basic sequence of ABBA. So Tannehill 1986, p. 292.

[11] 9.22, 44; 18.31; 22.22, 37; perhaps we should add 12.50 and 13.33.

[12] Schubert 1954, p. 176.

[13] ibid.

[14] B. P. Robinson (1984, p. 484) believes that both in Emmaus and in Jerusalem a meal in the normal sense is described. But what sort of meal would it be when the person who had so mysteriously assumed the role of host suddenly disappears? It is surely hard to imagine, or to expect the original reader to imagine, that Cleopas and his friend simply made the best of a strange situation and ate their dinner, only then deciding that return to Jerusalem was the best course. Similarly, it is true that parallels can be invoked for ἐνώπιον + appropriate noun or pronoun implying consumption of a meal. But this does not mean, surely, that this is implied in every case where this construction is employed.

[15] See Kodell 1988, pp. 106-10.

[16] The suggestion has been made once or twice in this essay that Luke wished to tie together fairly closely the end of his first and the opening chapters of his second volume. This proposal finds one of its strongest supports in the correspondence between 24.21a and Acts 1.6. Both seem to allude to a political possibility rather than to a spiritual one, and thus form part of a very thin line of evidence relating the expectation of Jesus and his disciples to contemporary politics. To that extent the taking up of the former utterance in the latter is striking. Another correspondence worth noting is that between Luke 24.19 and Acts 2.22, which show in common Ἰησοῦ (-ν) τοῦ (τὸν) Ναζαρηνοῦ/Ναζωραῖον . . . ἀνήρ/ἄνδρα; and the rest of both verses continue with less specific parallels: δυνατός/δυνάμεσι, and a miraculous activity in the presence of the people.

[17] Dillon (1978, p. 53) sees the anonymous 'others' who surround the Eleven in this chapter as perhaps 'representative of the Church'. For whatever reason, Acts 1.2, 13f. seem to exclude all others from the apostolic circle apart from Mary and Jesus' brothers. Here, then, the 'bridge' between the volumes is faulty.

[18] The relation between Luke 24.36–43 and John 20.19–29 is not clear. Marshall and Evans think that 'the same tradition is reflected in both Gospels' (Marshall 1978, p. 901; cf. Evans 1990, p. 917).

[19] An earlier draft of this essay was read at the conference of New Testament teachers in Britain at St Andrews in 1993, and I am grateful for the discussion that followed it. I am also grateful for several helpful comments made by Professor C. F. Evans.

BIBLIOGRAPHY

Cadbury, H. J. 1958. *The Making of Luke-Acts*. 2nd edn. London and Naperville, IL.

Dillon, R. J. 1978. *From Eye-witnesses to Ministers of the Word*. Rome: Biblical Institute Press.

Evans, C. F. 1990. *Saint Luke*. London: SCM Press.

Fitzmyer, 1985. *The Gospel According to Luke X–XXIV*. Garden City, NY: Doubleday & Company.

Flender, H. 1967. *St Luke: Theologian of Redemptive History*. London: SPCK.

Kodell, J. 1988. *The Eucharist in the New Testament*. Wilmington, DE: Glazier.

Marshall, I. H. 1978. *The Gospel of Luke*. Exeter: Paternoster Press.

Robinson, B. P. 1984. 'The Place of the Emmaus Story in Luke-Acts', *NTS* 30: 481–97.

Russell, D. A. 1989. 'Greek Criticism in the Empire'. Chapter 10 of *The Cambridge History of Literary Criticism*, vol. 1: *Classical*

Criticism, ed. G. A. Kennedy. Cambridge: Cambridge University Press.

Schubert, Paul. 1954. 'The Structure and Significance of Luke 24'. In *Neutestamentliche Studien für Rudolf Bultmann*, ed. W. Eltester. Berlin: Topelmann.

Tannehill, R. C. 1986. *The Narrative Unity of Luke-Acts: A Literary Interpretation*, vol. 1: *The Gospel according to Luke*. Philadelphia: Fortress Press.

4

The Women's Resurrection Testimony

Judith Lieu

The witness of the women to the resurrection of Jesus, silenced perhaps already by Mark, and certainly silenced in the long history of the Church's refusal to give a public voice to women, has in recent years been rediscovered and reclaimed with an undisguised triumphalism. While the male disciples slink away in the face of Jesus' arrest and trial, and Peter denies all knowledge of him, the women remain faithfully by the cross; they tend the tomb in which he is laid, are the first recipients of the resurrection message, and are appointed as the first 'apostles', commissioned to proclaim that message. For some this is the natural climax of a ministry in which Jesus consistently ignored contemporary devaluation of a woman's status: 'perhaps the most remarkable instance of Christ's confidence in women was when he gave the first revelation of his risen life to one or more women'.[1] Put in this way this is, admittedly, a rather curious argument if we stop to ask where the initiative lay or who is the proper subject of the resurrection event – the women surely came of their own volition to the tomb, while the New Testament would affirm that it was God who raised Jesus and revealed him. For many others it is the key to the independent and determinative role of women in the earliest, and so in the most authentic, moments of the life and ministry of the early Church. These Galilean women disciples, who had steadfastly remained in Jerusalem, played a decisive role in articulating the resurrection faith and in gathering together the scattered and disillusioned disciples: 'they, therefore, were empowered to continue the movement and work of Jesus, the risen Lord'.[2] Thus, the genitive of the title of this essay is both subjective and objective: the testimony by the women to the resurrection, the testimony to (the) women by the resurrection.

In this light, the much-discussed absence of the empty tomb tradition from the early sermons of Acts and from the Pauline tradition, especially 1 Corinthians 15.1–7, acquires a new, slightly sinister, complexion, well captured in Rosemary Ruether's 'midrash' on the gospel story:

> Peter declared '. . . We, the men, must be in charge of this revelation. We must not let Mary and the other women take too much credit . . . Only men can gather a true community of Israel.
>
> 'They will fashion the Risen Jesus into a new Lord and Master to represent the heavenly Father and to rule upon the earth . . .'
> Mary shuddered. 'Perhaps something of this other vision will still get through the distortion. Other people, even women like myself, will glimpse something of the true vision, and they will recognize me as their sister.'[3]

Yet, one might continue, the vision embodied in the discovery of the empty tomb by the women was doomed, even without the opportunism of the first male disciples or of a Paul seeking credibility in the Hellenistic world. Expanding on the biblical text (Deut. 17.6; 19.15), Josephus has Moses prohibit women as witnesses 'because of the levity and rashness of their sex' (*Antiquities* IV.8.15 [219]), a disqualification that would ensure the derogation of the empty tomb tradition and its dependency on women, especially in competition with appearances to male witnesses. Indeed – and here is the sting in the tail – this disqualification even allows modern scholars to contend that the primary resurrection traditions were the appearance narratives, and that the empty tomb traditions found in the Gospels developed later in conjunction with an emphasis on the bodily resurrection, with the presence only of the gullible women as a spurious apologetic for the tradition's late emergence.

If the latter conundrum makes the women fallible witnesses for their own significance in the continuity of the Jesus movement beyond Jesus' death and in the earliest history of the Church, we may, with some relief and with general trends in New Testament study, turn from the 'historical Jesus' to the message of the individual Gospels and their own witness, albeit male-authored, to the life of the earliest Christian communities. What testimony do they allow the women at the empty tomb to offer to women?[4]

Here Mark, because rather than in spite of the brevity of the Gospel's (original) ending, has seemed to offer the most, often allowing a blurring of the boundaries between his own tradition and the elusive 'historical moment'. Indeed, the celebration of the faithful Galilean women disciples just sketched owes much to Mark. It is

Mark, well-known for the ambiguity of his presentation of the (male) disciples, who draws to our attention the women's faithful discipleship, 'following', and 'ministering', from Galilee to the cross (Mark 15.40-1); the repeated lists of names then invite us to follow them to watching the burial, approaching the tomb with the spices they have prepared, and so discovering the rolled away stone and the 'young man' with his proclamation, 'He is risen' (15.47; 16.1): 'the women disciples emerge as examples of suffering discipleship and true leadership. They are the apostolic eye-witnesses of Jesus' death, burial and resurrection.'[5] Yet – as a growing bibliography demonstrates – it seems there is no less ambiguity here, for the story ends as the women flee in terror-stricken silence (16.8): is this a proper awe when faced with the divine revelation, a temporary fear that, as the reader must know, was soon overcome, or a bleak judgement on even their failure and faithlessness at that supreme moment? Do the women, in awe or in fear, offer a paradigm for all readers who, likewise, in the midst of failure must rely on the certainty of Christ's promise, 'I go before you', or does Mark already, both through the passivity of the women in the narrative and through their disobedience to the command to 'Go and tell', signal the incipient devaluation of the resurrection testimony to and by women?[6]

Faced with such uncertainty, we must look elsewhere for confirmation of the apostolic witness of the women. Here John may appear to offer grounds for a more secure verdict with the account, which bears all the marks of being deliberately crafted by himself, of Jesus' appearance to Mary Magdalene (20.[1-2], 11-18). This Mary has exerted a long fascination on the imagination of the Church: in some gnostic writings she rivals the male disciples in intimacy with Jesus and in true insight into his mission; there are later traditions in which she is credited with apostolic missionary travels, and in Rosemary Ruether's 'midrash' quoted earlier she is both the sister of Martha (Luke 10.38-42) and the sole recipient of the transforming resurrection vision which vests in her the future hope of redemption.[7] Will John's testimony bear the weight laid upon it?

Mary Magdalene is the last of a sequence of women who achieve a rare prominence in this Gospel, each offering a model of faith, women who invite speculation about their counterparts within the elusive Johannine community – the Samaritan woman, Mary and Martha, the mother of Jesus.[8] Already in the earlier tradition taking the leading position in the group of women at the tomb (Mark 16.1),

Mary has been singled out here to become the sole focus of the narrative and dialogue – a typical Johannine device and not necessarily a historical echo.[9] Yet in John too we have met her once before, without comment or further identification, at the foot of the cross (John 19.25). There, however, in contrast to the earlier Synoptic traditions (Mark 15.40 = Matt. 27.56; cf. Luke 8.2), she does not take first place: that is reserved for the mother of Jesus, a shadowy figure in the Marcan scene, if there at all.[10] In John the mother of Jesus is the only woman whom we know to have been with Jesus in Galilee from the start of if not throughout his ministry (2.1–10, 12). At the cross the attention focuses on her: this 'hour' now marks the end of what was promised at the beginning which she initiated (2.4), and we do not hear of her again; she brackets the earthly ministry of Jesus. Mary Magdalene, positioned last in the group before the cross, is the only one of the women who will move into the future. So, when she comes to the tomb – and we are not told why, for she neither observed the burial nor brings spices – we cannot think of faithful discipleship through ministry and suffering. Unlike her Marcan sister, we cannot even speak of witness – yet – for she stood but did not watch at the cross: there was another who saw and witnessed (19.35).

It would be attractive if we could find in her coming empty-handed to the tomb a deliberate contrast with Nicodemus' devoted but ultimately misguided superfluity of spices, but there is nothing of this in the text, which seems rather to be preserving only the essential minimum of the tradition. She is, at least, still the first to come to the tomb and to find the stone rolled away. Does this now make her a witness? Without angelic prompting she runs to tell Peter and his Johannine shadow, the Beloved Disciple – who, we recall, was also by the cross. Yet all she can tell them is that 'they have taken the Lord from the tomb' – surely only an inference, and of course a false one, for she has yet to look into the tomb and discover for herself that it is empty. Instead it is the two male disciples who run to the tomb and look, acting out as they do so their own personal rivalry which need not trouble us here. What they see – the folded grave-clothes untouched by grave-robbers' violence – presumably counts as valid testimony to the departed Jesus; it is the Beloved Disciple, the true paradigm for John, who makes the proper response to what he sees – without need for interpretation or explanation, he believes (20.8). Yet that is not the end: there is an ambivalence about the adequacy of this testimony and faith; moreover, the two disciples neither receive a commission – for there is no one to give one – nor announce to anyone what they have seen: they return back home (20.10).

Mary, who up to now has acted only to give priority to Peter and the Beloved Disciple without too much violence to the earlier tradition, comes into her own. The incoherence between the two episodes points to the redactional activity behind the text as it now stands. So, without reference to what has gone before, we find her once more by the tomb, weeping, ready once more to assume the theft of the body. Only now does she peer in; only now, therefore, can she see what her Synoptic sisters saw, the heavenly messengers sitting where the body had lain[11] – so presumably they were not there to be seen by Peter and the Beloved Disciple. Yet these are no messengers; they ask but do not tell her whom she is seeking, neither do they offer her comfort nor confirm either the empty tomb or the resurrection (ctr. Mark 16.6).[12] For John there is only one who can make himself known. Mary turns from the tomb and from the angels, neither of which has anything to offer, and sees, but is as yet unable to *see*, Jesus; the initiative is, of course, his. In a Johannine context the question, 'Whom do you seek?' (20.15; cf. Mark 16.6 by the angel) addresses her as a disciple as in 1.38, where it leads Andrew and his companion to remain with Jesus. From now on she is 'one of his own': only when he addresses her no longer as 'woman' (as he also addressed his mother, 2.4; 19.26!), but by name, does she recognize his voice and turn to follow him (cf. 10.3–4).

She is not, however, allowed to cling on to him, as, perhaps, she is already doing. This verse (v. 17) is notoriously difficult to interpret: how does this prohibition relate to the assertion that he has not yet ascended to the Father, or to his later invitation to Thomas to test for himself his physical reality? Is the 'ascending' here spoken of that of which Jesus speaks elsewhere (3.12; 6.62)? However, these cruxes are not central for our purposes. If Jesus has yet unfinished business, so too does Mary. She is to go and tell 'my brothers', 'I am ascending to my father and your father, to my God and your God.' Immediately, she goes. It is this commission, given not by mere angels but by the risen Lord himself, and her obedient fulfilment of it, that have won her the epithet 'apostle of the apostles'.[13] In words that echo Paul's proud claim in 1 Corinthians 9.1, 'Am I not an apostle? Have I not seen our Lord Jesus?', she proclaims to the disciples, 'I have seen the Lord!' Others will make that same confession

(20.28; 21.7, 12), and the affirmation of what 'we have seen' stands at the heart of the Johannine witness (John 3.11; [1.14]; 1 John 1.1–3), but Mary stands at the head of all who share it.

Yet even here we cannot escape some ambiguity. Although 'my brothers' *could* be inclusive, we can be far from confident that it should be so read. Just as the commission of Mark 16.7 is ambiguous as to whether the 'you' who will see him includes the women who take the message, or is reserved for the twelve male disciples who receive it, so here we may wonder whether Mary is excluded from the declaratory '*your* father . . . and *your* God'. It seems over-optimistic to see her included in the 'new family of faith'.[14] Instead, we must ask whether, once she has given her testimony to Jesus' new brothers, who now will experience for themselves the risen presence of Jesus and receive the apostolic commission (20.21–3), her mission is completed. What further value does Mary Magdalene's testimony have? Indeed, when we look ahead to chapter 21 we find again the pattern of the inability to recognize Jesus until he makes himself known, but this time it is the Beloved Disciple who proclaims, 'It is the Lord!' (21.4, 7). It is not enough to appeal here to a later redaction that seeks the deliberate balancing (?neutralizing) of the Mary Magdalene tradition by the (male) Beloved Disciple. The Johannine testimony to Mary/of Mary carries within itself the seeds of its own vulnerability.

We may turn more briefly to the other two Gospels to ask if they have further testimony to offer. Luke has sometimes been credited with an interest in women, among other dispossessed groups, although the claim is based more on the presence of narratives involving women in this Gospel alone than on any explicit statements in their favour. He maintains from Mark – we need posit no other source – the continuity of the women from cross to burial to empty tomb, even heightening that continuity by having the women follow the transfer of Jesus' body to the tomb and make their preparations immediately with only their sabbath observance intervening. However, it is not until they actually return from the empty tomb and convey the tidings to the Eleven that their names are given (24.10), perhaps because it is at this point, as witnesses and messengers, that they come into their own. They serve too as witnesses because they not only find the rolled away stone, but also fail to find the body whose deposition they had observed (24.3; 23.55) – something Mark had left the angel to indicate. More particularly, the two men in angelic garb – before whom they fall in proper awe – remind them of words that they themselves had heard Jesus speak while they were in Galilee. As is well known, Luke converts the promise of a future vision in Galilee (Mark 16.7) to a prediction made in Galilee; he also converts it from a reminder of a promise made to the disciples to a reproach for forgetting the prophecy of coming death which 'he told you'. Thus they are witnesses not just to the empty tomb and to the angelic proclamation of the resurrection, but also to the fulfilment of Jesus' own predictions of the necessity of his death and resurrection as Son of Man. The women allow the reader to make the same journey of memory and understanding, even before the apostles make it (ctr. the apostles' dismissal of the women's story in 24.11).

While Mark reminds us of their names, Luke, as we have seen, postpones naming them and considers it more important to repeat that these women have come with him from Galilee (23.49, 55), and in Luke we do find them there already during the Galilean ministry (8.1–3). Yet there these women have not been called to follow, but rather have been healed of demonic possession and other ailments. 'The twelve' are with Jesus as he preaches and proclaims the gospel, while these women, three of whom are named, minister *to them* from their possessions – their 'ministry' is one of financial support and care for those (men) who preach.

Will the resurrection testimony offer them more than this? It seems not. Already at the cross they stand not alone, but with Jesus' acquaintances, where the closer echo of Psalm 38.11 adds little in their favour.[15] It is true that the women, who do recall the prophecy heard in Galilee and without further instruction rush to tell the Eleven, compare favourably both with the disbelief with which they are met (24.11) and with the Eleven's slowness to believe when they see Jesus himself (24.41). Yet by the end it is to the Eleven that is given the confirmation of their role as witnesses and the commission to go out when clothed with power. The women were the first to discover the tomb; perhaps they should have been believed, but they had not been told to give any message, and the Eleven 'and the rest' suffer no disadvantage from their disbelief. Instead, the dynamic of the narrative of Jesus' appearances soon leads us to forget the women's testimony.

Despite Matthew's changes to his Marcan model, the role of the women is not fundamentally altered. Matthew simplifies the list of names, retaining only those he recognizes; moreover, the women come only to observe the tomb, perhaps because any thought of anointing a body incarcerated behind an enormous stone seemed already too implausible. Yet by behaving more appropriately, the women become simply agents in a cosmic drama: their fear is unsurprising, occasioned by the earthquake and by the angelic inter-mediary who rolls away the stone, and they carry out their commis-sion 'to tell his disciples that he has risen from the dead' with proper joy. All sense of climax is postponed, as it still is even when Jesus himself meets the women. Again they respond appropriately, in wor-ship – whereas later some of the Eleven will remain uncertain (28.17); but even more clearly than the angel's, Jesus' message only concerns 'my brothers'[16] – it is they who are to go to Galilee and see Jesus. This reinforcement in the mouth of the risen Lord himself leaves no doubt: it is the final appearance of Jesus to the Eleven that is the true climax of the resurrection witness.

Various strategies are possible for dealing with what we have dis-covered. We may draw attention to the contrast between the responses of the women and those of the male disciples, which is often to the former's advantage: they do not show the doubt that afflicts the latter (Matt 28.17; Luke 24.11, 16, 24, 37; John 20.24; 21.4).[17] So too, the priority of the women's experience both chronologically and for the disciples' subsequent experience persists despite the narrative tendencies to establish the independence of the two. Yet this leaves us with the dilemma whether it is a priority other than that of the mid-wife or of a John the Baptist destined to say '(they) must increase, (we) must decrease'.

We can, of course, seek for 'the hidden women' in the narrative. Did the Johannine 'disciples' who received the commission in John 20.22-3 extend beyond the Twelve? Was the Lucan Cleopas' anonymous companion on the Emmaus road his wife (Luke 24.18)? Are there among Luke's 'eleven and the rest' a number of women, just as Acts lists the Eleven and appends, almost apologetically, 'with women and Mary the mother of Jesus and his brothers' (Acts 1.13-14)? Yet these women will remain phantoms without a voice; they can neither give testimony nor receive it to the benefit of others.

We may, of course – and our other strategies will drive us in this direction – approach our texts with grave suspicion. Each of the gospel traditions, with the probable exception of Mark, who adopts different tactics, (re)asserts the authority of male leadership by propelling the narrative towards its 'proper' climax in Jesus' appearance to and commission of his disciples. Although both Matthew and John make the women (Mary Magdalene) recipients of an appearance of Jesus, both use it to give dominical authority to the command to 'tell my brothers'. Both John and Luke (24.24, [?12]) have male disciples authenticate the empty tomb, while at the same time removing from that scene the command to tell others. New Testament tradition has lost all traces of these women on the pages of the history of the early Church, even of Mary Magdalene, whose persistence in the tradition sounds the strongest ring of truth: only the mother of Jesus of those at the cross (in John at least!) reappears in Acts. Are we not encountering the deliberate minimizing of the testimony of the women? The tradition was too resilient to be effaced, but it could be confined; restrained and retained so that the women have a voice, but a voice which declares its own limitations. The resurrection witness of the women is a witness to their own confinement.

Can we then reach behind this to the liberating moment, to the authentic resurrection witness? To ask this is to ask the most fundamental question about the resurrection. Perhaps the women too must heed Leslie Houlden's words 'that treating the resurrection in the traditional way has often led to spurious hope', and recognize in it rather an invitation to make their own 'an audacious and total hope in the face of life's unintelligible ambiguities of pain and joy'.[18]

Notes

[1] Pape 1977, p. 57.

[2] See Fiorenza 1983, pp. 138–40 (quotation from p. 139).

[3] Ruether 1983, pp. 10–11.

[4] On the individual gospel narratives see Witherington 1988, ad loc., who often tends to a more optimistic interpretation than that taken here.

[5] Fiorenza 1983, p. 321.

[6] See Trompf, 1972; Lincoln 1989. I am grateful to Ms Bridget Upton for bibliographical advice on the ending of Mark.

[7] See Pagels 1982, pp. 84–5; Fiorenza 1983, pp. 304–7; Moltmann-Wendel 1982, pp. 61–92; Ruether 1983, pp. 1–11; I have not seen Haskins 1993.

[8] I am grateful to my former research student Ms Julie Harris for stimulation to think more about these women.

[9] There may be an echo of the earlier tradition in 20.2, 'We do not know.'

[10] A number of scholars have identified her as 'the mother of James the Less and Joses', but Mark certainly does not make this explicit.

[11] Of course, in Mark there is only one, and we are not explicitly told that he is an angel.

[12] So Mahoney 1974, p. 274, who, while focusing on 20.1–10, has some useful insights into vv. 11–18.

[13] Fiorenza 1983, p. 332.

[14] Just as it is reading too much into the scene at 19.25–7 to see the new family there inaugurated.

[15] In Psalm 38.11 the 'at a distance' is negative. Note also that in Luke the disciples do not flee.

[16] There may be some link here with the Johannine tradition; but a link in the tradition cannot establish the authenticity of the episode.

[17] Witherington 1988 draws attention to this and to other instances of male–female role reversal.

[18] Houlden 1986, pp. 151–2. It is a privilege to be able to offer this essay to Leslie as a much-valued colleague.

BIBLIOGRAPHY

Fiorenza, E. Schüssler. 1983. *In Memory of Her: A Feminist Theological Reconstruction of Christian Origins*. London: SCM Press.

Haskins, S. 1993. *Mary Magdalen: Myth and Metaphor*. London: HarperCollins.

Houlden, J. L. 1986. *Connections: The Integration of Theology and Faith*. London: SCM Press.

Lincoln, A. 1989. 'The Promise and the Failure: Mark 16:7,8', *Journal of Biblical Literature* 108:283–300.

Mahoney, R. 1974. *Two Disciples at the Tomb: The Background and Message of John 20.1–10*. Bern & Frankfurt/M.: Lang.

Moltmann-Wendel, E. 1982. *The Women around Jesus*. London: SCM Press.

Pagels, E. 1982. *The Gnostic Gospels*. Harmondsworth: Penguin.

Pape, D. 1977. *God and Women: A Fresh Look at what the New Testament says about Women*. London and Oxford: Mowbrays.

Ruether, R. 1983. *Sexism and God-Talk: Towards a Feminist Theology*. London: SCM Press.

Trompf, G. 1972. 'The First Resurrection Appearance and the Ending of Mark's Gospel', *New Testament Studies* 18:308–30.

Witherington, B. 1988. *Women in the Earliest Churches*. SNTSMS 59. Cambridge: Cambridge University Press.

5
The Hermeneutics of the Gospel Resurrection Narratives

Stephen Barton

The Christian doctrine of the resurrection of Christ is a cause of recurrent debate and controversy, and understandably so, given its central place in the creeds and in Christian worship and self-understanding.[1] Naturally enough, the testimonies to the resurrection in the four canonical Gospels continue to be a prime focus of popular and scholarly interest in this regard.[2] The aim of this essay is to survey three recent approaches to the gospel accounts from within the guild of New Testament scholarship, with a view to assessing their strengths and weaknesses from a hermeneutical point of view. My hope is that by so doing, light may be cast on the question, what constitutes true interpretation of the resurrection? One of the three approaches I have chosen is that of Leslie Houlden in a study published in 1987.[3] It was my privilege to hear Leslie present his findings a year earlier when he delivered the Holy Week Lectures at Salisbury and Wells Theological College, where I was a tutor. But our friendship goes back to earlier days when I was a postgraduate student at King's College London. So it is a privilege to present this short study in his honour.

The first approach to interpreting the resurrection that I wish to touch on is the approach from the perspective of *feminism*. A useful example is an article published in 1979 by the New Testament scholar Elisabeth Fiorenza.[4] In this article, and again subsequently in her major book *In Memory of Her* (1983),[5] Fiorenza argues for a 'hermeneutic of suspicion' approach to the accounts of the resurrection on the grounds that the role and position of women in early Christianity have been obscured by 'the androcentric traditioning and redaction of the early Christian authors'.[6] She points out, for example, that 1 Corinthians 15.3–5 makes no mention at all of women as witnesses of the resurrection, whereas in the Gospels, the role of women is prominent and Mary Magdalene is identified (in Matthew and John) as the first person to encounter the risen Lord. Even in the Gospels, however, strong androcentric tendencies are evident. The Gospel of Luke, commonly held to be particularly sympathetic to women, is a case in point. Fiorenza argues that Luke's account of the resurrection betrays a clear redactional tendency to play down the contribution of women in order that apostolic status and identity be accorded to men only. So she says:

> Luke does not know of any appearance of the risen Jesus to women. His androcentric redaction attempts in a subtle way to disqualify the women as resurrection witnesses. He emphasizes that the twelve who heard about the empty tomb from the women did not believe them but judged their words as gossip (24:11) . . . Not until the appearance of the risen Lord before Simon (24:34) did the men believe in the resurrection of Jesus.[7]

At first sight, Fiorenza's interpretation seems a plausible reading of the text. Certainly, Luke wants to provide his readers with grounds for confidence in the truth of the Christian proclamation of the Lordship of Christ, and one of the ways he does so is by highlighting the testimony of the twelve and casting them (including the handling of the appointment of a successor to Judas) in a mainly positive light. But has he done so at the expense of the resurrection witnesses who were women? And if he has, is this a deliberate part of his intention as redactor of the tradition, as Fiorenza argues?

A number of considerations give reason for caution. First, it is surprising, given Luke's widely acknowledged interest in the role of women in the ministry of Jesus and the life of the early Church,[8] that he should pull his punches when it comes to the resurrection. In fact, Luke, no less than the other evangelists, is quite emphatic about the presence of women and the significant role they play: they follow Jesus from Galilee; they take care to see the tomb where he is buried; they prepare spices; they observe the sabbath rest; they return to the tomb to embalm the corpse at the earliest opportunity allowed by law; they are the privileged recipients of an angelophany; they remember Jesus' teaching about his death and resurrection; and, unlike the women in Mark, they do not keep silent, but return and testify to the eleven 'and to all the rest' what they have seen (Luke 23.55–24.9). Nor does Luke submerge their identities for fear of distracting attention from the (male) apostles. On the contrary, as if to confirm the women's testimony to the resurrection, he concludes their account with a kind of signature: 'Now it was Mary Magdalene and Joanna and Mary the mother of James and the other women with them who told this to the apostles' (Luke 24.10). It is remarkable that Fiorenza has not drawn more careful attention to this very considerable amount of material, not least because it is the kind of material that can be read quite legitimately in a way that is by no means antagonistic to the feminist commitment to 'making women visible' which Fiorenza herself seeks to champion.

Second, it may be questioned whether the feminist agenda and the hermeneutic of suspicion Fiorenza brings to the text make possible an adequate hearing of what Luke is trying to say in his telling of the resurrection. For example, is the refusal of the apostles to believe the testimony of the women (Luke 24.11) really Luke's way of disqualifying the women as resurrection witnesses? Why, then, has Luke gone to such trouble to narrate at length the women's discovery of the empty tomb and the angelophany to them? Is it not the *apostles* who are cast in a negative light by their unbelief, a motif common to all four Gospels? And ought we not to read the Emmaus Road appearance story (Luke 24.13–35), with its *repetition* of the episode of the angelophany to the women (vv. 22–4), as a reinforcement and confirmation of what has been reported first by them? Such queries raise serious doubts about the adequacy of Fiorenza's interpretation. In brief, where Luke wants to bring his story of Jesus to a triumphant climax with the announcement of the resurrection confirmed by the multiple testimonies of both women and men to that event, Fiorenza reads the text as little more than a rather devious weapon for use in patriarchal power play in the Church at the end of the first century. One does not have to be unsympathetic to the concerns of feminism to be resistant to a hermeneutic of suspicion that results in a reading of Luke which runs so strongly against the grain of the text, restricts the interest of the text to the narrow (though not necessarily illegitimate) question of sexual politics, and paradoxically overlooks evidence conducive of a much more positive evaluation even in feminist terms.

What we have here, then, is a particularly clear case of a model for the interpretation of the resurrection that very clearly serves – or is *intended* to serve – the interests of a particular community of interpretation. There are grounds for thinking, however, that an adequate understanding of the resurrection is not best served by the method which Fiorenza has adopted, and that feminist interests themselves may not be best served by this approach either. The strength of

Fiorenza's approach is that she puts her hermeneutical cards on the table and raises for serious consideration an important issue that has largely been overlooked until recently, the effect of androcentric bias on resurrection tradition and on the formation of early church polity. The weakness of her approach is that the interests her interpretation is trying to serve lead to a very partial and tendentious reading of the tradition.[9] It is as if the search for largely hidden androcentric forces assumed to lie beneath the surface of Luke's narrative takes the place of attending in an open and sympathetic way to what lies on the surface.[10]

The reference just above to consideration of the surface level of the text brings us to a second way of interpreting the resurrection accounts that has come into vogue in the last decade or so. This is the attempt to interpret the resurrection of Jesus according to the canons of *literary criticism* rather than the canons of historical criticism. What is important here is not so much what lies behind the text, but what are the dynamics within the text itself, and what takes place on this side of the text, in the encounter between text and reader. To put it in terms of the issue of the meaning of the text, literary-critical approaches raise the question, is the meaning of a Gospel something only *extrinsic* to it (to do with what the author intended, or with the degree of correspondence between what the text says and what actually happened, for instance), or is it also something *immanent* to the text as text, where what is important is how the text communicates to the reader, its poetics?

There are significant gains to be had from this approach, not least for the interpretation of the resurrection. For instance, whereas Fiorenza's reading and others like it draw attention *away* from Luke's narrative, both by comparing it disparagingly with other texts and by situating it in relation to a hypothetical historical context of early church politics, a literary approach focuses attention on an appreciation of the text itself and how meaning arises in the encounter between the reader (including the feminist reader!) and the text. Also, whereas conventional interpretation of the resurrection tends to grind to a halt over disagreements of a historical kind about what actually happened and whether or not the texts (understood in this case as *sources*) are reliable given the 'disagreements' between them, a literary approach opens up the possibility that resurrection faith has at least as much to do with aesthetic appreciation and the acknowledgement of a story as 'followable' and 'habitable'.[11] Related to this is the further point that, because historical-critical approaches attempt to see *through* the text to the events they describe or to the traditioning process by which the text evolved into its present form, the tendency from a religious point of view is that the status of the text *as Scripture* is undermined. Literary approaches, precisely because they encourage a close reading of the text itself and an appreciation of how the text 'works' or 'speaks', are more amenable (in some ways at least) to a religious understanding of the Bible as God's lively oracles.[12]

But we need to look at a specific example to see what might be involved, and to consider its strengths and weaknesses. Our previous case study was Fiorenza on the resurrection in Luke. Now we turn to Mark Stibbe's very recent narrative-critical commentary on John, with particular interest in his interpretation of the resurrection stories in John 20-1.[13] This is clearly a new genre of biblical commentary. Gone are lengthy introductions on matters of authorship, purpose, theology, historical setting, history-of-religions background, text-critical matters, and so on – matters largely of 'background', and hence extrinsic to the text as text. In their place we find categories for the interpretation of texts drawn from narrative criticism: context (understood in literary more than historical terms); structure or literary design; form or genre; plot; time (both narrative and story time); author, narrator and (three kinds of) reader; characterization; literary devices; and irony. Consistent treatment of John in these terms makes up what Stibbe calls appropriately, a 'text-immanent perspective' on the Gospel.[14]

How does John's account of the resurrection look from this perspective? A preparatory answer comes in Stibbe's discussion of 'truth value'. After affirming that the truth value of the Gospel is related to its value as historical testimony to Jesus, Stibbe goes on to describe the *kind* of history represented by John as 'charismatic history' or 'poetic history'. He says:

> What is remarkable about John's story is its fusion of poetry and history, of the universal and the particular. John's story of Jesus is not just an historical account of the life of Jesus . . . It is also and above all a narrative in which the author, inspired by the Spirit of truth, evokes the transcendent significance of Jesus from the traditions concerning his earthly works and words. It is a work of poetic history.[15]

The reading that follows is full of literary insight and imagination that brings the text alive at almost every turn. We are introduced *inter alia* to ways in which John 20 and 21 form an inclusio with John 1; the parallelism between the conclusion of the Book of Signs at the tomb of Lazarus and the conclusion of the Book of the Passion at the (empty) tomb of Jesus; the way in which the various episodes at the tomb explore the theme of the relation between seeing and believing in the face of the elusiveness of Jesus; and the way chapter 21 resolves the tension surrounding the hitherto highly ambivalent portrayal of Peter. On the latter, Stibbe uses a psychological model to striking effect. Referring to Peter's decision to go fishing (in 21.3), he says:

> At a psychological level, the only explanation is that Peter is in a state of what is called 'denial'. Having failed Jesus so obviously in 18.15–27, he now seeks to suppress and even obliterate the shame in his life by reverting to 'life before Christ', to fishing. He seeks to deny the three denials. This attempt to fill his 'hole in the soul' with work fails dismally. The narrator laconically remarks that 'they caught nothing'. Peter's gesture is a futile one.[16]

There is no doubt that this way of reading John liberates us from a heavy literalism often tied to an empiricist agenda according to which the text gives direct access to 'what actually happened'. The appeal instead is to aesthetic appreciation of a story artfully told. But at this very point important questions arise. Stibbe claims that John's narrative is 'poetic history'. The overriding impression left by his commentary, however, is of poetry *rather than* history. And there is good reason why this is so. The tools of interpretation that Stibbe uses inevitably skew his reading in that direction. The result is a sense that something is missing. That 'something', putting it bluntly, has to do with history and theology. For it is not clear that (or how) narrative criticism is capable of putting us in touch with the astonishing realities to which the evangelist is attempting to bear witness – the resurrection of Jesus from the dead, the identification of Jesus as 'Lord' and 'God', the gift of the Holy Spirit, the call to mission, the communion with Jesus in the shared meal, the rehabilitation of Peter, the coming into being of a Christian scriptural testimony, and so on. Categories like characterization, context, plot, and 'reality effects' are interesting and illuminating in some ways, but in other ways they seem anodyne, almost banal, and in danger of what Brevard Childs describes as rendering the witness of the text 'theologically mute'.[17]

Clearly, the issue turns at least in part on what a particular reading of John and his account of the resurrection is for.[18] If the intention is literary and aesthetic appreciation, then literary-critical tools are appropriate and Stibbe's reading is a model of its kind. But if the intention is (say) of a more traditional Christian kind, where historical-existential questions and credal affirmations to do with Jesus and the resurrection are inescapable, then the referential and communal dimensions of the resurrection narratives have to be faced and tools of a more literary-historical-theological kind have to be used.[19] And it could be claimed with some justification that the latter approach is more appropriate for the interpretation of a text of Christian Scripture like the Gospel of John, itself a literary-historical-theological kind of text.

Our case studies so far have taken interpretations of the resurrection according to Luke and John. We turn now to one that focuses on the other two canonical Gospels, Matthew and Mark. I refer to Leslie Houlden's recent redaction-critical study, *Backward into Light*. At first sight, Houlden's work looks very different from that of Fiorenza in particular. Nevertheless, it is worth observing that they overlap in certain respects as well. For example, even though Houlden betrays no explicit interest in a hermeneutics of suspicion foundation for interpretation, he like Fiorenza uses (redaction-critical) tools that allow him to play one text or tradition off against another. Where Fiorenza plays Luke off against both Paul and the other evangelists, Houlden plays Matthew off against Mark. The result, it could be claimed, is an interpretation indebted to a hermeneutic of suspicion in all but name. The object of suspicion in Fiorenza's case is androcentric redaction of the tradition. In Houlden's case, the object of suspicion is Matthew's Gospel, or, more accurately, the kind of vision or spirituality represented by the way Matthew handles his Marcan source.

The thesis is presented with characteristic lucidity. The first clue is the title, *Backward into Light*. Working within the well-established redaction-critical consensus according to which Mark's Gospel is chronologically prior to Matthew's even though Matthew comes first in the New Testament canon, Houlden argues that Matthew's redaction of Mark represents a retrograde step, so that reading from Matthew to Mark is a movement 'backward into light'. The second clue is the chapter headings, which reveal the kernel of his thesis. According to Houlden, the move from Mark's earlier passion and resurrection narrative to the reworking by Matthew is a move 'from gift to assault' (ch. 3), 'from resignation to requital' (ch. 4), and 'from intimation to demonstration' (ch. 5). So, in the final chapter, significantly entitled 'Villains and Realists', Houlden sums up his case this way:

> In each of the comparisons made between Mark's and Matthew's telling of the story of Jesus' death and resurrection, and in the resulting reflections, Matthew has come off badly . . . I have found myself (there is no denying) awarding prizes to Mark and presenting Matthew as, however understandably, the villain of the piece, inferior and even reprehensible at almost every turn. Time and again, he has seemed to spoil the purity of Mark's teaching as embodied in his story.[20]

If we ask how Matthew has spoiled Mark's purity, Houlden answers along the following lines.[21] Whereas Mark's passion and resurrection appear to be shrouded in mystery and ambiguity – witness the cry of abandonment at Mark 15.34 or the tantalizingly abrupt ending at 16.8 – allowing faith to arise only as 'gift', in Matthew's reworking everything is much more explicit, public and indubitable – the apocalyptic portents, angelophany at the tomb, explicit appearances of the risen Christ, and so on – such that now faith arises not as gift: rather, it is bludgeoned out of his readers as a kind of 'assault'. So Matthew has spoiled Mark by satisfying the 'desperate will to know', by providing a clear basis for assurance, and by giving access to that corrupting power that comes from certainty. Houlden does not mince words here: 'Matthew, with his earthquakes and his angels descending from heaven, is a somewhat coarse protagonist of sheer and overwhelming grace, working on the senses first rather than the heart . . . Mark's unwillingness to insist tells us of a more godly kind of power.'[22]

It can be fairly concluded that Houlden's interpretation of the passion and resurrection in Matthew and Mark is indebted in its own way just as strongly to a hermeneutic of suspicion approach to the text as Fiorenza's. If her 'villain' is Luke, his is Matthew. The obvious question follows: is this approach justified? First, it is obviously not the only possible approach. Instead of a hermeneutic of suspicion, why not a hermeneutic of trust?[23] According to the latter, the Gospels would be approached differently. Instead of playing off one against the other, the interpreter might seek to discern how the gospel accounts *complement* one another. Arguably, this is appropriate given both the fourfold gospel shape of the New Testament canon and the traditional Christian reverence for the Gospels as Scripture. What this involves is not, however, a return to rationalistic attempts to harmonize the various details of the gospel accounts.[24] Rather, it is a question of asking, in a way that is sympathetic to the tradition, what each gospel testimony contributes to resurrection faith and Christian living.[25]

Second, Houlden's preference for the earlier Mark over the later Matthew seems to have as (unexamined) premises both a conflict model of Christian origins and a 'decline and fall' theory of church history. Mark represents light; Matthew is an obscuring of the light, a 'spoiling' of Mark's pristine 'purity'. Ironically, in terms of the spirituality Houlden is concerned to commend, with its strong preference for 'ambiguity and profound mysteriousness', 'complexity and unfathomability',[26] there is something 'fundamentalist' here: what Robert Wilken called 'the myth of Christian beginnings',[27] now in a more liberal, individualist guise, perhaps. Where the fundamentalist impulse is to go back behind the Church to the Bible, Houlden has just taken this impulse a stage further. Now it is a summons within the biblical corpus to go back behind Matthew to Mark! But the basic hermeneutical strategy is the same. Indeed, it may be no coincidence that Matthew is commonly described as 'the *ecclesiastical* Gospel'. Seen this way, going back behind Matthew to Mark is in itself a way of going back behind the Church to the earlier, apparently more authoritative source in the interest of individual conscience and modernist sensibility.

Third, Houlden's approach suffers from what Hans Frei called 'the eclipse of biblical narrative'.[28] The redaction-critical comparison of Matthew and Mark is used to identify the respective spiritualities of their authors in a way that *separates* the meaning of the resurrection narratives from their literary forms and imposes a *univocal* sense restricted to what the original author behind the text (is thought to have) intended. The result is that there is little scope left for the point made in more reader-oriented and also explicitly theological approaches that the text may have true meanings above and beyond that intended by the author. Instead of opening Matthew's narrative up in a way that is challenging and life-giving – which is what

Christian readers generally expect the reading of Scripture to do – Houlden's interpretation invites only a closing down and a turning away. The pre-eminence accorded (a particular reading of) Mark is bought at what many would view as too high a price.[29]

By way of conclusion, it is worth raising the question, what might constitute a way of interpreting the gospel resurrection narratives more adequate than those surveyed here? Clearly, this in turn begs the question, adequate for what? Answers to both these questions obviously demand more space than this short essay can afford. But I am impressed by the kind of position advanced by Nicholas Lash in his essay 'What Might Martyrdom Mean?'[30]

The import of Lash's argument is as follows. Understanding what an ancient text meant and what it might mean today are mutually interdependent activities. It is not a matter of approaching the text as a thing to be 'consumed' according to taste. Neither, to change the metaphor, is it a matter of seeking to understand the past like a tourist travelling in foreign lands. The act of interpretation is not like that. Meaning is not just 'there' to be observed and analysed. Rather, interpretation involves judging and being judged, and questions of truth cannot responsibly be passed over. The implication with respect to the gospel resurrection accounts is that understanding what they say cannot be done without some kind of *prior* understanding of what resurrection itself is about and a commitment to rendering the meaning(s) of the resurrection in a faithful way. To put it differently, a wise reading of the accounts of the resurrection requires that they be read in the light of a resurrection hermeneutic – that is, an understanding and experience both of the life of the resurrection and of 'communities of resurrection' which help to foster a life-transforming (rather than a reductionist or even nihilist) approach to the text.

Following on from this, it is crucial to recognize that basic to Christian interpretation is not abstract 'meaning' which can be held at arm's length, but *patterns of human action*. Lash puts it this way:

> I would wish to argue that the fundamental form of the Christian interpretation of scripture is, in the concrete, the life, the activity and organization of the Christian community, and that Christian practice consists (by analogy with the practical interpretation of dramatic, legal and musical texts) in the performance or enactment of the biblical text: in its 'active reinterpretation'.[31]

With respect to the resurrection, this implies that interpretation is primarily a practical issue, and that judgements about the meaning and truth of the Gospels' witness to the resurrection need to be made in the practical and communal domain, over and above (but by no means excluding) considerations of a historical, literary, or theoretical kind.[32]

Notes

[1] I am grateful to several Durham colleagues for reading and commenting on an earlier draft of this paper: Colin Crowder, Walter Moberly, and Peter Selby.

[2] For a recent survey article, see G. R. Osborne, 'Resurrection', in Joel B. Green et al. (eds), *Dictionary of Jesus and the Gospels* (Leicester: IVP, 1992), pp. 673–88.

[3] J. L. Houlden, *Backward into Light: The Passion and Resurrection of Jesus according to Matthew and Mark* (London: SCM Press, 1987).

[4] E. S. Fiorenza, '"You are not to be called Father": Early Christian History in a Feminist Perspective', *Cross Currents* 39 (1979), pp. 301–23.

[5] E. S. Fiorenza, *In Memory of Her* (London: SCM Press, 1983).

[6] Fiorenza, 'You are not to be called Father', p. 306.

[7] ibid., p. 308.

[8] For recent discussion and further bibliography, see M. R. D'Angelo, 'Women in Luke-Acts: A Redactional View', *Journal of Biblical Literature* 109 (1990), pp. 441–61.

[9] For more extended discussion along similar lines, see A. C. Thiselton, *New Horizons in Hermeneutics* (London: HarperCollins, 1992), pp. 442–52.

[10] Striking by contrast is another interpretation of the resurrection which is indebted also to a liberationist hermeneutic, that of Leonardo Boff, *Jesus Christ Liberator* (ET; London: SPCK, 1980), pp. 121–

38. Of course, his concern is not a specifically feminist one. But it could be argued that his interpretation, focusing as it does on central theological issues of Christology, eschatology, and anthropology, provides a more adequate (systematic theological) model for feminist hermeneutics of the resurrection to follow.

11 Cf. the seminal work by S. E. Fowl and L. G. Jones, *Reading in Communion* (London: SPCK, 1991).

12 See further R. Morgan with J. Barton, *Biblical Interpretation* (Oxford: Oxford University Press, 1988), chs 6–7.

13 M. W. G. Stibbe, *John* (Sheffield: Sheffield Academic Press, 1993), pp. 198–215. The theoretical basis for his narrative-critical reading of John is to be found in his earlier monograph, *John as Storyteller: Narrative Criticism and the Fourth Gospel* (Cambridge: Cambridge University Press, 1992).

14 Stibbe, *John*, p. 18.

15 ibid., p. 19.

16 ibid., p. 210.

17 B. S. Childs, *The New Testament as Canon* (London: SCM Press, 1984), p. 209.

18 See further M. G. Brett, 'Four or Five Things to do with Texts: A Taxonomy of Interpretative Interests', in D. Clines et al. (eds), *The Bible in Three Dimensions* (Sheffield: JSOT Press, 1990), pp. 357–77.

19 A good example of the latter would be P. Carnley, *The Structure of Resurrection Belief* (Oxford: Clarendon Press, 1987).

20 Houlden, *Backward into Light*, p. 66.

21 Due to the word limit for the essay, I will focus on ibid., ch. 3, 'From Gift to Assault'.

22 ibid., p. 36.

23 Cf. F. Watson in his Introduction to F. Watson (ed.), *The Open*

Text: New Directions for Biblical Studies? (London: SCM Press, 1993), p. 10.

24 A recent example of this genre is J. Wenham, *Easter Enigma: Are the Resurrection Stories in Conflict?* (Exeter: Paternoster Press, 1984).

25 For one attempt along these lines, see S. C. Barton, *The Spirituality of the Gospels* (London: SPCK, 1992).

26 The phrases come in Houlden, *Backward into Light*, p. 34.

27 R. L. Wilken, *The Myth of Christian Beginnings* (London: SCM Press, 1971).

28 H. W. Frei, *The Eclipse of Biblical Narrative* (New Haven, CT: Yale University Press, 1974).

29 For an argument along similar lines, see D. C. Steinmetz, 'The Superiority of Pre-Critical Exegesis', *Ex Auditu* 1 (1985), pp. 74–82.

30 The essay was first published in 1981 and republished subsequently in his collection of essays, *Theology on the Way to Emmaus* (London: SCM Press, 1986), pp. 75–92.

31 ibid., p. 90.

32 For earlier discussion along these lines, see Peter Selby, *Look for the Living: The Corporate Nature of Resurrection Faith* (London: SCM Press, 1976), and Rowan Williams, *Resurrection* (London: Darton, Longman & Todd, 1982).

6

Did Jesus of Nazareth Rise from the Dead?[1]

Michael Goulder

The Christians of the New Testament believed in the resurrection of
Jesus for two quite distinct reasons: first, a series of people thought
that they had *seen* him; and second, there were reports of a more con-
cretely *physical* kind – the tomb was empty and his body had gone, or
his disciples touched him, or he ate with them, and so on. The evidence for the first basis, the appearances, is very early: it goes back
at least to what Paul was taught when he was converted, a couple of
years after the crucifixion. The stories about the empty tomb, the
touching and the eating, all come to us from much later – the empty
tomb is first spoken of in Mark, writing about forty years after the
crucifixion. There are excellent reasons for being sceptical about both
of these two bases of belief, but they are quite different. The
appearances are to be explained psychologically; the concrete physical
details arise from disputes within the Church.

If someone tells us they have seen a friend from another world, we
may speak of an appearance, if we accept what they say, or an appari-
tion if we doubt it. How do we decide which? Well, we may know of
similar events that we think we do understand; and we will follow the
general principle that it has proved sensible to trust this-worldly
explanations rather than ones with ghosts, demons, etc. Here is a
statement by Susan Atkins, who was involved with Charles Manson in
a dreadful series of murders in California in the 1970s:

> The thoughts tumbled over and over in my mind. Can society for-
> give one for such acts against humanity? Can it take this guilt off
> my shoulders? Can serving the rest of my life in prison undo
> what's been done? Can anything be done?
>
> I looked at my future, my alternatives. Stay in prison. Escape.
> Commit suicide. As I looked, the wall in my mind was blank. But
> somehow I knew there was another alternative. I could choose the
> road many people had been pressing on me. I could follow Jesus.

As plainly as daylight came the words, 'You have to decide. Behold, I stand at the door and knock.' Did I hear someone say that? I assume I spoke in my thoughts, but I'm not certain, 'What door?'

'You know what door and where it is, Susan. Just turn around and open it, and I will come in.' Suddenly, as though on a movie screen, there in my thoughts was a door. It had a handle. I took hold of it and pulled. It opened. The whitest, most brilliant light I had ever seen poured over me. In the center of the flood of brightness was an even brighter light. Vaguely, there was the form of a man. I knew it was Jesus. He spoke to me – literally, plainly, matter-of-factly spoke to me in my 9-by-11 prison cell: 'Susan, I am really coming into your heart to stay.' I was distinctly aware that I inhaled deeply, and then, just as fully, exhaled. There was no more guilt! It was gone. Completely gone! The bitterness, too, instantly gone! How could this be? For the first time in my memory I felt clean, fully clean, inside and out. In 26 years I had never been so happy.[2]

We may speak of Susan Atkins' experience as a *conversion vision*. Psychologists would say she had hallucinations, both in hearing voices and in seeing things.[3] But the point is that she was able to achieve a deep and satisfying new orientation to life, a conversion, which expressed itself in the form of a vision. We often read about this sort of experience in religious literature – Isaiah's vision of God in the Temple, for instance – but it is also common with non-religious conversions, like Arthur Koestler's conversion to Marxism in 1931.[4] That is what was experienced by Peter on Easter Day, when he saw the Lord, or by Paul outside Damascus. We speak of the conversion of Paul, and we might well speak of the conversion of Peter, for Jesus said to him, 'When you are converted, strengthen your brethren' (Luke 22.32) – he was no longer a boastful, sleeping denier of his Lord, but a courageous champion of the faith, to martyrdom.

Psychologists have suggested various theories to account for such conversions, the cognitive dissonance theory,[5] for instance; but we do not for the moment need to claim that we fully understand such experiences; it is enough that we see the general thrust of what is happening. Faced with such a bleak future, Susan Atkins found a resolution that enabled her to see herself in a different light, and lose her burden of guilt. Guilt may quite often be associated with such dramatic conversions.[6] Koestler says:

> Pacing up and down in my bedroom, I had the sudden impression that I was looking down from a height at the track along which I had been running. I saw myself with great clarity as a sham and a phoney, paying lip-service to the Revolution that was to lift the world from its axis, and at the same time leading the existence of a bourgeois careerist, climbing the worm-eaten ladder of success, playing poker and landing in unsought beds.[7]

Perhaps Peter had a similar experience on Easter Saturday. He might well see himself as a sham and a phoney, paying lip-service to the kingdom of God which was to lift the earth from its axis, and climbing the worm-eaten ladder of self-preservation. So even if we do not have a full theory to explain conversion, we know what we are talking about; as Starbuck said, 'however inexplicable, the facts of conversion are a natural process'.[8]

Another feature often found in association with conversion is the accumulation of pressures.[9] Susan Atkins had been through the trauma of the trials, and was now facing a life in gaol. Koestler had just lost three months salary at poker, found his newly mended car frozen, and gone to bed with a woman he disliked. Peter had been humiliated for his boasting at the Supper, for his sleeping in Gethsemane, by his triple denial in the High Priest's courtyard – and then found that Jesus, whom he had thought to be the Christ, had been crucified to death. Paul was making a considerable journey, and it was midday. Or another important consideration is the upheaval of a recent bereavement. It is quite a common occurrence for widows and widowers who have been deeply attached to their partners to have experiences of them soon after their death; a Welsh GP reports that as many as 45% of his patients recently widowed have seen or heard their dead partners.[10] Peter and the others were certainly very attached to Jesus. Or again, violent conversions are correlated with matters like being easily hypnotized,[11] or having had an intense religious upbringing.[12] Both Peter and Paul are reported as having had other visions – Peter at the Transfiguration and at Cornelius' visit; Paul by his own account had 'an excess of revelations' (2 Cor. 12.7). Paul also tells us that he had been a Pharisee in his youth (Phil. 3.5).

Of course, not all of these features apply to both Peter and Paul. We know less about Peter as a character, but more about the events immediately before his conversion; the series of blows to his self-image, the guilt, the bereavement, all make a conversion vision a plausible explanation for his experience. We know less about the immediate events of Paul's conversion, but more about him as a character. His upbringing, his intensity, his liability to visions are all testified in his own writing. Furthermore, we know that he was going to Damascus to persecute the Church there, and this level of intense feeling is also correlated with conversion. Carl Gustav Jung writes about Paul:

> Fanaticism is only found in individuals who are compensating secret doubts. The incident on the way to Damascus marks the moment when the unconscious complex of Christianity broke through into consciousness. Unable to conceive of himself as a Christian on account of his resistance to Christ, he became blind, and could only regain his sight through complete submission to Christianity. Psychogenetic blindness is, according to my experience, always due to unwillingness to see; that is, to understand and to realise something that is incompatible with the conscious attitude. Paul's unwillingness to see corresponds with his fanatical resistance to Christianity.[13]

Some New Testament scholars would rather trust Heikki Räisänen than Jung; and he has rightly derided the unwillingness of Pauline scholars to consider psychological motivations.[14] He cites J. C. Beker, 'How could the Christophany have been so traumatic and so radical in its consequences unless it lit up and answered a hidden quest in [Paul's] soul?'[15] He thinks that the passages about the law as a yoke, and of 'not receiving a spirit of bondage to be again in fear' suggest that Paul had experienced Judaism as bondage and fear himself. My own suspicion is that Paul had had a Gentile friend in his youth, and that the connection of his conversion with his call to evangelize the Gentiles has to do with some such experience. The fact that we cannot provide a full account of a psychic event two millennia ago does nothing to commend theological dogmatism; even if speculative, a natural explanation is to be preferred.

We may speak of Peter's and Paul's experiences as primary; they both started from scratch, so to speak – the appearances to the apostles or the five hundred brethren that Paul mentions are secondary in the sense that these groups have already heard, and perhaps credited, the reports of Jesus being alive. We have many instances of this kind of experience – large groups of people who have seen the statue of Mary at Knock moving, or UFOs, or experiments with groups where expectation affects perception in ways that can be repeated. I cite here a series of appearances of Sasquatch, or Bigfoot, an eight-foot hairy, evil-smelling monster, over three months in the autumn of 1977 in S. Dakota.[16] Sasquatch had been a legend for a century further west, and his exploits were shown in a B film in S. Dakota in the summer of 1977. He was then sighted in the area, first by Indian youths, then by white ranchers, then by hundreds of people. His giant footprints were found in the mud. The police went after him. Experts from the Bureau of Indian Affairs were unable to explain the phenomena. Traps were set for him, with recordings of women's voices being played all night; but Bigfoot was clever. He was reported at length in the local papers daily, and even made national television.

The Bigfoot phenomenon is explained as *collective delusion* by Smelser's value-added theory.[17] Such things cannot happen without (1) a close-knit community in which rumour can spread easily, and which is isolated from the sceptical normal world. This was the case in the settlements in S. Dakota, and also in the primitive Church. (2) There has to be structural strain – anxiety, the lack of clear criteria; and the presence of poorly educated people, and of women, helps. The early Church was anxious; its doors were locked for fear of the Jews; and it was not well-educated either. (3) It has to be easy for a generalized belief to become specific. The Sasquatch legend was part of Indian culture, and the film was recent. In the same way, many Jews believed the dead would rise when God's kingdom came, and Jesus had recently proclaimed the advent of the kingdom. (4) There have to be precipitating factors – the film, the press with Bigfoot; Jesus' execution, Peter's conversion vision with the Church. (5) The community has to mobilize for action. There were constant meetings over Bigfoot, the setting of traps, police-hunts, etc. The Church met constantly for prayer in Acts 1.

(6) There has to be a pay-off for the sightings. If you sighted Bigfoot, you were the centre of attention; people spoke about you; the press sought you out. If you sighted Jesus, you confirmed the Church's hopes, and your own. You were an accepted member of the kingdom of God. Instead of accepting that you had been totally mistaken, that all Jesus' talk of the kingdom had been eyewash, that you must go back to the old life amid the derision of sceptics, another

prospect opened. Despite the crucifixion, Jesus was right after all! The end of the world had begun! The first of the dead had been resurrected! It is not difficult to see that such a visionary experience would have an enormous pay-off; and it is easy to parallel cases where people have had similar hallucinations with much less to gain.

The response of religious people to such explanations is usually rather undisturbed. You have shown a possible psychological mechanism, it may be said; but you have not affected the substance of the resurrection claim. The apostles actually saw the Lord risen from the dead, and that experience changed them from beaten men to heroes. I need to stress, therefore, that the psychological explanations make the supernatural claims otiose. It is as if two people were looking at a man foaming on the ground. One says, 'He has epilepsy', the other, 'He has a demon.' The first man calls a doctor, who administers a drug, and the patient recovers. The second man may say, 'I agree that he has epilepsy; but he also has a demon.' But the demon has now become unnecessary, and should be dispensed with. We do not need the physical resurrection of Jesus to explain the apostles' change from beaten men to heroes; that is fully accounted for by their having been converted – that is what conversion means.

For the empty tomb, the touching and eating, we move into a different area. At first, it seems, the explanation accepted in the Church for the visions of the first weeks after the crucifixion was that Jesus had risen from the dead (1 Cor. 15.5ff.). But by the middle 50s there were Jewish Christians[18] who said that there was *no* physical resurrection – neither for the dead generally, nor, we must suppose, for Jesus in particular. There was *spiritual* resurrection, for they thought it worthwhile to be baptized a second time on behalf of their dead relatives; but they laughed at the idea of a physical resurrection – 'How are the dead raised?', they asked, 'and with what body do they come?' As Gerhard Sellin has shown, we find such beliefs of spiritual resurrection in the Jewish-Greek author Philo.[19] In this way the idea of spiritual resurrection goes back to very early times; and it is in fact not far from what many Christians believe today, including Bishop David Jenkins.

This spiritual theory was not a passing fad. We find it continuing, still among Jewish Christians, in the letters of Ignatius, about 115. Ignatius writes to the Christians in Smyrna:

For I know and believe that [Jesus Christ] was in the flesh even after the resurrection; and when he came to Peter and his company, He said to them, *Lay hold and handle me, and see that I am not a demon without body.* And straightway they touched him, and they believed, being joined unto His flesh and His blood . . . And after His resurrection He ate with them and drank with them as one in the flesh, though spiritually He was united with the Father.[20]

Of course, when debating with those holding the spiritual resurrection theory, it was no good stressing how many people had *seen* Jesus, because they could always reply that they had just seen the risen spirit; what were necessary were reports of touching and eating, because touching and eating require *physical* presence.

Now the stories that Ignatius draws on are from Luke's Gospel, which was written about 90, sixty years after Jesus' death. Such details come in no earlier source, though they are elaborated by John, about 100, with the famous story of Thomas. It is Luke who first tells us that Jesus said to the apostles, 'Handle me and see, for a spirit has not flesh and bones,' and that he ate some fish (24.39, 42–3). Wasn't that lucky for Ignatius, that he had just the right kind of story to hand, just in time! It seems rather too good to be true that such a story should have been circulating orally for *sixty years* after Jesus' death, and have recently come to light. The obvious explanation is that the Lucan church felt certain that the resurrection was a physical event, and they interpreted the tradition of the visions with the extra details of touching and eating to make the point.

Now exactly the same motive underlies the creation of the empty tomb story in Mark, which was written about 70, forty years after Jesus' death. Paul never mentions an empty tomb. No doubt Mark had a tradition that Jesus had been buried by Joseph of Arimathea, and that Mary Magdalene and other women had meant to anoint the body, but had not been able to. But his story supplies the exact need of a Pauline church that believed in a physical resurrection. The women come with their spices, and are met by an angel who says, 'You seek Jesus of Nazareth, the crucified one; he is risen, he is not here – behold the place where they laid him' (16.6). So Mark has solved three problems in one. The women's failure was not due to failure to find the tomb in the dark, or to feebleness; the body had been taken away by the angel. This was Jesus of Nazareth, the crucified, who had been raised; no question of a spirit being unable to suffer, and so different from Jesus the crucified. Third, the women saw the place where he had been laid, now without the body; so he had been raised *physically*.

This view of the empty tomb story as the creation of the Marcan church is not just the speculation of a sceptic; there is a contradiction built into the story that gives it away. Mark says the angel told the women to give the message to Peter and the others to go to Galilee, where they would see Jesus; so the reader is led to think that all is smooth – the disciples got the message, he supposes, and went to Galilee, where the resurrection appearances took place. But now Mark thinks of a difficulty. What are people going to say who hear this story for the first time in 70 – especially Jewish Christians, who will be deeply sceptical of physical resurrection stories? Will they not say, 'I've been a Christian for forty years, and it is the first time I have heard such a tale. Why have I never heard this before? It is a pack of lies.' So Mark thinks of an answer to this problem. He ends the tale, 'And [the women] went out and fled from the tomb, for trembling and astonishment seized them; and they said nothing to anyone, for they were afraid' (16.8). You know what women are like: they were seized with panic and hysteria, and kept the whole thing quiet. That is why people have not heard all this before. The only trouble with Mark's ingenious solution is that he is left with the problem of how the apostles got the message to go to Galilee. But he did not need to worry about that too much. Matthew and Luke soon supplied the missing message; and orthodox commentators on Mark do not usually notice the problem two millennia later.

Belief in Jesus' resurrection does not rest on a fraud. Peter and Paul and the others had genuine conversions which they experienced as visions; in the circumstances of the time, when there was a widespread belief that the kingdom of God was coming, and that the dead would be raised, these were quite naturally interpreted as evidence that Jesus had risen from the dead. At first people accepted this without much question; but from the 50s, and for perhaps a century, two theories were competing in the Church. The Paulines, Mark, Luke, and John, elaborated the traditions of appearances with an empty tomb story, and the details of touching and seeing. But it is now obvious that these were interpretative additions to counter the spiritual theory; and it would be helpful if Christian scholars would admit that, and tell their churches that the tale of the resurrection of Jesus has no dependable basis, and is not worthy of serious consideration.

Notes

[1] This paper was delivered at a meeting of the British Section of the SNTS at Sheffield in September, 1991, in a debate on the resurrection of Jesus with Prof. James Dunn. It received a brilliant riposte from Leslie Houlden at the Section's succeeding meeting at Exeter in 1992; and I have given it a new and simpler title to avoid any further misunderstanding! Leslie's paper will be published as 'The Resurrection and Christianity' in *Theology* 97 (1994). His support and generosity have been a light through my life, and the piece is offered in warm appreciation.

[2] M. J. Meadow and R. J. Kahoe, *Psychology of Religion* (New York, 1984), p. 90. I am grateful to my colleague, Dr Carolyn Hicks, who has directed my thinking in various excursions into psychology, but who is not to be held responsible for any errors.

[3] ibid., p. 91.

[4] *Arrow in the Blue*, cited by W. Sargant, *Battle for the Mind* (Garden City NY, 1957), p. 85.

[5] Meadow and Kahoe, *Psychology of Religion*, pp. 101f.; L. Festinger et al., *When Prophecy Fails* (New York, 1956).

[6] F. J. Roberts, 'Some Psychological Factors in Religious Conversion', *British Journal of Social and Clinical Psychology* (1965), pp. 185-7, reports that sudden conversions among 43 theological students showed no higher incidence of reported guilt than among gradual converts; but such samples do not include mass murderers like Susan Atkins, or people driven to psychological blindness like St Paul.

[7] See n. 4.

[8] E. D. Starbuck, *The Psychology of Religion* (New York, 1903), p. 143.

⁹ Sargant, *Battle for the Mind, passim*; Meadow and Kahoe, *Psychology of Religion*, pp. 99f.

¹⁰ Dr W. D. Rees, *British Medical Journal* 4 (Oct. 1971), pp. 37–41, cited in Timothy Beardsworth, *A Sense of Presence* (Oxford, 1977), pp. 12f.

¹¹ D. Gibbons and J. DeJanrette, 'Hypnotic Susceptibility and Religious Experience', *Journal for the Scientific Study of Religion* 11 (1972), pp. 152–6; G. Matheson, 'Hypnotic Aspects of Religious Experiences', *Journal of Psychology and Theology* 7 (1979), pp. 13–21.

¹² W. H. Clark, *The Psychology of Religion* (New York, 1958), p. 204; G. E. W. Scobie, 'Types of Christian Conversion', *Journal of Behavioral Science* 1 (1973), pp. 265–71.

¹³ C. G. Jung, *Contributions to Analytical Psychology* (ET; New York, 1945), p. 257.

¹⁴ Heikki Räisänen, *Paul and the Law* (London, 1982), p. 232.

¹⁵ J. C. Beker, *Paul the Apostle* (Philadelphia, 1980), p. 237.

¹⁶ J. R. Stewart, 'Sasquatch Sightings in South Dakota', in G. K. Zollschan et al. (eds), *Exploring the Paranormal* (Bridport/Lindfield NSW, 1989), pp. 287–304. I am grateful to Dr Mark Fox for the reference.

¹⁷ N. Smelser, *Theory of Collective Behaviour* (New York, 1962), pp. 12–22.

¹⁸ That they were *Jewish* Christians is indicated by their exposition of the two men of Gen. 1.27/2.7, countered by Paul at 1 Cor. 15.45ff.; and by their devotion to *the Law* (1 Cor. 15.56). The view that Paul was a total obsessive, who introduced a hit against the Law whatever the topic being covered, like Cato on the destruction of Carthage, is quite without foundation. Where is the evidence for such an obsession elsewhere?

¹⁹ G. Sellin, *Die Streit um die Auferstehung der Toten* (FRLANT 138; Göttingen, 1986), esp. pp. 21ff.; Philo is fond of Paul's word ἄφθαρτος. Cf. H. C. C. Cavallin, *Life after Death* (CB NT 7:1;

Lund, 1974), pp. 135-9. Cavallin comments that Philo can hardly not
have known Dan. 12 and 2 Macc. 7, and seems to interpret resurrection as identical with immortality (p. 139). See now E. P. Sanders,
Judaism: Practice and Belief 63BCE-66CE (London/Philadelphia,
1992), pp. 298-303.

[20] Smyrn. 3.

7

'They discussed among themselves what this "rising from the dead" could mean' (Mark 9.10)

Anthony Harvey

The implications of this sentence deserve to be taken seriously. The evangelist clearly expected no one to be surprised that a representative group of Jesus' disciples simply did not understand what Jesus could have meant by his 'resurrection'. Innumerable modern discussions of the subject start out with the bold assertion that 'the Jews believed . . .', and fill in the content of this belief from later rabbinic doctrines concerning resurrection. Only the Sadducees are allowed to hold a different opinion. The question about Jesus then becomes: when and how was he known to have been the subject (or the object) of this 'resurrection'? But our text suggests a quite different scenario. Jesus talks about 'rising' at some moment in the near future. Far from being able to slot this prediction into their existing beliefs, the disciples are puzzled. What could Jesus mean?

It has to be said that such evidence as we have on this difficult topic supports the evangelist more than it supports the dogmatism of the modern interpreter. Beliefs about life after death which may be extracted from writings roughly contemporary with the New Testament show much diversity and (in the nature of the case) little precision. And in the New Testament itself there is a wide range of options: there are even clear, if seldom acknowledged, traces of a belief in reincarnation;[1] indeed Josephus apparently attributes some form of this belief to the Pharisees.[2] Which is, after all, just what one ought to expect. Popular beliefs about the after-life may share certain very general premises; but these may amount to no more than that *some* form of existence after death may be looked forward to, at least by some. In detail they will necessarily be vague and often contradictory. We would do well to heed the warning issued many years ago by that wise and erudite scholar A. D. Nock: there is 'a widespread tendency of language about the after-life to admit inconsistencies'.[3]

If popular belief in these matters is necessarily imprecise, it is also extremely conservative. In 1955 John Mavrogordato was able to demonstrate from modern Greek folk-songs that in two thousand years 'the Christian churches had never succeeded in making the slightest impression on popular belief' with regard to the after-life, which continued to be conceived of exactly as in the time of Homer – a place of shadowy existence and gloom, except for the very few who were destined for something better.[4] Very similar is the picture of Sheol painted in the Old Testament: there is no question of different destinies for the just and the wicked, for all alike descend to a pit where the dead cannot even praise God (Ps. 115.17). A people who continued to use the Psalms as their prayer book must have found it hard to think of the after-life in any other way. When writing in Greek, it was natural and appropriate to call it 'Hades' (Matt. 16.18 and elsewhere).

Yet alongside this belief, and by no means brought into harmony with it, was another equally fundamental one that was slow to appear in the Hebrew Scriptures but is virtually taken for granted in apocalyptic literature, namely that the after-life makes provision for the reward of the righteous and the punishment of the wicked. This too is clearly reflected in Jesus' parable of the rich man and Lazarus (Luke 16.23). It is not difficult to suggest an explanation for this development. As any prospect of material rewards for the Jewish people became increasingly unreal under foreign occupation, some compensation after death for the sufferings of the righteous in this life became a necessary postulate if the world was to yield any moral sense at all. We are reliably informed that the Sadducees took exception to this, and refused to recognize any after-life other than 'Sheol'. The reason for this is hardly likely to lie (as is often suggested) in a particularly blinkered approach to Scripture: the Sadducees do not come over in other respects as strict fundamentalists. It is more likely that they saw any preoccupation with rewards in the after-life as tending to weaken people's resolve to pursue material advantage by political action here and now. It is often said, doubtless with some truth, that the reason why the preaching of the Church today makes so little reference to heaven and hell is that, in a sense, they are already here: the possibility of material satisfaction in this life, and the struggle for a more equitable distribution of available goods in the world, has displaced the desire for rewards and the fear of punishment in the hereafter. Conversely, the Sadducees may have been alarmed by a growing preoccupation with the 'world to come' when their own energies were devoted to ameliorating things in 'the world as it is'. However this may be, the function of the after-life in redressing the balance of undeserved wrongs in this life and providing for reward and punishment in the next was well established in popular belief, and became the basis for speculation in both apocalyptic and rabbinic writings.

In what shape or form the individual would be available to receive these posthumous benefits or punishments was of course a matter that intellectuals might discuss at great length: we have just such a discussion in 1 Corinthians 15. But we need not assume that the question was of great interest at the popular level. In these matters, the touchstone of popular belief is not so much the endorsement of theories as the tenacity of burial customs. These too tend to be conservative. The Hebrew Scriptures show a consistent concern for careful and reverent burial, and there is a notable emphasis on being buried in the right place – with one's family and in one's own land. Unlike the Greeks, the Jews never admitted cremation; and the only modification to traditional custom in later times was one that was doubtless forced on them by the practical constraint of space in rock-tombs: skeletons were dismembered and tightly packed in small stone ossuaries. Even then, care had to be taken not to fracture the bones.[5] Burial rites showed a consistent concern to preserve the physical remains somehow *intact*.

These practices may have helped to give rise to the Pharisaic doctrine of the resurrection of the body, which in turn may have reinforced the practices. It can be argued, for instance, that it was their anxiety to preserve the bone-structure intact which caused them to modify the procedure of death by stoning;[6] hence also the evangelist's interest in recording that Jesus' legs were not broken on the cross (John 19.33). This, of course, would depend on how far their views were generally known and accepted – Jesus seems to distance himself from them when he describes dead persons as (presumably incorporeal) 'angels in heaven' (Mark 12.25). Yet the consistent respect which was accorded to the bones of the deceased does suggest that in popular thought individuals after death might be recalled by God in a form related to their physical existence in life. There is no evidence that the Greek conception of survival in the form of a disembodied soul ever penetrated the Jewish mentality – indeed it is questionable whether it was ever popular in Greece outside philosophical and literary circles.[7] Rather, the continued personal identity of the individual that is required for any belief in posthumous rewards and punishments was felt to reside somehow in the one durable part of the human body: the bones. And Ezekiel's vision of dry bones being brought back to life (however different its original intention) provided a reassuring image of the way in which God could reverse the brute facts of physical corruption and decay. At his call, the dead (carefully preserved so far as their bones were concerned) would 'rise'.

In some such way as this the popular mind may have rationalized the respect accorded to the bones of the deceased. Not that such rationalization was often articulated: the inscriptions on the ossuaries of Beth She'arim show little explicit faith in a significant after-life and no consistency in describing it – in this respect those in Greek are startlingly similar to the tombstones that lined the street of an ancient Greek city.[8] Certainly there was no preference for words meaning 'rise' or 'be awakened'. In Greek, these words (*anastēnai* and *egeiresthai*) would normally have meant simply being 'restored to life', as is the case many times in the Gospels and Acts. They could also mean being 'raised from the dead', in the sense of what might be the ultimate destiny of a nation or an individual.[9] But the use of them was neither consistent nor precise (how could it be in a matter that is by definition beyond human knowledge?), and many other express-ions were in use: several are attributed to Jesus.[10] Standardization in such matters could arise only within a clearly defined school or move-ment.

It is precisely such standardization that confronts us very early in the Christian movement. The disciples are reported to have been puzzled by Jesus' use of 'rising from the dead', and no wonder. Jesus appeared to be taking a speculative notion about the after-life – 'being raised' – and abruptly inserting it into the calendar of imminent events to signal the moment at which they would be free to speak about the transfiguration. Not long afterwards his followers did some-thing very similar. They identified an extraordinary event they had experienced by using words that were more appropriate either to life after death or to a temporary bringing back to life. What enabled them to agree on this standard terminology so rapidly?

We need to make a fresh start from another direction. Jesus had died; but his followers believed in him. What did they believe? They certainly believed that his life, his authority, his teaching, were evidence that God was 'with him' (Acts 10.38); his execution could not represent God's final judgement on him. He was, in some sense at least, a 'Son of God'; this meant that God must rectify the human misjudgement in the next world, in heaven. He must vindicate Jesus. The more profoundly one believed in Jesus, the more firmly one would believe that this vindication had taken place. No 'resurrection' (outside heaven) would be necessary: the impact of Jesus' authority, power, and goodness would be enough to inspire faith that he, if anyone, was rewarded by God, and that this rewarding would inaugurate a new period of history and release a new spirit among his followers. Such a theology is articulated in the Christ-hymn in Philippians 2, where there is no mention of resurrection: God has simply 'exalted' Jesus; what more could be required? The same is true of Hebrews (where the resurrection is never mentioned). It is true also of Peter's sermon in Acts 3, where Jesus' resurrection, though referred to in parenthesis (3.15), plays no part in the argument: God had caused prophecy to be fulfilled by allowing the Messiah to suffer (3.18); in response to repentance and prayer he would send this designated Messiah, who in the mean time had been received into heaven (3.21); the hearers of the sermon were the inheritors of the blessing promised to the descendants of Abraham, namely the opportunity to turn from their evil ways so that 'times of refreshment' might come with the return of the Messiah. No belief in the resurrection is called for; only that the Christ, after his suffering, is now in heaven, ready to return.

Whether or not the author of Acts was reporting a style of preaching that had actually been used in the Church, we must at least credit him with having placed in Peter's mouth words that would have been read as a plausible account of such a sermon. Presented in this way, the gospel does not require faith in the resurrection as such, but only in the vindication and exaltation of Jesus in heaven and the prospect of his return. Such a faith could certainly have been the consequence of the kind of conversion experience described by Michael Goulder (pp. 58–68): a vision of Jesus raised in heaven to the right hand of God would have been well in the line of the ecstatic experiences that inspired a number of apocalyptic writers (including the author of Revelation), and accords well with the tantalizingly brief accounts which Paul gives of his own 'conversion experience'. It would have been perfectly appropriate to refer to this exalted Christ-figure as having been 'raised from the dead': this was (as we have seen) a necessary condition for entering into any kind of heavenly existence. And such a 'resurrection', we know, had a powerful metaphorical (or 'mystical') appeal for Paul: just as we can be said to share Christ's crucifixion or burial through a 'death to sin', so we can share his heavenly life by being 'raised with him'. No reference to a resurrection experience *on earth* is required. The entire discussion in 1 Corinthians 15 concerns the possibility of resurrection *in heaven*. 'How are the dead raised?' is a speculative question, open to philosophical and analogical arguments on either side. It has nothing to do with a physical 'raising up' on earth, and the same goes for the (possibly pre-Pauline) formula, 'He was handed over for our transgressions and raised for our justification' (Rom. 4.25). The place where we are justified is in heaven: by being united with him in his resurrection we share his justification, which was in the spiritual (not bodily) realm. For he was

> manifested in the flesh,
> justified in the Spirit,
> taken up in glory.
>
> (1 Tim. 3.16)

Here, then, are a number of instances – some of them in apparently ancient credal formulae – in which the Christian faith was summarized without any reference to 'resurrection': Jesus' exaltation in glory into heaven, not his brief posthumous appearance on earth, was the object of faith and hope; and the guarantee of its truth was not the witness of the apostles to an experienced event, but the outpouring of the Spirit on the Church. This is also good Johannine theology. In the Fourth Gospel we have, of course, resurrection appearances; but none of them is recounted as an aid to belief in the way that pre-resurrection events are – we are even told that it is those who have *not* seen who are blessed. We now have to ask: if this was at some stage or in some circles a valid way of presenting the Christian story, what caused the 'resurrection' to move into a central position in the Christian proclamation?

A possible answer is that even the 'exaltation' of Jesus after his death was felt to have implications with regard to his physical body. If the point of carefully preserving the bones of the deceased was to maintain the continuing physical identity of each individual whom God would 'raise' on the last day, it might be difficult to believe that Jesus had already been 'raised' in heaven if his corpse was still visible on earth. But for this it would have been sufficient for the bones simply to disappear. Indeed it was precisely because of the possibility of a fraudulent claim of this kind that the chief priests and Pharisees asked for the tomb to be guarded (Matt. 27.64); the alleged disappearance of the body would have been a sufficient ground for the disciples to claim that Jesus 'had been raised'. No 'appearances' would have been necessary to justify the claim.

This is logical enough. It is the kind of logic which may have inspired the story that 'tombs had been opened' at the moment of Jesus' death: if this moment was the signal for a more general 'resurrection of the just', the bones of these persons would have been required for the purpose, and their tombs would have had to be 'opened' (Matt. 27.52). In other words, we are still within the bounds of popular belief; given the care taken over the preservation of mortal remains, and the widespread belief in an eventual 'raising up' for judgement and reward, the statement that a person had been 'raised' would have invited questions about the whereabouts of the corpse. It is to answering these questions that the story of Jesus' empty tomb seems to have been addressed – a story usually thought to belong to a later stage in the formation of the tradition but, on this analysis, being an essential ingredient of any telling of Jesus' 'resurrection' whatever.

But we have already noted that logic is an unreliable guide in these matters. Those, for instance, who believed that being raised up by God would take the form of reincarnation in another human being did not presumably think that the first body had somehow to disappear: Herod wondered if John the Baptist had been 'raised' and was alive in Jesus, but we hear of no rumour of John's body having left the tomb in which his followers had devoutly placed him. We cannot be certain that the disciples *could* not have proclaimed Jesus' resurrection – in the terms of Philippians 2, for instance, or 1 Timothy 3 – if his tomb had remained sealed and uninspected. Still less can we say that their proclamation required resurrection 'appearances'. Indeed, these appearances were something of a complication. The most obvious sense of 'Jesus was raised on the third day' was that he had been exalted into heaven. Yet for a while he was still seen on earth. How was the one to be reconciled with the other? Again, we must not assume a logical consistency that would be inappropriate to such mysterious happenings. Yet the author of the Fourth Gospel seems to have seen the problem: 'Touch me not, for I have not yet ascended to the Father' (20.17). That is to say, the appearances were perceived to be essentially transitional: Jesus was on his way. Matthew and Luke each seek to clarify things: Matthew by allowing only for a brief scene of recognition and commissioning, Luke by recording an interim period on earth terminated by the 'ascension into heaven'. The appearances were something for which there was absolutely no precedent: the phenomenon of a person being brought back to life in order to be exalted in heaven.

If, then, these appearances were neither necessary for proclaiming Jesus' resurrection nor easily reconcilable with normal notions of what such a resurrection might involve, what we have to account for is the enormous emphasis placed on them, and on the witnesses to them, by Paul and by the author of Acts. Jesus had been 'seen' (1 Cor. 15.5-7); witnesses could be named; and examples (apparently not exhaustive) of these sightings are recorded by three of the evangelists. If it was a 'collective experience', such as has been observed from time to time by social anthropologists, it was of such an unprecedented and unexpected kind that one may be pardoned for not being satisfied with an explanation purely in terms of group psychology. But what is equally striking is the way in which the terminology for describing these extraordinary events became rapidly standardized. What was it that enabled the disciples to identify and describe both Jesus' posthumous appearances and his exaltation into heaven as 'resurrection'?

As so often, we may gratefully accept a clue from the Fourth Gospel. The dialogue between Jesus and Martha after the death of Lazarus turns on the ambiguity of the word for 'rising' (*anastasis*). What Martha and her sister were hoping for was that Jesus would bring Lazarus back to life. For this, a perfectly intelligible expression was 'to be raised' (*anastēnai*, Luke 16.21). Jesus in fact promises to do this ('your brother will rise', 11.24); but, in disbelief, Martha assumes that he means 'at the last day'. The irony depends entirely on *anastasis* having *both* meanings: coming back to life, and being summoned back to some form of existence by God on the 'last day'. The author of the Fourth Gospel exploits this ambiguity in the interests of his theology of (eternal) 'life', which begins now and continues through and in spite of death. That Jesus can be said to 'be' the *anastasis* means, at the very least, that, in him, both senses of the word coalesce: returning to life, if it is the life of faith, is not essentially different from the life that is the gift of God after death. But for our purposes the important point is that the word *anastasis* was clearly perceived to have both meanings. And the same is true of *egeiresthai*, being 'wakened' or 'raised'. It could mean 'being brought back to life', but it could also mean being summoned back into existence for God's final judgement and assignment of reward.

We may plausibly guess that it was the double reference of these two words which caused them to be adopted by the church, to the exclusion of other possible candidates, as the standard vocabulary for proclaiming what had happened to Jesus. What were needed were terms that would convey both the immediate personal experience of the 'witnesses' that Jesus had returned to life, and the faith of all his followers that the victim of a criminal condemnation and execution had been vindicated by God and given a place in heaven. It is likely that no other words from the whole repertory of speculation about life after death carried the same invaluable ambiguity. But this in turn allows us to say something about the resurrection appearances that these words were also used to describe. If, as the result of a vision, a disciple was to have said, 'Jesus has been raised,' there was nothing in the semantics of this expression to distinguish it from 'Lazarus has been raised' (John 12.1) – that is, that he had been brought back to life. But this was not what the disciple would have meant. His primary faith was that Jesus had always had God 'with him', and that God must have vindicated him by 'raising' him to an honoured place in heaven. A vision of Jesus on earth which was felt to confirm this was not strictly comparable to the 'Bigfoot' phenomenon cited by Michael Goulder: the Christian movement was not inspired by strange sightings of a supernatural figure *on earth*, but by the conviction that Jesus was *in heaven*. The resurrection experiences were clearly felt to give enormous support to this conviction; but they were essentially *transitional*. The risen Jesus was not simply a person brought back to life: his body had been 'raised' by God, not for continued activity on earth, but for the purpose of a new existence (though with the same identity) in heaven; and whether by attributing to him paranormal powers (miraculous appearances and disappearances), or by creating a limited timescale for these appearances ('forty days'), or simply by the statement that he was on his way ('I am going to the Father'), the evangelists made it clear that, in the case of Jesus, 'resurrection' always had this double meaning. When we ask what actually happened, any answer we give must be one that accounts for a new precision in the Christian vocabulary: from not knowing what 'rising from the dead' could mean, Jesus' followers moved in a remarkably short time to a usage that was standard, intelligible, and flexible enough to describe the varied and unprecedented experiences that had given rise to it. It is of course possible to describe all this as a collective delusion. But the phenomena of which this is claimed to be an explanation seem to me, even on linguistic grounds, to be curiously resistant to any such simple analysis – a modest but not insignificant conclusion that I believe may be congenial to the scholar to whom these essays are gratefully dedicated.

Notes

[1] Mark 6.14: Herod does not think that Jesus is John the Baptist come back to life, but that the effect of his 'rising from the dead' is that 'his powers are at work' in Jesus.

[2] A. E. Harvey, *Jesus and the Constraints of History* (London: Duckworth, 1982), p. 150, n. 147.

[3] A. D. Nock, *Essays* (Oxford: Clarendon Press, 1972), p. 507, n. 19.

[4] John Mavrogordato, 'Modern Greek Folksongs of the Dead', *Journal of Hellenic Studies* 75 (1955), pp. 42–53, at p. 52.

[5] *Semaḥoth* 49a (*Babylonian Talmud, Minor Tractates*, ed. A. Cohen, 1971, vol. 1, p. 390). Bone-packing is referred to in the Mishnah, *Moed Katan* 1.5.

[6] D. Daube, *The New Testament and Rabbinic Judaism* (London: Athlone Press, 1956), pp. 303–8.

[7] E. Rohde, *Psyche* (ET; London, 1925), p. 538: 'Theology and philosophy remained the sole repositories of the belief in the immortality of the soul'.

[8] See *Beth She'arim*, vol. 2: *The Greek Inscriptions* (Israel Exploration Society, 1974), esp. no. 127. One of the most common epitaphs is: 'Take courage, no one is immortal.'

[9] As in Isaiah 26.14 (LXX); Dan. 12.2 (LXX, Θ); Mark 12.23, 26.

[10] e.g., *palingenesia* (Matt. 19.28), *paradeisos* (Luke 23.43).

8
Early Objections to the Resurrection of Jesus

Graham Stanton

Recent studies of early Christian traditions about the resurrection of Jesus have generally overlooked the objections that were raised by opponents of Christianity in the first and second centuries. This is somewhat surprising. Historians know how important it is to consider evidence or arguments that are an embarrassment to the eventual 'winners'. Astute theologians always listen carefully to the voices of 'outsiders'.[1]

Criticisms of early Christian claims concerning the resurrection of Jesus give us some limited insights into the variety of ancient attitudes to life after death. They help us to appreciate more keenly the ways Christian proclamation of the resurrection was understood or misunderstood by both Jews and pagans. By paying attention to early criticisms, we may be able to trace more readily the points at which early Christian traditions about the resurrection have been shaped by apologetic concerns.

The potential value of this approach will be obvious. So why have the voices of the critics not been heard? They have been ignored mainly because it is undeniably difficult to uncover their views. We have much more extensive evidence for early polemical comments on the actions and teaching of Jesus than on the resurrection.[2] However, by casting the net widely I believe it is possible to make a number of observations that are relevant to inquiries into the setting, development, and reception of early resurrection traditions, observations which stimulate further theological reflection today.

Since it is often helpful in studies of earliest Christianity to work back from later, clearer evidence to more problematic earlier evidence, I shall start with objections to the resurrection of Jesus made in the second half of the second century and work back, where appropriate, to New Testament evidence. I am starting outside the canon for the further reason that it is all too easy to use the New Testament texts as a mirror to find opponents and rivals under every canonical bed. Evidence from outside the canon may help us to avoid some of the pitfalls of mirror-reading.[3]

THE PAGAN CELSUS AND A JEW

The first pagan comments on earliest Christianity come from the early decades of the second century. Although Suetonius, Tacitus, Pliny, Epictetus, Hadrian (in his imperial rescript), and Fronto provide invaluable insights into the ways Christians were perceived by pagans, they do not help our quest for objections to the resurrection of Jesus. They tell us that the odd behaviour of Christians raised many eyebrows, but they say little or nothing about what Christians believed or taught.

In the second half of the second century, however, some pagan writers do comment on Christian beliefs.[4] Lucian of Samosata noted that Christians associated with Peregrinus (a Christian convert who died about AD 165) 'were poor souls who convinced themselves that they would all be immortal and live forever, on account of which they think lightly of death'. Galen of Pergamum also commented on the contempt Christians showed towards death. Lucian and Galen both remind us that belief in life after death (whether resurrection or immortality) was by no means universal in the pagan world of their day, and that Christians were known for their distinctive hopes for the future. However, neither writer refers explicitly to the resurrection of Jesus.

For the first extended pagan objections to the resurrection of Jesus, we must turn to Celsus' extended attack on Christianity, which was written between 177 and 180. Some seventy years later Origen recognized that Celsus' trenchant voice could neither be silenced nor ignored, and wrote a lengthy reply. Fortunately, Origen's reply includes quotations from as much as 70% of Celsus' now lost book.

Celsus' wide-ranging attack includes comments on the resurrection of Jesus, and on Christian beliefs in life after death. In the first sections of his book, the Platonist philosopher repeatedly quotes the views of a Jew. Origen insists that Celsus' Jew is an 'imaginary character . . . who addresses childish remarks to Jesus', and claims that the views attributed to him are not consistent with those of a Jew (*Contra Celsum* I.28).[5]

However, there are good grounds for concluding that on this issue even Origen has nodded. Some of the critical comments attributed to

Celsus' Jew concerning the birth, actions, and teaching of Jesus are also found in polemical Jewish traditions and independently in other early Christian writings.[6] Celsus has clearly drawn on earlier traditions: it is impossible to say just how early they are, but their value as evidence for the views of Jewish opponents of Jesus and his followers can hardly be over-estimated.

Although it is not always possible to decide whether Celsus is setting out his own objections to Christianity, or those of the Jewish opponent whom he quotes, Celsus and the Jew have quite different views on life after death and also on the resurrection of Jesus. As in Luke-Acts – I shall discuss the evidence below – it is possible to distinguish between pagan and Jewish objections.

Celsus claims that a dead man cannot be immortal (II.16) and that Christians worship a corpse (VII.68): for the pagan philosopher the very notion of resurrection is absurd (V.14; VI.29), though he is willing to discuss the possibility of some form of immortality (V.14; cf. IV.56). Celsus insists that 'the fact that hope of the resurrection of the dead is not shared by some Jews [presumably Sadducees] and some Christians [presumably gnostics] shows its utter repulsiveness, and that it is both revolting and impossible' (V.14). However, he does not relate this observation to the resurrection of Jesus. Hence it is not surprising to find that he does not discuss the resurrection of Jesus at length: he leaves extended criticism to the Jew whom he quotes.[7] In contrast to Celsus himself, however, the Jew insists that 'Jews hope to be resurrected in the body and to have everlasting life' (II.77), a view that Origen accepts and expounds at some length (V.14–26).

At a later point in his attack on Christianity, long after he has stopped quoting a Jew, Celsus returns to the evidence for the resurrection of Jesus and mentions in passing the presence of *women* at the empty tomb, not one hysterical woman, as in the objection of the Jew (cf. II.55 and V.52). Celsus himself makes nothing of the fact that Christian claims rest on the evidence of women; instead, he points out scornfully that the alleged Son of God 'was not able to open the tomb, but needed someone else to move the stone' (V.52). This is an objection that Celsus' Jew is unlikely to have made; in a Jewish context, 'Son of God' did not necessarily denote divinity.

In short, the pagan Celsus and his Jewish ally raise rather different objections to the resurrection of Jesus. Celsus uses the Jew's specific objections to supplement his own scornful comments on the whole notion of post-mortem resurrection.

Pagan parallels to the resurrection of Jesus are discussed in a particularly interesting passage in II.55–8. At this point Celsus' Jew is addressing Jews who believe in Jesus. He claims that six Greek legends provide parallels to the resurrection of Jesus. 'Do you think that the stories of these others really are the legends which they appear to be, and yet that the ending of your tragedy is to be regarded as noble and convincing?' The implication is that Christian Jews believe that the resurrection of Jesus cannot be put on a par with other stories about individuals brought back to life. But nothing is made of this.

Origen's own defence is striking: whereas the heroes in the Greek legends disappeared secretly and then returned to the men they had left, 'Jesus was crucified before all the Jews and his body put to death in the sight of their people.' However, he goes on to claim that there are important biblical parallels: the raising to life of the young boys by Elijah (1 Kings 17.21–2) and Elisha (2 Kings 4.34–5). The resurrection of Jesus, he insists, was more remarkable because of the greater benefits it brought to mankind.

No doubt this latter comment is valid, but Origen misses a far more important point: the young boys to whom he refers, along with Jairus' daughter, the widow's son at Nain, and Lazarus, were restored to this life. The evangelists, for all their differences in emphasis, did not claim that the body of Jesus was resuscitated only to die again at a later point. Perhaps in their refusal to appeal to parallels to the resurrection of Jesus, the Christian Jews addressed by Celsus' Jew saw this more clearly than either Origen or Celsus. One hopes so.

Celsus' Jew advances vigorously the theory that the followers of Jesus 'saw' their recently crucified leader in a dream or hallucination. Origen's response is not very persuasive: 'Celsus's idea of a vision in the daytime is not convincing when the people were in no way mentally disturbed and were not suffering from delirium or melancholy. Because Celsus foresaw this objection he said that the woman was hysterical; but there is no evidence of this in the scriptural account . . .' (II.60).

This discussion reminds us of the ultimate futility of trying to seek proof one way or the other. 'Vision' or 'hallucination', how can one decide? Surely the matter can be settled only on the basis of wider considerations that are theological rather than historical or psychological.

Three of Celsus' objections elicit a similar theological response from Origen. Celsus claims that if Jesus really wanted to show forth divine power, he ought to have appeared to those who maltreated him, to the man who condemned him, and 'to everyone everywhere' (II.63, 67). In reply to this strong challenge, Origen insists that when Jesus was sent into the world, he did not merely make himself known; he also concealed himself (II.67). Similarly (with reference to the baptism as well as the resurrection appearances), 'the divine voice is such that it is heard only by those whom the speaker wishes to hear it' (II.72). Perhaps the sharpest objection raised by Celsus' Jew is his jibe, 'Where is the risen Jesus, that we may see and believe?' In response, Origen turns the tables on his Jewish opponent and asks for proof that Israel is God's 'portion' (II.77). Origen's riposte is terse and to the point: God's self-disclosure to Israel was not openly accessible to all and sundry on a permanent basis, and its reality cannot be proven. So too with the appearances of the risen Jesus.

A theological thread runs through these responses to Celsus which is as important for current theological reflection as it was in the middle of the third century. Origen sees clearly that although some of Celsus' objections were based on misunderstandings and others were mischievous, he could not offer clear-cut historical proof of the resurrection of Jesus (see especially II.77): God is not at the beck and call of men and women.

Origen knows full well that proof of the historicity of an incident in the Gospels is difficult and in some cases impossible (I.42). He knows that he cannot sidestep allegations that the text of the Gospels has been tampered with (II.27) and that the resurrection narratives contain discrepancies (V.55–6). He repudiates 'mere irrational faith', and insists that readers of the Gospels need an open mind and considerable study. 'If I may say so,' he writes, 'readers need to enter into the mind of the writers to find out with what spiritual meaning each event was recorded.' Is this the way faith and reason should be held together in discussion of the resurrection narratives? Is there still a place for discerning 'spiritual meaning' by Origen's own method of allegorical interpretation? If so, what criteria will guard against 'irrational faith'?

Nearly all the objections to the resurrection of Jesus that have been raised since the Enlightenment were anticipated by the pagan Celsus, or by the Jew whom he quotes. There is only one notable exception, the theory that the disciples stole the body of Jesus from the tomb.[8] Most of the objections to the resurrection of Jesus that are pressed by Celsus' Jew are likely to have been made long before Celsus wrote between AD 166 and 170. Their importance for serious discussion of New Testament resurrection traditions cannot be overestimated. Some of Origen's replies carry little or no persuasive power today, but some are (or should be) still on the agenda of current theological discussion.

TRYPHO THE JEW

Just over a decade before Celsus launched his attack on Christianity, Justin Martyr wrote his *Dialogue* with the Jew Trypho. Four passages are of particular interest.

1. Justin and Trypho, just like Origen and Celsus' Jew, and (as we shall see shortly) Luke's Paul and his Jewish opponents, can agree that there will be a resurrection of the righteous (45.2–3).

2. Justin, just like Celsus, knows that there are some so-called Christians (presumably gnostics) who say that there is no resurrection of the dead. He is confident that Trypho will agree that Sadducees (and some other Jewish groups) who deny the resurrection should not be considered true Jews (80.3–4). We shall see below that Luke also sees hope for resurrection from the dead as a line of continuity between Judaism and Christianity.

3. In one passage a Christian credal summary is put into the mouth of Trypho. 'You say many blasphemous things,' says Trypho, 'thinking to persuade us that this man who was crucified has been with Moses and Aaron, and has spoken to them in a pillar of a cloud, that he then became man and was crucified, and has ascended into heaven, and comes again on earth, and is to be worshipped' (*Dialogue* 38.1). Just as in several New Testament passages (e.g., Phil. 2.5–11; 1 Tim. 3.16; Eph. 4.7–10; Rom. 10.5–8), this 'creed' moves directly from the crucifixion to the exaltation of Jesus without referring to resurrection.

4. I noted above that the only major objection to the resurrection of Jesus which is not mentioned by Celsus is the claim that the disciples stole the body of Jesus. By a curious irony, this is the only Jewish criticism of Christian claims about the resurrection that Justin

mentions. Justin claims that on hearing that Christ had risen from the dead, Jewish leaders

> appointed chosen men and sent them into all the civilized world, proclaiming that 'a certain godless and lawless sect has been raised by one Jesus of Galilee, a deceiver, whom we crucified, but his disciples stole him by night from the tomb, where he had been laid after being unnailed from the cross, and they deceive men, saying that he is risen from the dead and has ascended into heaven'. (*Dialogue* 108)[9]

Some of the phraseology of this alleged anti-Christian Jewish propaganda comes from Justin himself, some of it possibly from Matthew 28.13, 15. However, there are good reasons for supposing that Justin may here be drawing on an earlier source for these Jewish allegations, and not simply on New Testament passages. (i) At this point at least, Justin is not setting up Trypho as a straw man who lists Jewish objections in order to allow Justin to refute them one by one, for Justin does not respond to them anywhere in the *Dialogue*. (ii) The reference to Christianity as a 'sect' is striking and unique in Justin: he uses the term elsewhere to refer to factions *within* Judaism (62.3; 80.4) and *within* Christianity (35.3; 51.2), but not to Christianity *per se*. (iii) The reference to Christianity as a godless and lawless sect raised by Jesus does not come from the Gospels, nor does the reference to the disciples as deceivers.

While it is impossible to confirm that a Jewish counter-mission of this kind took place, there is nothing inherently improbable in the reference to Jewish messengers being sent 'into all the civilized world'.[10] Justin is probably drawing on (as well as filling out himself) early Jewish allegations. Certainly *Dialogue* 108 sets out what Justin *felt* to be the heart of Jewish arguments against the resurrection of Jesus. This chapter confirms that Christians were aware of and sensitive to Jewish claims that the disciples stole the body of Jesus from the tomb. But, unlike the evangelist Matthew, Justin does not bother to refute this obvious objection to Christian claims. Perhaps he felt that it was so absurd that refutation was unnecessary.

In some versions of the Jewish polemical traditions known as the *Toledoth Jeshu*, there is an interesting variant of the theory that the body of Jesus was stolen from the tomb. The body of Jesus is stolen, not by his disciples as in Matthew and in Justin, but by his opponents: they drag the body through the streets of Tiberias. These traditions almost certainly stem from a time after the conversion of the Emperor Constantine: by then Jews and Christians were no longer rivals, and Jews were all too aware of the heavy hand of Christian oppression. This form of polemic falsifies at a stroke Christian claims; there is no need for the elaborate ruses Matthew alleges (27.62–6; 28.11–15).

The fact that the passage quoted above from *Dialogue* 108 is the only reference to Jewish objections to the resurrection of Jesus, and that there is no debate between Justin and Trypho on this topic, is striking. Why do Justin and Trypho share convictions about a general resurrection of the dead, but fail to discuss the resurrection of Jesus? For them both, Christology and the law are more important issues. Their central dispute concerning Jesus of Nazareth is not his resurrection, but whether or not Jesus fulfils Scripture; as we shall see in a moment, this was also Luke's view.

As in other Jewish polemic from this period, the claim that Jesus was a magician and a deceiver who led Israel astray is much more prominent than objections to the resurrection of Jesus. Perhaps the latter was not an easy issue to debate. After all, many Jews accepted that one day God would raise the (righteous) dead: how could one decide whether or not this general resurrection had been anticipated in the case of Jesus? As in Justin's *Dialogue*, debate could be neatly side-stepped by the claim that the disciples had stolen the body of Jesus.

GENTILE AND JEWISH RESPONSES IN ACTS

I turn now from Justin to an earlier Christian apologist. Luke is aware of rather different negative reactions to Christian proclamation of the resurrection of Jesus. I shall start with his presentation of Gentile objections to the resurrection of Jesus.

Paul ends his speech to the 'men of Athens' in the Council of the Areopagus with the claim that God has raised from the dead the man whom he has designated to judge the world (Acts 17.31). Paul's listeners do not comment on his proclamation of God the Creator who does not live in shrines made by human hands, but some of them scoff at his reference to resurrection from the dead (17.32). From Luke's point of view, Gentiles find the notion of resurrection quite incomprehensible.

There may be a further reference in Acts 17.18 to a negative response in Athens to Paul's proclamation of the resurrection, but I am not as confident about this as most translators and commentators. Luke opens his account of Paul's visit to Athens by noting that he argued in the market-place every day with passers-by, some of whom were Epicurean and Stoic philosophers. As is often the case in Acts, there is a division of opinion. Some said, 'What does this babbler want to say?' Others said, 'He seems to be a proclaimer of foreign divinities.' In most editions of the Greek text and in modern translations, Luke then explains in an aside to the reader that these critical comments were responses to Paul's proclamation of 'the good news about Jesus and the resurrection' (17.18).

There is now a general consensus that in this verse Luke claims that the Athenians totally misunderstood Paul's proclamation of Jesus and the resurrection (*anastasis*) as a reference to two divinities, 'Jesus and Anastasis'. This ingenious explanation has an impressive pedigree which goes back to Chrysostom; it is supported by the NEB's translation in 17.18, 'Jesus and Resurrection'. But this is unlikely, for it implies in an un-Lucan way either that Paul was a completely ineffective communicator, or that his listeners were stupid. In addition, in Codex Bezae (supported by the old Latin codex Gigas) there is important though often overlooked evidence for omission of the whole aside at the end of verse 18: a very early copyist may have noted Luke's failure to indicate the content of Paul's initial proclamation to the Athenians, and inserted the aside on the assumption (based on 17.32) that Paul must have preached about 'Jesus and the resurrection' and been totally misunderstood.[11]

In the second passage in Acts that refers to Gentile reaction to Christian proclamation of the resurrection, the Roman governor Festus informs Agrippa that he had been surprised by the accusations the chief priests and elders of the Jews had brought against Paul: 'they merely had certain points of disagreement with him about their religion, and about someone called Jesus, a dead man whom Paul alleged to be alive' (Acts 25.19, REB). Festus concedes that he is out of his depth in such discussions.

Luke then draws a careful contrast between Gentile and Jewish responses to proclamation of the resurrection. When Paul defends himself before Agrippa, he assumes that the Jewish king will not find it incredible that God should raise the dead (26.8). He then claims that in his preaching he asserts nothing beyond what was foretold by the prophets and by Moses: 'that the Messiah would suffer and that, as the first to rise from the dead, he would announce the dawn both to the Jewish people and to the Gentiles' (26.22-3, REB). At mention of the resurrection of the Messiah, it is not Agrippa, but the Roman governor Festus who intervenes: 'Paul, you are raving; too much study is driving you mad.' Paul does not attempt to enlighten Festus on the subject of the Messiahship of Jesus and the resurrection. Instead, he draws Agrippa into the discussion and repeats his claim that since Agrippa is a Jew, he is well versed in these matters (26.24-6). This passage is the final reference to the resurrection in Acts. In it Luke sets out clearly his belief that while Gentiles are completely baffled by Christian proclamation of the resurrection of Jesus, at least some Jews responded (or should have responded) much more sympathetically.

This latter point is developed by Luke in a rather subtle way that is well worth exploring, for it raises important theological issues. Luke first isolates Sadducean denial of the resurrection of the dead as a minority Jewish opinion (Acts 4.1-4; 5.17; 23.6). Luke believes that other Jews, including the Pharisees, do not have a fundamental objection to Christian claims concerning the resurrection of the dead. Hence, so the argument runs, they ought not to dismiss Christian claims concerning the resurrection of Jesus.

In the trial of Paul by the Sanhedrin (Acts 23.1-10), Paul emphasizes that he is himself a Pharisee, a son of Pharisees, and then singles out 'the hope and resurrection of the dead' as the central issue at stake. The Sanhedrin is divided. Luke reminds the reader that the Sadducees say that there is no resurrection, and then notes that 'some scribes of the Pharisees' defend Paul: 'We find nothing wrong with this man' (23.9). They even concede the possibility that the appearance of Christ to Paul outside Damascus was a reality: a spirit or angel has spoken to him.[12]

A similar point is made in Paul's defence before Agrippa (26.2-23). Luke's Paul refers once again to his membership of the 'sect' of the Pharisees. An important switch from the singular to the plural in verse 8 (missed by many translators) indicates that Paul is addressing not merely Agrippa, but Jews generally: they should not think it incredible that God raises the dead! From the context it is clear that the resurrection of Jesus is in view. The line of argument is bold, to say the least. Luke's Paul is claiming that on the basis of Jewish (especially Pharisaic) beliefs about the resurrection from the dead, the resurrection of Jesus is not at all problematic. In Luke's view, 'resurrection' is one of the lines of continuity between Judaism and Christianity.

This reading is consistent with the earlier chapters of Acts. In numerous passages Luke records the objections Jews raised to Stephen's and Paul's preaching. Although the resurrection of Jesus is prominent in the preceding 'sermons' (or, better, 'speeches'), with the exception of Sadducees and their allies, objections are not raised by Jewish opponents.

However, in two passages Luke makes a theological point that he could hardly have expected non-Christian Jews to accept: the resurrection of Jesus is the first example of the resurrection of the dead. In rather terse Greek, at Acts 4.2 Luke insists that the resurrection had come to pass in the person of Jesus.[13] He repeats the point in his final reference to the resurrection: Paul proclaims to Agrippa 'that the Messiah must suffer, and that, by being the first to rise from the dead', he would proclaim light 'both to our people and to the Gentiles' (26.23). Luke believes that as a Jew Agrippa will not find the notion of resurrection from the dead absurd (26.8). However, the claim that 'Jesus is the *first* to rise from the dead' must be asserted vigorously, for it will not find a ready welcome.

Luke sets the resurrection of Jesus into an eschatological framework that is distinctively Christian. In addition to the two passages just referred to, the four passages that refer to the hope of Israel make this clear. In 23.6 ('the hope and the resurrection of the dead'); 24.15f.; 26.6f.; and 28.20, Luke's Paul insists that the resurrection of Jesus should be seen as the climax of the messianic hopes of Israel.[14]

For Luke the resurrection of Jesus is the fulfilment of 'what the prophets and Moses said would take place' (Acts 26.22). The same points had already been made strongly in Luke's Gospel: 24.21, 26–7, 32, 44–6. Perhaps somewhat optimistically, Luke believes that most Jews will not have fundamental objections to the resurrection of Jesus. What separates most Jews and most Christians from one another is not the historical evidence for the resurrection of Jesus, but whether or not Jesus fulfils the messianic hopes of Israel. To the surprise of many Christians, the contemporary Jewish theologian Pinchas Lapide defends a similar position. He openly accepts the resurrection of Jesus as a historical event and as an act of God. But for Lapide, as for Luke, it is the Messiahship of Jesus that marks the division between Christianity and Judaism.[15]

OTHER FIRST-CENTURY OBJECTIONS

In the light of the preceding discussion, several further New Testament passages need to be reconsidered, though in each case the dangers of mirror-reading, to which I drew attention above, should be borne in mind. I noted above that Celsus presses the objection that if Jesus had really wanted to show forth divine power, he ought to have appeared to those who put him to death, and to everyone everywhere (II.63, 67). Perhaps similar objections lie behind Acts 10.40-2. Luke's 'answer' to the objection that the risen Jesus was not seen by the whole people is striking: the chosen witnesses to whom Jesus had appeared were commanded to proclaim him to the people.

John 14.18-22 may also reflect similar consternation over the resurrection appearances. In these verses it is not clear whether resurrection appearances or the parousia (or both) are in view. In verse 22, however, the question of the 'other' Judas certainly refers to the resurrection appearances: 'how is it that you intend to disclose yourself to us, and not to the world?' From the immediate context, John's answer to this possible objection is that Jesus will disclose himself to those who love him and keep his commands (v. 21).[16]

Mark 15.44-5 may also be related to an early objection to the resurrection of Jesus. Although Matthew and Luke follow Mark closely in this pericope, these two verses are not found in either Gospel. I think it is probable that they were added very early to the version of Mark used by Matthew and by Luke in order to underline the reality of the death of Jesus and so rule out a claim that Jesus had not really died on the cross, but had revived in the cool tomb. The 'swoon' theory, like most modern objections to the resurrection of Jesus, may have been anticipated in antiquity.

By now some readers of this chapter will have recalled the objection mentioned by Paul in 1 Corinthians 15.12: 'If . . . we proclaim that Christ was raised from the dead, how can some of you say there is no resurrection of the dead?' (REB). I do not think that this verse reflects any doubt on the part of the Corinthians about the resurrection of Jesus: there is no hint either in the immediate context or elsewhere in 1 Corinthians that this was the case. For reasons which we need not discuss here, some Christians in Corinth denied that believers could or should look forward to a general resurrection.

The early objections to the resurrection of Jesus remind us of the varied views of both Jews and pagans on post-mortem existence. Not surprisingly, some of the New Testament resurrection traditions have been shaped in the light of a range of apologetic concerns. More surprising, however, are the ways in which the evangelists and those who earlier transmitted resurrection traditions offered hostages to fortune: in most of the traditions, the discovery of the empty tomb is bewildering; the risen Jesus appears only to a small number of his followers – and their doubts are not excised from the traditions. Several obvious objections are not countered: resurrection traditions are transmitted and proclaimed, doubts and all.

Early objections to the resurrection hardly ever seem to have been made in isolation from negative assessments of the teaching and the actions of Jesus.[17] Opponents and followers alike saw that claims about the resurrection of Jesus raised the same issues as his actions and his teaching: for opponents, the whole story was riddled with trickery and deceit; for followers, the story was God's story.

An even more important issue emerges from this study of early objections to the resurrection of Jesus. For some early opponents of Christianity, the theological claims about the risen Jesus that were made by his followers raised far more fundamental issues than did allegedly implausible details in the resurrection traditions. The opponents who saw this still deserve to be listened to.

Notes

[1] Leslie Houlden always goes out of his way to listen to those whose viewpoints differ from his own. He has heard an earlier version of this chapter, unaware, I hope, of its ultimate destination. It is a pleasure to offer this study to a good friend and valued colleague who will be missed keenly at King's College.

[2] See Stanton 1994, pp. 166–82.

[3] See Barclay, pp. 73–93.

[4] See Benko 1980, Wilken 1984, and Whittaker 1984.

[5] Quotations are from Chadwick 1953.

[6] See Stanton 1992, pp. 171–2, 185–9.

[7] See Bammel 1986, pp. 265–83. Bammel concludes that since the comments of Celsus' Jew come from the time of the apostolic fathers and the later writers of the New Testament, they are of unsurpassed value.

[8] In I.51 Origen mentions, but only in passing and not in response to an objection raised by Celsus, Matthew's attempt to rule out the claim that the disciples stole the body of Jesus (28.13–14). Origen even claims that the soldiers who guarded the tomb and were later bribed were *eyewitnesses* of the resurrection, as in the Gospel of Peter 9–10!

[9] Justin refers to this 'counter mission' near the opening of the *Dialogue* (17), but at that point he gives only a summary of its contents without mentioning the objection to the resurrection; there is an even briefer reference at 117.

[10] Following formal declaration in Jerusalem of observation of the new moon, messengers were sent to the diaspora. My research student Eileen Poh has drawn my attention to references to letters on other matters which were sent to the diaspora: Jer. 29.4–23; 2 Baruch 78–87; 2 Macc. 1.1–10a; 10b–2.18; Esther 9.20–32.

[11] Since Codex Bezae (and the so-called western text) includes a large number of additional words and phrases in Acts (often as explanatory comments), in some of the small number of places where this codex offers a shorter reading it may well retain the original wording. It is less easy to account for later omission of the phrase than for a later addition.

[12] So Haenchen 1971, pp. 638–9.

[13] So also Haenchen 1971. NRSV echoes the terse Greek: 'they were proclaiming that in Jesus there is the resurrection of the dead'. REB attempts to unpack the Greek and almost misses the point: 'they were proclaiming the resurrection from the dead by teaching the people about Jesus'.

[14] On these passages, see Haacker 1985, pp. 437–51.

[15] Lapide 1984.

[16] I am grateful to the Rev. Roger Larkinson, a research student at King's College, for pointing out to me the possible relevance of this passage for my approach.

[17] For the latter, see Stanton 1994.

BIBLIOGRAPHY

Bammel, E. 1986. 'Der Jude des Celsus' in his collected essays, *Judaica: Kleine Schriften I*, 265–83. Tübingen: Mohr.

Barclay, John. 1987. 'Mirror-Reading a Polemical Letter: Galatians as a Test Case', *Journal for the Study of the New Testament* 31: 73–93.

Benko, S. 1980. 'Pagan Criticism of Christianity During the First Two Centuries', in *Aufstieg und Niedergang der Römischen Welt* II, 23:2, ed. W. Haase, 1055–118. Berlin: de Gruyter.

Chadwick, Henry. 1953. *Origen: Contra Celsum*. Cambridge: Cambridge University Press.

Haacker, K. 1985. 'Das Bekenntnis des Paulus zur Hoffnung Israels nach der Apostelgeschichte des Lukas', *NTS* 31: 437–51.

Haenchen, E. 1971. *The Acts of the Apostles*. Oxford: Blackwell.

Lapide, Pinchas. 1984. *The Resurrection of Jesus*. London: SPCK.

Stanton, G. N. 1992. *A Gospel for a New People: Studies in Matthew*. Edinburgh: T. & T. Clark.

Stanton, G. N. 1994. 'Jesus of Nazareth: A Magician and a False Prophet who Deceived Israel?' in *Jesus of Nazareth: Lord and Christ*, FS I. H. Marshall, eds. J. B. Green and M. M. B. Turner, 166–82. Grand Rapids: Eerdmans.

Whittaker, Molly. 1984. *Jews and Christians: Graeco-Roman Views*. Cambridge: Cambridge University Press 1984.

Wilken, R. L. 1984. *The Christians as the Romans Saw Them*. New Haven and London: Yale University Press.

Williams, A. L. 1930. *Justin Martyr: The Dialogue with Trypho*. London: SPCK.

9
'He is not here':
Towards a Theology of the Empty Tomb

Francis Watson

It is possible to imagine a situation in which one looked back on the time of belief in the raising of Jesus from the dead as a closed historical epoch. Historically, human beings have persuaded themselves of the truth of an extraordinary profusion of incompatible and (to outsiders) unlikely beliefs about their gods, and belief in the raising of Jesus would simply be another item to add to the collection, an object of idle curiosity or scholarly study, but extinct as a matter of living religious concern. Yet, while such an unambiguously post-Christian situation as this is certainly imaginable, it is not the situation in which we happen to find ourselves. To place this belief alongside other ancient beliefs as the object of a serenely dispassionate gaze is currently only possible if one abstracts oneself from social contexts in which it remains a matter of fundamental religious concern. Belief in the raising of Jesus remains a social reality, along with the dissension that such fundamental religious traditions often generate within the communities that preserve them. Christ is still preached as raised from the dead, and the debate about the proper interpretation of the basic assertion is usually perceived by participants as of central rather than merely peripheral significance. It is not at all the case that only 'traditionalists' really care about this issue. 'Revisionists' – those who advocate a substantial modification of Christian understanding in this area – may care about it no less deeply.

The labels 'traditionalist' and 'revisionist' are convenient ways of identifying two ends of a spectrum which in fact traverses a variety of shades of opinion. The labels simplify the debate by representing it as a straightforward polarization between two internally consistent positions, but they do not wholly *mis*represent it: for there is indeed a series of either/or theological choices in place here. In particular, attention has come to focus on the question whether what we call 'the resurrection' involves the physical body of Jesus as the vehicle of his

new life, or whether it is to be understood primarily as an interpretation of the experience that restored his disciples' faith and hope. The
second position necessitates a downgrading of the significance of the
empty tomb story (which is, ironically, the only stable element in the
fourfold gospel presentation), whereas the first regards this story as
indispensable testimony to the 'physical' or 'bodily' nature of Jesus'
resurrection, understood both as an empirical occurrence within space
and time and as a transcendent divine act. On one view, the
archaeological discovery of the bones of Jesus intact within his tomb
would destroy Christian faith; on the other view, it would not affect it
in the slightest.

If we construe this as a debate about whether or not Jesus' physical
remains might in principle be available for archaeological identification (as the remains of some of his contemporaries already are), the
'traditionalist' position may appear to have slid into the realm of the
fantastic and the absurd, from which its 'revisionist' dialogue-partner
has a duty to try to rescue it. But in fact neither position is concerned
solely with the empirical question whether on the third, fourth and
fifth days after the crucifixion the normal processes of physical decay
continued unchecked – in fulfilment of the divine decree, 'You are
dust, and to dust you shall return' (Gen. 3.19). In both positions the
empirical question – which confronts us with an utterly concrete
either/or choice – is relocated within an overarching theological
framework, so that the question is no longer simply whether an
alleged paranormal event did or did not take place, but the capacity of
what we call 'the resurrection' to help to shape our understanding of
the being of God in relation to the world. The two conflicting
opinions over an empirical matter of fact only make sense within the
theological frameworks of which they are respectively a part. While it
is true that theologies are in practice far more fluid than my construction of two opposing 'positions' acknowledges, it seems worthwhile
to identify some of the theological ingredients that tend to cohere with
the respective points of view.

The 'traditionalist' position belongs within a theology 'from
above', primarily concerned with divine *action* in relation to the
world. The triune God is conceived as a differentiated personal
agency disclosed especially in the complexes of acts that in the biblical narrative comprise 'creation' and 'redemption'. In this model,
divine action is 'personal' not only in the sense that any 'act' presupposes a personal agent, but also in the sense that divine action is

primarily oriented towards the human persons whom it initially calls into being, and whose relations with one another and with their divine origin it aims to restore and perfect. God's act in the raising of Jesus is therefore not an isolated, freak phenomenon, but belongs within the pattern of divine action reflected in the biblical narratives. In all its particularity and concreteness as the culmination of the story of Jesus, its scope is universal; it aims at restored and renewed divine–human communion and community, the human love of God and of neighbour. The Church's mission 'to the ends of the earth', stemming from the outpouring of the Spirit at Pentecost, is conceived as the uncompleted historical actualization of this potentially universal import, as ripples spread outward towards the margins from a highly localized central point.

The 'revisionist' position finds such talk of 'personal divine agency' frankly incredible, an anachronistic survival from a time when, in the absence of the complexities and immensities disclosed by modern knowledge, the world was a simpler and a smaller place. The proper response to this qualitatively new situation is (it is said) a theology 'from below' that renounces over-confident talk of divine action and speaks instead of the human apprehension, in and through particular religious traditions, of the divine mystery that encompasses the world and comes to expression in religious experience and in liberating praxis. To speak of God as raising Jesus from the dead is therefore a mythological or symbolic way of referring to the particular historical apprehension of God in which the life and death of Jesus issued, and to the new and fruitful possibilities for living in the world that this opened up. Local cultural factors determined the interpretation of this apprehension in terms of 'resurrection'. Its abiding significance within the Christian tradition is unquestionable, yet it must not be understood in such a way as to undermine the integrity and value of other apprehensions of God both inside and outside the Christian tradition. We must resist at every point a Christian totalitarianism committed to devaluing everything that is other than itself and therefore blind to the possibility that the divine mystery is greater, richer, and more manifold than our limited and insular conceptual frameworks allow. The interpretation of a particular, localized event as a divine action with universal significance is at the heart of this totalitarianism, and a reinterpretation of this event that reduces its pretensions is therefore a demand of theological responsibility as well as of intellectual honesty.

It would be possible to argue that the first position is not quite as vulnerable to the critique of the second as might appear at first sight. Revisionist theologies make life too easy for themselves when they treat what may be serious and nuanced theological positions as nothing more than a symptom of an underlying dogmatism, fundamentalism, androcentrism, or other such unforgivable sins. However, in this context it is more important to note the potential *hermeneutical* role of the two theological positions: both may function as interpretative frameworks or paradigms, guiding although not necessarily controlling or dictating the way in which the New Testament texts are read. If, for example, the texts are read along redaction-critical lines, with the emphasis placed on the supposed concerns of their authors rather than on the event of the resurrection itself, this presupposes the theological legitimacy of a revisionary view of the resurrection traditions as the relatively autonomous constructions of human religious imagination.

Over against this, I wish to explore the interpretative possibilities of the alternative position, according to which the truth-claim that 'God raised Jesus from the dead' is irreducible to assertions about the disciples' faith or early Christian tradition, but means what it says. Is it possible to read the gospel narratives, in all their fragmentariness, as a truthful witness to the meaning and significance of this divine act? I shall attempt a positive answer to this question, by way of a reading of the Marcan and Matthean empty tomb stories that is sensitive to the distinctiveness of narrative mediation of theological truth.

Biblical narrative is rarely well interpreted if one understands it as a direct, neutral transcript of a prior empirical reality, and such an approach is particularly problematic in the case of the gospel post-resurrection narratives, granted the obvious and well-known divergences between them. It cannot be said that each Gospel preserves a fragment of such a transcript and that if we reassemble the fragments we gain a clear idea of what actually happened. Quite apart from its other difficulties, this harmonizing view is forced to treat the fourfoldness of the gospel testimony as an unfortunate accident: each Gospel would then contribute a few random pieces to the jigsaw-puzzle, and the pieces would make no sense at all in their native contexts. It is, however, premature to conclude from the obvious impossibility of harmonizing the narratives that in their divergences they undermine their own testimony to the raising of Jesus and compel us to accept some greatly reduced revisionist account of this event.

Let us consider the hypothesis that the New Testament's claim that God raised Jesus from the dead is irreducible to any prior statement about the disciples' experiences within a given cultural context, and that this claim is therefore ultimately *true*. What if we link this true claim with the further claim that the Gospels' divergent testimony to the raising of Jesus is inadequate and self-contradictory? The result would be a somewhat odd account of divine action: God raises Jesus from the dead but fails to ensure the production of adequate testimony to this event, with the result that its disclosive capacity is seriously impaired. It is theologically preferable to ask whether the gospel narratives can be read as an appropriate testimony to the raising of Jesus precisely *in* their fragmentariness, and not *in spite of* it. On this view, the narratives and the traditions from which they stem would be included within the sphere of the event itself, so that the generation of an appropriate testimony to itself would be integral to the event. What kind of interpretative findings would such an approach open up?

The fragmentary nature of the gospel post-resurrection tradition is most obvious in the case of Mark 16.1–8, especially if with some manuscripts and most recent scholars verse 8 is taken as the original ending of Mark. The women's encounter with a young man in white, seated in the tomb, generates only the terror to which this text allows the final word. Yet before the women's panic-stricken flight, the text has succeeded in pointing to a future event beyond its own horizons – a reunion with the disciples in Galilee, the presupposition of which is that Jesus is risen. The event is not narrated, but its occurrence is guaranteed not just by the young man's promise ('there you will see him . . .'), but by the grounding of this promise in the prior word of Jesus ('. . . as he told you'). The women's failure to pass on the young man's message to the disciples might be read as an indication that the promised reunion never took place, and that this is the reason why the narrative of reunion that verse 7 leads the reader to expect is not forthcoming. But since the reunion is guaranteed by the word of Jesus, the reader is led to conclude that the reunion *must* have taken place somehow, even if the narrative appears to make it impossible. The fundamental impossibility of the promised reunion between Jesus and his disciples arose from the event of his death; and if even this impossibility has been overcome by the fact that he is risen, then the lesser impossibility arising from the women's silence will surely not prevent the reunion from taking place.

On the view that the reunion in Galilee is not narrated because the failure of the women meant that it never happened, the Gospel of Mark ends not in mystery, but in sheer banality and anti-climax. On the view that the narrative points towards the real occurrence of an apparently impossible event lying beyond its own horizons, the situation is much more interesting. Why is it that the narrator refuses to meet his readers' demand that the story of the reunion should be told? It is part of the contract between narrator and reader that a story should be brought to a proper conclusion. Yet this narrator has written a cliffhanger that refuses even the consolation that the story will be resumed next week or next month. He has left his readers poised on the brink of a precipice beyond which lies only empty space – the empty space of a page which tantalizes by remaining obstinately unwritten. (Another biblical writer at least has the grace to offer his disappointed readers an explanation of his failure to write: 'I was about to write, but I heard a voice from heaven saying, "Seal up what the seven thunders have said, and do not write it down"' [Rev. 10.4].) Were those early readers of Mark who added the alternative endings right to feel a certain frustration with the text as it stood before them? Or had they missed the point?

They perhaps failed to see that the Marcan empty tomb story is not only followed by an unexpectedly blank page, but that it is also preceded by one. The story is located in the gap between the two unnarrated events that nevertheless together form the climax of the Marcan narrative: the event of the resurrection itself and the reunion with the disciples through which the event was definitively disclosed. Both events (or rather, both the past and the future dimensions of the single event) are spoken of only indirectly, through the young man's speech to the women. The non-narration of the disclosure-event is of a piece with the non-narration of the resurrection itself. In this narrative, the resurrection of Jesus is always spoken of as a future or as a past event (cf. 14.28 and 16.6, respectively). It never occupies the narrative's present, so that the reader could say: *now* he is being raised. It appears that the resurrection is *both* a datable event, occurring 'on the third day' or 'after three days', *and* that in some sense it cannot be incorporated into the relatively straightforward chronological sequence of the narrative. This is all the more remarkable in that the women visit the tomb 'very early [*lian proi*] on the first day of the week' (16.2). Will they not arrive just in time to behold the great event itself? Coincidences of this kind – a fortuitous arrival at the precise moment when something momentous is taking place – are a commonplace of narrative technique. Yet, just as the coincidence is about to occur, this narrative swerves away from it; the women are very early, but Jesus rose earlier still, and they encounter not Jesus himself, but a surrogate with whom he has left a message. Wishing to testify to the twofold event of the resurrection and its authoritative disclosure through Jesus' appearance to his disciples, this narrative refuses to subject the event to the order and comprehensibility of narrative form, but speaks only of that which lies at the margins of the event: an empty tomb, a communication at second-hand. The refusal stems, it seems, from the narrator's reticence in the face of the mystery of the divine act. To narrate an event is to enclose it within a verbal structure that aims to make it intelligible and imaginable; narrative presupposes the *reproducibility* of the event in the mind of the reader by way of the words on the page. In speaking of this event only in the form of a non-narration, the Marcan narrator indicates that the divine act of raising Jesus from the dead is not intelligible, imaginable, and therefore reproducible as other events are. Narrative testimony to it must therefore be indirect and fragmentary.

The fragmentary nature of this particular narrative is therefore not an accident, but is integral to its meaning; it is an expression of the narrator's reticence in the face of the mystery of the divine action. The reader's eyes must be diverted from trying to penetrate too directly into the heart of the mystery, which must therefore always be located in the future or in the past and never in the narrative's present. Two broader implications suggest themselves at this point. First, the fragmentary nature of the fourfold gospel resurrection tradition as a whole may similarly be seen not as subverting its own authority, but as essential to the peculiar nature of its testimony. Second, a revisionist interpretation of the event of the resurrection in terms of the disciples' experience of renewal has in effect rejected Marcan reserve by locating this event within the general category of 'religious experience', thereby asserting its essential clarity and intelligibility to critical reason. But it then becomes a fundamentally different event to the one that lies just beyond the bounds of the Marcan narrative. In Mark, even a second-hand report of the event is so destabilizing and disorienting that a terrified distancing of oneself from it is the natural if not the appropriate reaction. There are few footholds here for critical self-assurance.

Matthew's narrative is distinguished from its Marcan equivalent by its story of the guard at the tomb, by the spectacular angelophany, and by two appearances of the risen Lord – one to the women on their way back to the city, the other to the eleven disciples in Galilee. Does Matthew, along with much modern criticism, abandon Marcan reticence for the sake of clarity and intelligibility? If the Marcan narrative can be seen as an appropriate response to the mystery of the divine action, can the same really be said of the Matthean one? If the fourfold canonical testimony to the event of the resurrection belongs within the sphere of the event itself, then one should be reluctant to play off one of the accounts against another. Is it possible to read the Matthean and the Marcan accounts as, in their different ways, speaking of the same thing, together and not against one another?

In Matthew as in Mark, the women are again at the tomb very early; but here they arrive in time to see something worth seeing. This narrator deploys the narrative convention of coincidence that his co-narrator unexpectedly refused. The horizontal movement of the women towards the tomb is matched by the vertical movement of the angel of the Lord, and the arrival of the two parties is apparently simultaneous: as the women arrived in the garden, 'behold, there was a great earthquake; for an angel of the Lord descended from heaven and came and rolled back the stone, and sat upon it. His appearance was like lightning, and his raiment white as snow' (Matt. 28.2–3). Presumably the stone has been rolled away so that the reader and the women who represent the reader within the text may together *watch* as the Lord arises from death in triumphant Easter glory? Why are we kept in suspense by the rather conventional description of the angel's glory when it is *Jesus* we wish to see? Perhaps there will be a voice from heaven, calling Jesus out of the tomb? A divine voice acknowledged Jesus as Son at his baptism and his transfiguration, and this would be still more appropriate here.

This is the train of events that the narrator might seem to have set in motion by bringing the women to the tomb at precisely the moment when the tomb is opened by an angelic hand. And yet, of course, there is no divine voice, and Jesus does not emerge. The angelic glory does not prepare the way for the manifestation of Jesus' far greater glory, it is a *substitute* for it. 'He is not here', the angel tells the women; he has already left, secretly, while the stone remained in place. Defying the narrative convention according to which the opening of a door should be immediately followed by an entrance or an

exit, Jesus has evidently made his exit *before* the door is opened. As
in Mark, the women leave the garden with a second-hand message of
the resurrection, and even their encounter with Jesus – whose
appearance seems to be quite normal, much less impressive or alarm-
ing than the angel's – does not make up for the fact that they have
missed the great event itself, which they know of only indirectly. As
the women see not the resurrection of Jesus, but the gaping hole
where he lay, so for the reader there is a gaping hole in the narrative.

The fact that in Matthew's narrative the stone is rolled away in the
women's presence means that this evangelist goes still further than
Mark in creating an expectation which the narrative at the last
moment refuses to fulfil: the expectation that the event of the resurrection will be narrated. Acts of angelic power and glory can be narrated, but the raising of Jesus from the dead is different. It is
shrouded in secrecy and silence, and only its after-effect – a vacant
tomb – can be reported. The Matthean narrator diverges from his
Marcan counterpart in being willing to recount appearances of the
risen Jesus: in isolation, the Marcan *via negativa* is perhaps too
stringent, tending to emphasize the mystery of the divine action to
such an extent that its disclosive character is underplayed. But the
narratives are agreed in their refusal to dispel the mystery by pene-
trating into its heart. The tomb of Jesus remains a holy of holies,
separated from the reader by an impenetrable veil until, after the
event, the veil is removed and there is nothing to be seen.

If the gospel narratives are themselves among the after-effects of the
event to which they indirectly testify, then the unnarrated event lies
not only in the margins of the texts but also in the midst of a comprehensive historical reality that also encompasses both texts and
readers. A 'literary' reading that postulates an enclosed, self-
sufficient text cannot do justice to a text whose genre is 'Gospel', the
proclamation of the good news of Jesus Christ the Son of God (cf.
Mark 1.1). A theological reading must be oriented towards the event
itself, although this event can only be approached through the mediation of the tradition it generated, formalized in the New Testament
texts. Since in the New Testament reflection on the theological significance of the event takes a variety of forms, it would be a mistake
to conclude that the category of 'narrative' in itself holds the key to
this event. In comparison with other modes of discourse, narrative
does some things well and other things less well; what it has to say
about the raising of Jesus will be partial, and should not be played off

against the more conceptual approach of the Pauline tradition. Yet it does have its own distinctive theological contribution to make. In the light of the preceding reflections on the Marcan and Matthean empty tomb story, four more general theological points are worth noting.

1. The non-narration of the event establishes it as an event *sui generis*. Its uniqueness does not stem from the fact that its subject-matter is a divine act; this consideration does not normally inhibit the four evangelists or any other biblical narrators from describing an event. This is not merely one divine act among others; it is the goal towards which the entire story of Jesus has been moving, a story which itself grows out of and completes the earlier scriptural testimony to the past and future acts of God in relation to creation and covenant. The manner of the narration suggests an ultimacy which in Mark is left undefined, while in the Matthean narrative it eventually takes shape in the commission to make disciples of all nations, baptizing them in the name of the Father, the Son, and the Holy Spirit, and in the promise of the risen Jesus' eternal presence in fulfilment of his appointed role as 'Emmanuel, that is, God with us' (Matt. 28.19–20; cf. 1.23). The ultimacy of this event is not directly related to eschatology, as it is by Paul in 1 Corinthians 15, and the Pauline view of the risen Christ as the first-fruits of the general resurrection should therefore not be regarded as normative for our understanding of the early Christian testimony to the resurrection.

2. That the divine action is represented as a mystery beyond the scope of narrative is significant for our understanding of God. Talk of divine mystery is commonly divorced from talk of divine action. 'The God who acts' is often devoid of mystery, a supernatural agent whose actions are relatively more powerful than anyone else's but are still readily assimilable into the sphere of personal action in general. The indirect presentation of the bodily resurrection of Jesus is in agreement with the doctrine of creation *ex nihilo* in representing divine action as qualitatively different from finite human action. On the other hand, where mystery is the primary defining characteristic of the divine, the notion of divine action begins to seem anthropomorphic and mythological. Where that is the case, the divine mystery is conceived as ultimately non-personal, an unknowable element within which our own burdensome personhood can be surrendered and dissolved. This (pantheistic?) approach to the divine mystery is, in fact, the product of an alienated view of human personhood. The doctrine of the raising of Jesus has to do with a relation between divine

Creator and human creature which is fundamentally and irreducibly personal, and the mysteriousness of this event bears witness to its origin in an agency which is at the same time personal and non-finite.

3. The empty tomb story understands the divine act as the presupposition of the human faith that it eventually generated, and it is the divine act rather than the human faith that is the primary theme of the story. Faith is thus characterized in terms of its object, and the fact that the divine act is left shrouded in mystery leaves faith inherently vulnerable. It is wrong to characterize the raising of Jesus as an exceptionally well-attested historical event. Within that frame of reference, Celsus' objections remain hard to answer:

> If [the risen] Jesus desired to show that his power was really divine, he ought to have appeared to those who had ill-treated him, and to him who condemned him, and to all people universally . . . But when he might have produced a powerful belief in himself after rising from the dead, he showed himself secretly only to one woman and to his own friends. (Origen, *Against Celsus*, ii.63,70)

The testimonies of Caiaphas, Pilate, and a range of other contemporaries would have constituted a more impressive 'historical evidence' than the few fragments that have survived. There is no security for Christian faith in 'historical evidence', and that this is the case is no accident, but derives from the nature of the unseen, unknowable act in which God raised Jesus from the dead. The Matthean narrative acknowledges the vulnerability of Christian faith to the challenge of so-called 'historical evidence' when in its story of the guard it addresses itself to the problem of the continuing reality of an alternative account in which an all-too-human action renders the hypothesis of a divine act unnecessary: the story that, according to the testimony of the guards, the disciples came by night and stole Jesus' body, which 'has been spread among the Jews to this day' (Matt. 28.15). In tracing this counter-claim back to Easter day itself, the narrative acknowledges that the Christian proclamation of the risen Lord is from the very first open to the possibility of a disbelief that can justify itself in terms that are entirely reasonable within their own frame of reference. Yet this inherent vulnerability of Christian faith need not issue in anxiety and uncertainty, for faith is ultimately grounded not in a personal judgement about the veracity of certain witnesses, but in the promise that 'I am with you always, to the close of the age'

(Matt. 28.20). It is this that has the last word, and not the counter-proclamation or the disciples' own doubt (cf. Matt. 28.17).

4. This talk of 'vulnerability' implies that we are still burdened with what looks very like an empirical claim, in principle falsifiable. On the one hand, the event of the raising of Jesus is unobservable and shrouded in mystery; on the other hand, the fact that after the event the body of Jesus is no longer there suggests that his body is the indispensable vehicle of his risen life. When various 'revisionist' alternatives are widely available, why would anyone prefer a position so exposed to the theoretical if not the practical possibility of empirical falsification? Is this preference based only on a theory about the inseparability of text and event, itself perhaps stemming from a desire to insert oneself within what calls itself 'orthodox Christian belief', at whatever cost to intellectual integrity? Theologically, the significance of this obstinately empirical element lies in what might be called the *materiality* of divine action: its consistent orientation towards the material reality out of which human beings along with other creatures are constituted. The basic paradigm of this materiality is obviously the act of creation itself, where (in the biblical account) the divine creator is not too spiritual and transcendental to sully his hands with matter. Unlike the more refined and fastidious deity of Neoplatonism, he shapes and moulds it and pronounces the results to be very good. Thus, in the fullness of time, the Word became *flesh*, and this enfleshment is not to be seen as a mere interlude followed by a return to the security of a transcendental, inhuman spirituality. The doctrine of Jesus' bodily resurrection is therefore of a piece with the doctrines of creation and incarnation; the culmination of the biblical narrative of creation, fall, and redemption is in fundamental conformity to the beginning. The empty tomb story is a stumbling-block to all forms of theological docetism, and since docetism has proved the most pervasive and insidious of all the temptations that have afflicted Christian theology, resistance to the doctrine of the bodiliness of Jesus' resurrection is only to be expected.

In this necessarily tentative exploration 'towards a theology of the empty tomb', I have tried to avoid the myopic positivisms that cannot see beyond the marshalling of so-called 'historical evidence' for or against the actuality of the raising of Jesus. An alternative seemed to be to allow reflection on the meaning and actuality of the resurrection to arise out of the manner of its narrative mediation, on the assumption that the narrative form of the central biblical testimony to the raising of Jesus is a factor of real although not exclusive significance. Naturally this reading, like any other, reflects a particular set of theological commitments. But that observation would only reduce and relativize its claim if one knew *a priori* that these commitments were inappropriate and that any attempt to explore their possible truth content was therefore doomed to failure. A negative dogmatism of this kind would face a range of counter-questions about its own certainties.

10

Why Does the Resurrection of Christ Matter?

John Barton

Christians agree that the resurrection of Jesus is essential to their religion: 'If Christ has not been raised, your faith is futile' (1 Cor. 15.17). But if we ask *why* it is so important, the trumpet gives an uncertain sound. More people, I would guess, believe that it is an indispensable part of the Christian faith, than can give any sort of account of why that is so. What was plainly a structurally essential part of the faith for most New Testament writers is thus sometimes experienced now as not much more than one in a check-list of 'doctrines' to which assent is required by anyone who wants to be described as a Christian.

In what follows, I shall not attempt to satisfy the reader's perfectly reasonable expectations and say why the resurrection does matter. I shall simply try to unpack the problem. Leslie Houlden has so often shown, by precept and example, that we cannot answer questions we have not yet properly formulated, and in contributing this essay in his honour I will try to show a similar restraint – though perhaps not to the very end. My debt to his own discussion in *Connections* will be obvious.[1]

1. To begin with what I think is the weakest Christian interpretation of Jesus' resurrection: it can be said that it demonstrates that God is powerful, more powerful even than death. It is essentially the *ne plus ultra* of the miraculous, like the gospel healings or exorcisms, only more so. From within a Christian faith that has something more than this to say about the resurrection, this is acceptable; but as a complete account it seems inadequate. How do we know that the resurrection of Jesus was not a freak event, an unusual but marginal occurrence? The Bible reports other raisings to life, both by Jesus himself – the widow's son, Lazarus – and by Elijah and Elisha. What is it about the resurrection of *Jesus* that makes it a *unique* witness to the power of God? Why do the creeds insist that Jesus rose from the dead but make no reference to these other 'resurrections'?

2. Christians often claim that Jesus' resurrection matters because proves that there is life after death.[2] The creeds might be thought to support this, although 'the resurrection of the body' is not explicitly linked to the resurrection of Jesus, which is treated as part of the sequence from his incarnation to his second coming. 'Life after death' as now sometimes conceived, where the person is thought of as living on, unproblematically, after the death of the body, seems quite a long way from the giving of fresh life to someone who is extinct. It fails to catch the sense of radical disjunction between old body and new that the resurrection narratives, for example, seem to imply, in harmony with Paul in 1 Corinthians 15. (The New Testament stresses the continuity between pre- and post-resurrection body, too; but 'life after death' does not do justice to what it has to say.) Much that used to be written about the contrast between the resurrection of the body and the immortality of the soul was simplistic and cannot be defended. But it remains true that the two concepts, though compatible in principle and often held together in practice, are not simply identical.

An argument from the resurrection of Jesus to the resurrection of all believers is already found in Paul, in 1 Corinthians 15. But this is much more complex than modern use of Jesus' resurrection as a warrant for life after death. Paul does seem to deploy the Christian belief that Jesus rose from the dead to counter those who say there is no resurrection at all, reasoning that if they are right, then Christ cannot have risen – which for him constitutes a *reductio ad absurdum* of such people's arguments. But he goes a stage further: 'if Christ has not been raised, then our preaching is in vain and your faith is in vain' (15.14); 'if Christ has not been raised, your faith is futile and you are still in your sins' (15.17, already cited). It is not so much that Christ's resurrection matters because it proves there can be resurrection in general. Rather, there must be a general resurrection, or else Christians would not be experiencing forgiveness of sins and other aspects of salvation, for there would be no risen Christ to impart them. The focus is thus on Christ's resurrection as the source of salvation, rather than on its probative value for 'life after death'.

3. In Acts, and also in the creeds, Jesus' resurrection appears with much less sense of surprise than in the Gospels, where the resurrection narratives strike even the casual reader as an unexpected addition to the aesthetically satisfying passion narratives. It is difficult to imagine how Bach would have set the St Matthew Passion if it had been deemed to include Matthew 28. The sense of violent disjunction

and resurrection narratives may, indeed, be a very
about them. Christian liturgy in some measure
sense – Easter Eve is not at all like Christmas Eve; it
for a moment of climax, but for a moment of reversal.
ds simply provide a list, in which resurrection follows
pass͞ ost routinely; and something similar might be said of the speeches in Acts.

Take Acts 3.12–26: God had foretold that the Christ would suffer (v. 18), and he fulfilled this by raising Jesus to life when the Jews had had him executed (vv. 13–15). The reason why all this – cross and resurrection – matters, is that it achieved the goal of exalting Jesus to heaven, whence he is to come as the final Judge (vv. 20–1). If, as is sometimes claimed, this passage represents a primitive stage in Christian thinking at which resurrection and ascension were not distinguished, it may mean that God reversed Jesus' death *by exalting him to his right hand* in order that he might be his agent at the end. In this scheme, the resurrection does not matter in itself, perhaps does not really occur. The sequence of events is aimed at getting Jesus into heaven, and so ready to come again. Some versions of the '*Christus Victor*' theory of the atonement are also concerned with resurrection/ascension as the events that 'opened the gate of heaven'. This has little to do with the restoration of human life to the dead Jesus, much more with Jesus' progress from earth to heaven.[3]

4. Already implied in this third way of thinking about the resurrection is some kind of eschatological scheme. God has a plan for human history, within which Jesus is central; and his resurrection belongs to the last phases of that plan. When Paul calls Jesus the 'first fruits of those who have fallen asleep' (1 Cor. 15.20), he can only be understood against a background of thought in which the resurrection of the dead belongs to the end time, and Christ's being raised to life was the long-awaited sign that the end was near, the harvest about to be reaped.

These ideas are seldom in the minds of modern Christians, even when reading 1 Corinthians 15, where verses 20–8 spell out the order of events leading up to the final scene in which even the Son will become subject to the Father – important (and difficult) for Christology as well as for the doctrine of the resurrection. Pannenberg, indeed, made the eschatology of early Christian thinking about Christ's resurrection central to his Christology, arguing that the resurrection marked Jesus out as uniquely God's 'Son' precisely because it was appropriated by the disciples in the context of Jewish eschatological hopes as expressed in the later Old Testament and 'inter-testamental' literature.[4] Jesus' being raised from the dead mattered to his first disciples because it meant that one of the signs of the end had arrived. If the dead were being raised – even if only this one man had so far experienced resurrection – then the final hour for death and decay had struck at last. That the dead would rise in the end-time was not novel, no one needed convincing of that; the news (good news for frightened disciples, and potentially for all oppressed Jews, if only they could have been convinced of it) was that the end-time had now arrived. That is why the resurrection of Jesus mattered so much.

Some Christians still accept an eschatological scheme like that in 1 Corinthians or contemporary Jewish works. But many do not, and it is a question how far Paul's approach to Jesus' resurrection is tenable outside such a scheme.[5] The metaphor of 'firstfruits' becomes meaningless, and there is no longer a coherent context within which to interpret what happened to Jesus. Nor is it any longer possible to argue (with Pannenberg) that his resurrection shows him to be crucial in God's scheme of salvation. Where there is no longer a belief in an eventual restoration of all creation (*apokatastasis*), Jesus' resurrection lacks the intelligibility it had for some early Christians.

5. Two further accounts of the resurrection interpret it in terms of Jesus' identity or character. As we have just seen, for Pannenberg who Jesus was (and is) depends on the resurrection, for it is the resurrection which shows him, in Paul's words, to be 'the Son of God in power' (Rom. 1.4). But the reverse can be argued, and commonly was argued in antiquity. The resurrection matters because it is the Son of God who was raised to life. The resurrection of just anyone, startling as it would be, could be some kind of freak event. What matters is that it is *his own Son* whom God raised to new life. This makes the resurrection seem almost inevitable: God surely could not have abandoned his own Son to final death! Jesus was raised from the pangs of death 'because it was not *possible* for him to be held by it' (Acts 2.24).

This way of thinking quickly runs off into docetism if it is not kept very carefully in check. How can the resurrection be good news for us, people ask, when the one person so far to experience it was not like us, but was the Son of God? If the story of how this man lived, suffered, and died, but then was miraculously raised to life again, ends with the footnote 'and he was, of course, the Son of God', the audience is all too likely to feel deeply let down. *Of course* he wouldn't stay dead if he was the Son of God: why didn't you say so before? What we need is an ordinary human being to rise again from the dead – that would be worth celebrating. The orthodox 'two natures' Christology has of course provided a sophisticated way of meeting this objection, without giving up a belief that Jesus is God's Son. But if we stress that the resurrection matters because it was the resurrection of the Son of God, we do very easily fall into the trap of appearing to make it wholly unsurprising and largely lacking in comfort or consolation.

6. A more subtle and more distinctively modern appeal to 'who Jesus was' can be found in John Austin Baker's account of the resurrection in *The Foolishness of God*.[6] The resurrection matters, he maintains, because of the kind of person Jesus was – his moral character and personality. Such an idea is present in embryo in the New Testament, where it is stressed that Jesus was a man who 'went about doing good and healing all that were oppressed by the devil': *this* is the one whom 'God raised on the third day' (Acts 10.38, 40). And we could see most of the stories in the Gospels – in principle, all that precedes the passion narratives – as intended to give readers a picture of Jesus of Nazareth which will show them why it is good news that he, and not someone else, was the first to rise from the dead. As Baker writes:

> The nature of existence is such that the only credible God is one whose values are those exemplified in Jesus. If Herod the Great had risen from the dead, this would not have been tolerable to reason as a testimony to God. For a God who ratified monstrosity might explain the evil in the world; he could never satisfy us as a source of goodness. But the God who ratifies the values incarnate in Jesus . . . can be seen as having a good purpose which gives meaning to the evil in the world. The vindication of Jesus alone supplies the crucial testimony.[7]

There is no theory about the significance of the resurrection that I find more persuasive than this. Its concentration on the human character of Jesus (which does not mean that it is incompatible with traditional Christology) roots the Christian faith in tangible goodness and prevents it from becoming a 'myth'. It coheres with an essentially Abelardian interpretation of the atonement, in which it is the

Moral person + moral commitment ✗

attractiveness of Jesus' moral vision, and its perfect exemplification in his own life, that save us, and do so by opening our hearts, not by working some cosmic trick behind the scenes. (This is a travesty of other theories, but is how they tend to feel for those who prefer Abelard.) It tells us that if we find Jesus' character admirable, so does God, and that is why he is the only person (so far) to have been resurrected. The God it presents us with is God as we should like him to be or (to put it in a way much more convincing to me) God as he must be, if he is to be believable at all. Thus the resurrection as evidence for the type of person God is willing to 'eternalize' becomes the resurrection as evidence for what God himself is like. It shows that God is like Jesus. And that is very good news indeed.

In all this discussion I have not asked what we mean by the resurrection of Jesus anyway. Leslie Houlden has surveyed the possibilities and problems in *Connections*, chapter 9. There is obviously a spectrum of possible meanings, and the theories discussed here do not necessarily operate with the same understanding of what it is to be resurrected. For example, the 'eschatological' interpretation (option 4, above) thinks in terms of resurrection life as one of the conditions of the end-time, perhaps discontinuous with present experience; option 3 thinks of it as the 'glorification' of Jesus, which may not be quite the same thing; while those who see it as a supreme healing-miracle (option 1) presumably understand it as a restoration, as nearly as can be imagined, to pre-death, earthly life.

But it is worth mentioning as a potential problem for Baker's approach that it requires the greatest possible continuity between the crucified Jesus and the risen Jesus – in particular, recognizably the same character. It is essential that the risen Christ manifests just the same moral commitments as he did during his life and passion. Raising Jesus to life but making him significantly a different person would not fulfil the basic requirement of this model.

It can be said that the creeds, with their simple listing of events and no sense of distinction between the Jesus who died and the Jesus who rose, meet this requirement. So do the gospel narratives, most heart-stoppingly in the story of the walk to Emmaus (Luke 24.13–35), but also in other narratives where everything turns on *recognition* of the stranger as the already known Jesus. But in both cases it would be hard to show that there is much attention to Jesus' character or personality in the modern sense – indeed, to expect it would be anachronistic. The New Testament evidence that Jesus was raised to life because he was the kind of person dearest to God's heart is not plentiful. Baker's theory remains, I think, a modern interpretation of the resurrection considered as a fact attested *by* the New Testament, rather than as a modern version of a theory that is clearly already present *in* the New Testament. This is not meant as a criticism of it! Good theology need not be merely a reappropriation of something already present in the Bible – indeed, there is little point in it if that is all it is.

My intention in this essay has not been to answer the question why the resurrection matters, but to illustrate the variety of defensible answers that have been and can be given. Their diverse character, however, prompts one observation in conclusion. From earliest times, Christians have been convinced that Jesus of Nazareth was 'raised from the dead'. But they have never come to a common mind either on what this amounted to – except that his risen body was both continuous with and different from the body that had died – nor, perhaps more extraordinarily, on why it mattered anyway. The New Testament and the creeds record several different theories, not all mutually compatible, and subsequent theology has added others.

Is this not good evidence that belief in the resurrection preceded all the interpretations of it? If it were clear what place resurrection belief plays in the Christian scheme of things, one could imagine that it might have been fabricated for the purpose. There would be a logical hole in Christianity which could only be filled by the resurrection of Jesus, and that resurrection 'must' therefore have happened. This cannot be the correct explanation when there are numerous different, sometimes not even compatible, accounts of what Jesus' resurrection was and why it matters. An academic essay may be the wrong place to draw the conclusion that the resurrection of Jesus did, as a matter of fact, occur; especially since, as we have seen, there is no agreement about what it was that occurred, if it did. But we might say at least that a belief that Jesus had been raised certainly preceded any attempt to explain why that was such excellent news for the human race.

Notes

[1] See J. L. Houlden, *Connections: The Integration of Theology and Faith* (London: SCM Press, 1986), esp. ch. 9.

2 ibid., pp. 148–9.

3 See J. L. Houlden, *Patterns of Faith* (London: SCM Press, 1977), p. 58.

4 W. Pannenberg, *Jesus: God and Man* (London: SCM Press, 1968), pp. 66–73.

5 cf. Houlden, *Connections*, p. 145, and p. 193 n. 22.

6 J. A. Baker, *The Foolishness of God* (London: Darton, Longman & Todd, 1970).

7 Baker, *The Foolishness of God*, p. 278. I have argued in a similar way myself in J. Barton, *Love Unknown: Meditations on the Death and Resurrection of Jesus* (London: SPCK, 1990), pp. 46–8.

11
A Naked Pillar of Rock

Maurice Wiles

Leslie Houlden's writing on Christian theology has not received the recognition that the acuteness of so many of its observations merits. This is no doubt due, in part at least, to the relaxed and unpretentious way in which those observations are characteristically expressed. But his way of putting things is not just stylistically attractive; it often embodies memorable images. Book reviews are a relatively utilitarian form of composition, not the place where one expects to come across images of haunting power. Yet it was in a book review by Leslie, which appeared ten years ago, that I encountered the image that constitutes my title, an image that has stayed with me ever since as a focus of reflection about the issue of resurrection in contemporary faith. The context in which it came reads as follows:

> Moreover, the isolation of incarnation and resurrection for treatment as prime and crucial instances of direct divine action, while it may seem a concession to modernity, effectively falsifies the role they formerly played. Once peaks in a landscape full of hills, all seen as such instances, they now stand out like naked pillars of rock in a plain.[1]

Resurrection and incarnation have many features in common. Both are major Christian doctrines linked to particular moments in history, for which a highly specific form of divine initiative is claimed. Moreover, each is associated, though not wholly identified, with a clearly miraculous occurrence, on any definition of the much-disputed word 'miracle'. The other peaks in the landscape of earlier days sometimes resembled them in both respects, more frequently in one or the other. Thus some took the form of important historical events, ascribed to divine initiative but not associated with any particular miraculous event – such as the sack of Jerusalem by Nebuchadrezzar or its restitution following the rise and military successes of Cyrus. Others were miraculous happenings, but ones of far less religious or theological significance – such as some of the other gospel miracles or those of Peter and Paul, like the raising of Dorcas or the blinding of Elymas. While many conservative Christians continue to assert the truth of all these purported divine initiatives and less central miracle stories without alteration, more critically minded Christians, even quite orthodox ones, have come to discount many, if not all, of them. They have been cleared away as blots on the intellectual landscape. The question I want to pursue here is: what are the implications of such clearing for the two remaining naked pillars, in particular for belief in the resurrection? To keep the discussion of so vast a topic within the bounds of a relatively short paper, I shall concentrate on Anglican thought.

The creeds speak of the incarnation in terms of Christ's conception by the Holy Spirit and birth of the Virgin Mary, and of the resurrection as something that happened 'on the third day'. But the ways in which the two theological claims are related to their associated miraculous events are not identical. The existence of a difference at this point is indicated by a difference in linguistic usage. The word 'resurrection' is one we use equally naturally to refer either to the theological concept or to the miraculous event. But the word 'incarnation' is a more purely theological term, and is not, in a parallel way, a synonym for 'virginal conception' or 'virgin birth'.

That difference in linguistic usage is reflected in a difference between the ways in which the links between historical claim and theological affirmation are regarded in the two cases. The virgin birth has proved much more detachable from the doctrine of incarnation than has the miraculous nature of the resurrection event from the doctrine of resurrection. On the issue of the virgin birth and belief in the incarnation, the 1938 report *Doctrine in the Church of England* acknowledged two different views among its members. 'Many' held

> that belief in the Word made flesh is integrally bound up with belief in the Virgin Birth, and that this will increasingly be recognised.

'Some', on the other hand, took the view

> that a full belief in the historical Incarnation is more consistent with the supposition that our Lord's birth took place under the normal conditions of human generation. In their minds the notion of a Virgin Birth tends to mar the completeness of the belief that in

the Incarnation God revealed Himself at e   point in and through human nature.[2]

The first position no doubt continues to be held by the increasing number of Christians who maintain a strongly conservative understanding of Christian faith as a whole. But among Christians who accept a broadly critical approach to faith, the latter view has surely gained ground. In such circles, doubt in the literal truth of the virginal conception no longer shocks. Nor does the issue play a significant role in discussions about the doctrine of the incarnation. In the debates set in motion by *The Myth of God Incarnate* (to which Leslie and I were both contributors),[3] it played virtually no part. In the index to the subsequent volume, *Incarnation and Myth: The Debate Continued*,[4] in which seven critics of the initial book's challenge to traditional incarnational doctrine also had their say, 'virginal conception' has only one entry – and that is to a piece by Michael Goulder, not by one of the book's critics. In the case of one of the two 'naked pillars', the element of identifiable miraculous event has largely disappeared.

In the case of the resurrection, there has been a similar detachment of the theological conviction from its associated historical miraculous event; but for the most part it has been more hesitant and much less widely accepted, even outside the circles of those strongly conservative believers for whom any such questioning of the miraculous event is virtually ruled out on principle. The parallel between the relation of the historical and the theological aspects in the two doctrines is evident enough. The historical evidence in the case of the resurrection may be more broadly based and more central to the New Testament than in the case of the virgin birth, but it shares many of the legendary characteristics and the less than public character of the other. 'Stories of the empty tomb', as John Macquarrie puts it, 'look like examples of the usual mythologizing tendency, which seeks to express the faith that God has acted in terms of objectifiable and empirically verifiable phenomena.'[5] The 1938 Doctrine Report makes an acknowledgement in relation to the resurrection similar to that about the virgin birth – but more cautiously, and only in an appended note. In this case some thought it

essential to the full Christian hope that the physical dissolution of life should be reversed by resurrection.

But others, who understood the empty tomb to be of symbolic significance only, claimed support for their view from the fact

> that both in the Apostles' Creed and the Pauline Epistles the resurrection of the dead and the Resurrection of Christ are made correlative the one to the other, and that the beliefs are connected not only by their historical origin, but also in their essential nature.[6]

A striking feature of the way in which these differences of opinion are described is the importance given to positive doctrinal reasons in favour of the position adopted. This is characteristic not only of the Doctrine Report in particular, but of Anglican scholarship generally, at that time and subsequently. Oliver Quick's *Doctrines of the Creeds* was published in the same year as the Doctrine Report. In relation to both the virgin birth and the resurrection, it emphasizes the indecisiveness of the historical evidence. The first sub-heading in the chapter on the virgin birth is 'The Determining Considerations are Doctrinal', and with respect to the resurrection Quick argues that the decisive factor in determining Christian belief in the resurrection of Jesus is the Christian's prior belief in his absolute uniqueness.[7] Michael Ramsey argues in similar vein that when the evidence suggests 'a supernatural event at the climax of the story of Christ', we might well react with incredulity, were it not that 'the Christ Himself is a unique and transcendent fact in history'.[8] John Burnaby's book, *The Belief of Christendom*, which was in many respects a successor to Quick's book a generation later, also adopts a similar line of reasoning, though less concerned about whether it will lead to historically conservative conclusions:

> It is with the Empty Tomb as with the Virgin Birth: if we believe it, we believe it because we believe that the Son of God who came down from heaven to be born as a man has overcome death in the manhood he has made his own.[9]

The use of such doctrinal arguments as the decisive ground for rejecting the historicity of the empty tomb story and a physical resurrection of Jesus, tentatively adumbrated in the Doctrine Report, has grown with the passage of time. Geoffrey Lampe argued that the belief 'that Christ's Resurrection is the assurance that we too shall rise from the dead . . . implies that his Resurrection was not different in kind from what we may hope for from him'. Moreover, Lampe suggests, a physical resurrection preventing the dissolution of Christ's body would (like a virginal conception) be a docetic denial of Christ's full humanity; it would mean that Christ did not share our human lot to the very end.[10]

But it is hard to see how such doctrinal arguments can play the decisive role for which they have been cast. They can be developed impressively to either effect. The most appropriate role for doctrinal argument to fulfil in cases of this kind is that of enabling us to see the wider significance of what we apprehend on other grounds to be the case. They can help us to see the facts in a new light, and while there is admittedly a grey area between seeing facts differently and seeing different facts, we need to be very wary of doctrinal arguments that claim to determine for us facts for which we otherwise lack sufficient evidence. If they have been given special weight in these discussions because of the inconclusiveness of the historical evidence, they have proved ill-suited to the task assigned them. They have their own distinctive kind of inconclusiveness.

Faced with the failure of this attractive and characteristically Anglican blend of critical history and doctrinal reflection, two contrasting strategies seem to have emerged. One strategy is to acknowledge that the resurrection *is* to be seen as a naked pillar of rock, an isolated phenomenon, but to insist that that is no embarrassment; the isolation of the naked pillar is a glorious isolation. Anthony Hanson expresses this view with robust vigour. He writes:

> With one all-important exception, the process of recognizing God in Christ . . . does not necessarily involve the acknowledgement of any superhuman element.

But there is the one exception. God's self-disclosure

> needed a superhuman event, the resurrection of Jesus Christ, in order to identify it and complete it.

He sums up his position with these words:

> With the all-important exception of the resurrection of Jesus Christ, which we have claimed was an essential act of divine vindication, this has been an exposition of the incarnation which has not at any point relied on miracle, on anything superhuman, for its evidence.[11]

In similar vein, John Polkinghorne points to the fact that today little appeal is made to miracle 'as a *primary* ground for belief', but adds a qualifying clause:

> except for the critical role that the resurrection plays in Christian thought, as the vindication of the crucified Messiah and of the God who allowed his chosen one to die a shameful death.[12]

Neither Hanson nor Polkinghorne rules out the possibility of other miracles. The surrounding peaks are scaled down and moved out to the periphery of the landscape rather than demolished altogether. But Leslie's evocative image gives imaginative expression to the difficulties inherent in such a position. If the resurrection of Jesus is required to provide such indispensable evidence for Christian belief, it will have to do so without recourse to that which it is intended to establish. But the more isolated a phenomenon it is understood to be, the more difficult the process of establishing its truth becomes. Despite the efforts of Wolfhart Pannenberg,[13] the historical evidence seems quite unable to bear the enormous weight that such an approach demands of it.

The other strategy is much more elusive in character. In broad terms, it can be seen as a more sophisticated version of the approach represented by Quick, Ramsey, and Burnaby, in which it is primarily conviction about the resurrection that is determined by the wider structure of Christian belief rather than the other way round. Hardy and Ford acknowledge that while 'there are "hard data" associated with [the resurrection] which need assessment, . . . they are inevitably ambiguous'.[14] With 'inevitably ambiguous' data one has to rely on other considerations to determine how to read them. The context which makes for a positive reading of the evidence is described as the trinitarian structure of knowledge of the resurrection: 'a God who can do this, an historical person who is the object of it, and a spiritual and social experience of justified trust'.[15] Rowan Williams provides a characteristically self-reflective account of what motivates such an approach and what it involves. His aim is to chart a middle way 'between the Scylla of critical pedantry and the Charybdis of vaguely religious psychology'.[16] In other words, the middle way that he seeks lies between one that tries to resolve the problem by overcoming the historical ambiguities that characterize our records of the resurrection, and one whereby resurrection becomes simply a metaphor for grace, or triumph over adversity, or hope, or any other general human phenomenon, without its being related very clearly to the actual execution of a supposed rebel and/or blasphemer by the Roman colonial administration.[17]

The heart of the matter is 'the continuity of Jesus' identity through death';[18] the disciples encounter 'a Jesus who is, now as hitherto, a partner in dialogue, a material other, still involved in the fabric of human living while also sovereignly free from its constraints'.[19] Williams describes himself as opting for

a fairly 'objectivist' account of the resurrection, taking seriously the empty tomb as a sign of God's historical act of raising Jesus 'as a person' (as a 'body' in some sense).

But he goes on:

I find this extremely perplexing, and cannot give any very satisfactory theological or philosophical account of it.[20]

The same option, and the hesitation about it, are reflected in the cautious double negative with which he qualifies his insistence that 'the tomb story is not a sufficient condition for resurrection faith'. He continues:

but that is not to say that the evangelists are mistaken in seeing it as a *necessary* condition.[21]

Indeed, it is hard to see how he can maintain what is for him the heart of the matter without some such historical (or quasi-historical) claim. But, as he himself tells us, his position is, by 'a deliberate choice', characterized by a 'vagueness on the substantive point of "What Really Happened?"'.[22] The sense in which Jesus is encountered as 'a material other' remains highly elusive. For Jesus, it is said, 'can in some measure "inhabit" the material world beyond the limitations of his biological existence'. The language of materiality seems primarily designed to ensure that the human transformation that is integral to resurrection faith is not seen as 'merely a change in attitude' but as involving, for example, economic relationships, for in that way 'material reality will have become charged with the life of Christ risen'.[23] So it is not clear whether or not there is a naked rock left standing; the whole landscape is so suffused with the shimmering light of the rising sun that the outlines of particular objects are hard to make out. A hostile critic will be puzzled to know whether to regard such an approach as a conservative attempt to maintain a fully miraculous resurrection, of the same kind as Anthony Hanson's, but shirking his robust confrontation with the difficulties raised by the disappearing peaks in the surrounding landscape, or whether to see it as a move towards a more agnostic account, using the language of mystery to throw dust in the eyes of more conservative believers (and dust in a desert may sometimes contribute to the glory of a hazy sunshine). It certainly sees itself in a very different light, as offering a constructive middle way. But there are difficulties in being clear about just what that way really is. So to question its viability is not necessarily evidence of a critical pedantry, blind to the mysterious truths to be learned only on the road to Emmaus.

If the naked pillar of a distinctively miraculous resurrection does go the way of the other peaks, and disappear from the landscape, what will be left? Will there be just a bare plain of such uniform dullness that no landmarks remain to guide the journey of faith, no vestige of inspiration to encourage it? Once again, the twin pillar of the incarnation offers some guidance about the possible scenarios.

'Incarnation', as we have seen, has always been more readily separable from its attendant miraculous features. Loss of belief in the virgin birth has not necessarily had any effect on the way in which incarnation has been believed and affirmed. Whether there is anything logically incoherent in the strong incarnational claim made by the tradition, which identifies the personal core of the being of Jesus with that of the second person of the Trinity, may be a matter for dispute. But if there is not, there is certainly nothing logically incoherent in affirming it to be true without any supernatural element in its implementation. And there are those who do that. The difficulty such a position has to face is an epistemological one: how can we know it to be true? Second, the term can be used to affirm the unique character and significance of Jesus, without being intended to imply any particular understanding of the nature of God's presence to or in him. On such an understanding, for example, an 'adoptionist' view would be seen as one form of incarnational view, rather than as a rival to it. Third, it can be used to express the general truth of the potential immanence of God in every human spirit, of which Jesus is seen as a focal example. 'Incarnation', on such an interpretation, is a more vivid expression of God's presence to human life, combining the notions of regularity and continuity suggested by the term 'immanence' with the more vigorous imagery of the term 'inspiration'.

These three ways of understanding the term 'incarnation' seem to me to be usefully distinguishable, even though the dividing lines between them may sometimes be hard to draw. Their relative appropriateness for a contemporary incarnational theology is a contentious issue, but it is not my purpose to discuss that now. They are outlined in this brief form here simply in order to raise the question: are there analogous possibilities for a non-miraculous understanding of 'resurrection'?

It seems to me that there are, and that all of the three analogous views in the case of resurrection are to be found within the community of believers. The first position is quite close to that of Hardy and Ford, or of Williams. While reading the 'inevitably ambiguous' data in a more firmly negative way, it would still maintain the heart of the matter, 'the continuity of Jesus' living identity through death'. We can say of such a position, as we said of its incarnational counterpart, that if there is nothing logically incoherent in the general notion of continuity of personal identity through death, there is certainly nothing logically incoherent in affirming it to be true of Jesus without any supernatural element being involved in its implementation. But if the ambiguous data *are* read in this negative way in respect of any supernatural character, then, as in the parallel incarnational case, the epistemological difficulties are formidable. Does the character of Christian faith as a whole, without any appeal to miracle, warrant the conviction that there is a distinctive continuity of personal identity through death in the case of Jesus? It may be that it does; but the process of establishing that it does is likely to involve an erosion of the difference between this position and the other two.

The second position would be to use the term 'resurrection' to indicate the positive and distinctive nature of the aftermath of the life and death of Jesus without intending to imply any particular understanding of how that creative aftermath came about. As with the equivalent understanding of incarnation, the etymologically straightforward meaning of the word will be played down. New life out of death is a familiar, but still powerful image for the resilience of human life, both personal and corporate, out of apparent destruction and despair. The creative transformation following from the death of Jesus (whether or not that involves and is empowered by the continuity of Jesus' personal identity through death) may be seen as a unique embodiment of this divine life-giving power within the world.

Third, 'resurrection' may be used with less specific attention to the figure of Jesus, as a general term either for continued personal identity through death or for that potentiality in human life as a whole for the emergence of new life out of old – or, of course, for both. Jesus would then be a focal example of either or both of these senses of 'resurrection', but not in a way that is different in kind from what may also be apprehended through the wider experience of life and can be properly, if tentatively, affirmed on that wider basis. This may seem to be a radical move away from Christianity's traditional insistence on the resurrection of Jesus as the miraculous reversal of all human possibilities and expectations. But it is not quite so radical a move away from Christianity's roots as it may at first appear. As Leslie's initial image reminds us, belief in the resurrection of Jesus arose in an age when hope of resurrection was already alive in some forms of Judaism, and when other miraculous, if more temporary, raisings from the dead were also affirmed. Moreover, not all early Christian assertion of resurrection was directly linked to that of Jesus. Joanne McWilliam comments on this feature of early Christian writing, even in relation to that most substantive of claims – the resurrection of the body. She writes:

> If belief in the resurrection of the body was the distinctive feature of Christian hope, the basis of the teaching of that belief presents a puzzle. It is often assumed, wrongly, that the Christians of the first centuries reiterated the tight Pauline link between Christ's resurrection and their own hope, but in fact, as I found, to my surprise, when I examined the question some years ago, few of the apologists for the resurrection make this connection.[24]

These reflections, to which Leslie's image has given rise for me, do not lead to any particular resolution of the problems concerning resurrection. What I hope they may have done is to suggest that for those for whom it no longer seems possible to affirm the ostensibly miraculous claims about the resurrection of Jesus, various lines of constructive possibility for a theological treatment of resurrection still lie open. Moreover, even if the pursuit of those lines takes them away from much traditional Christian affirmation, there are still significant positive links with the early tradition. Perhaps the disappearance of the last naked pillar will free our gaze from its more superficially impressive grandeur and teach us to apprehend the less immediately evident glories of the wider landscape.

Notes

[1] Review of W. J. Abraham, *Divine Revelation and the Limits of Historical Criticism* in *Journal of Theological Studies* 34.1 (April 1983), p. 378.

[2] *Doctrine in the Church of England* (London: SPCK, 1938), p. 82.

[3] John Hick (ed.), *The Myth of God Incarnate* (London: SCM Press, 1977).

[4] Michael Goulder (ed.), *Incarnation and Myth: The Debate Continued* (London: SCM Press, 1979).

[5] John Macquarrie, *Principles of Christian Theology*, 2nd edn (London: SCM Press, 1977), p. 288.

[6] *Doctrine in the Church of England*, p. 87.

[7] O. C. Quick, *Doctrines of the Creeds* (London: Nisbet, 1938), p. 156; pp. 146–50.

[8] A. M. Ramsey, *The Resurrection of Christ* (London: Geoffrey Bles, 1945), p. 56.

[9] J. Burnaby, *The Belief of Christendom* (London: SPCK, 1959), p. 102.

[10] G. W. H. Lampe and D. M. MacKinnon, *The Resurrection* (London: Mowbray, 1966), pp. 58–9.

[11] A. T. Hanson, *Grace and Truth* (London: SPCK, 1975), pp. 20, 63, 77. Hanson is an illuminating example of the contrasting attitudes to the virgin birth and the resurrection of Jesus to be found in so much contemporary thought. The virgin birth is irrelevant to the question of how the Word became flesh, because 'if it does provide an answer to the question, we now know that it provides the wrong answer' (p. 95).

[12] John Polkinghorne, *Science and Providence* (London: SPCK, 1989), p. 57.

[13] W. Pannenberg, *Jesus: God and Man* (London: SCM Press, 1968).

[14] D. W. Hardy and D. F. Ford, *Jubilate* (London: Darton, Longman & Todd, 1984), p. 133.

[15] ibid., p. 132.

[16] R. D. Williams, *Resurrection* (London: Darton, Longman & Todd, 1982), p. 120.

[17] ibid., pp. 119–20.

[18] Hardy and Ford, *Jubilate*, p. 132 (summarizing Williams' view).

[19] Williams, *Resurrection*, p. 106.

[20] ibid., p. 118.

[21] ibid., p. 106.

[22] ibid., pp. 118–19.

[23] ibid., pp. 111–12.

[24] Review of B. Daley, *The Hope of the Early Church*, in *Theological Studies* 53.4 (Dec. 1992), p. 748.

12

'I Believe in the Resurrection of the Body'

John Muddiman

Leslie Houlden's special calling and talent has been to make connections[1] between New Testament studies and the wider culture of theology in university and Church. He has refused to be confined to a ghetto where specialists only speak to other specialists; and he has maintained his right as a historian to ask questions about truth. So I will not have to apologize, at least to him, for the form and subject of this essay, which is offered with warm affection and respect on the occasion of his retirement.

The formula of the Nicene Creed, 'I believe in the Resurrection of the Body', and even more bluntly its parallel in the Apostles' Creed, 'I believe in the Resurrection of the Flesh', seems to have been intended originally to emphasize the distinctive Jewish doctrine of resurrection against prevailing Greek ideas of the immortality of the soul. It is, however, toned down by the addition of an extra phrase 'and in the Life Everlasting'. This is one example of a recurring phenomenon in the history of doctrine. The Church erects and reinforces a doctrinal boundary against outsiders, at the same time as permitting some room for manoeuvre to those already inside. Or, to put the point more generously, the Creed oscillates between claim and qualification, between the assertion of revealed truth and the vagueness of an unimaginable future; and hints at a more complex interrelation between the physical and the spiritual in its doctrine of resurrection than the demands of apologetics allow it to articulate.

Both these phrases of the Creed are metaphorical. It is clear that everlasting life must be a metaphor, for the one sure characteristic of life in the literal sense is that it will not last for ever. We cannot be referring to life simply going on and on; that would be 'eternal aging' (perish the thought). Nor can we be speaking about ordinary life arrested at its prime – eternal youth (perish that thought too!). So, we must be speaking of a certain quality of literal life transposed on to another plane of discourse, that is 'life' in the age to come, which indeed is not limited in duration, but that is only one of its character-istics and not a particularly interesting one.

If everlasting life is clearly a metaphor, it is perhaps not so obvious that resurrection is also a metaphor. Languages like English which borrow classical words for their technical terms run the risk of obscuring their original sense. It might have been healthier for theol-ogy if, instead of the apparently literal term resurrection, we had translated the Latin into Anglo-Saxon and spoken instead of the 'upstanding' of the body. This idea of 'standing up', 'rising to one's feet', 'getting up', is one of the metaphors used of resurrection in the New Testament; the other, used almost as frequently, is 'waking up'. Waking up and standing up are almost synonyms; that is perhaps because ordinary folk in the first century got up as soon as they woke up – unlike us! There was no possibility of lying in bed in the morn-ing; the floor space was needed for a living room. The root of this metaphor is a very natural comparison between death and sleep; sleep is a small-scale instance of death.[2] And just as we rise from sleep anew every morning, so we may hope to wake up and get up from the last big sleep.

The terms of the Christian doctrine of resurrection are metaphors certainly, but they have a literal referent; they are not merely a provocative way of speaking about a belief which might be more soberly described as the immortality of the soul. They are derived from a tradition of Jewish apocalyptic that described a future, public, and collective vindication of the saints at the end of this age. The language is modified, however, by being applied also to a past, indi-vidual, and more private event, the resurrection of Jesus of Nazareth. It is this, more than any tendency to accommodate its beliefs to Greek ideas, that produces the curious vacillation in the Christian doctrine of the after-life which we noted above, and which can be illustrated from St Paul's sharply contrasting statements: 'Each in their turn; first Christ, then at his parousia those who belong to Christ' (1 Cor. 15.23) and 'I would rather die and be with Christ, for that is much better' (Phil. 1.23).[3] While not uprooting itself from Jewish apocalyp-tic, Christian belief in the unique resurrection of Jesus allows other ideas to flourish that put its origin under strain. Thus, Paul can again argue in both directions simultaneously, from Jesus' resurrection to future hope (1 Cor. 15.12), and vice versa (1 Cor. 15.13).

The aim of this paper is to offer a way of exploring this complex interrelationship between Jesus' resurrection and ours, with particular attention to the question of how 'bodily' the resurrection is thought to be in each case. I will spend a little time on the historical evidence for Jesus' resurrection before looking at the topic for which there is not yet any evidence, our own resurrection. Christian doctrine has usually assumed that a straight line can be drawn from the one to the other; what happened to him will eventually happen to all the redeemed. But although I believe there is an important correlation between them, it does not seem to me that it is a case of straight correspondence. In other words, it is not just the timing that is different – Jesus, back then, in AD 30 or so, and the saints at some future date called the end of the world; the character of the event in each case is also different.

To help make this point, I want to distinguish two senses of the phrase 'resurrection of the body', as follows: resurrection *from* body – i.e., that it is the body one possesses and is, which is raised; and second, resurrection *into* body – i.e., that the resurrection existence itself is bodily existence. The first has to do with physical continuity; the second with the physicality of some future existence. It is for instance quite possible to argue that the body (the corpse, the mortal remains) is raised (translated, transfigured, glorified) into something which is no longer body at all. That would be 'from body' but not 'into body'. And it is equally possible to argue that the original body has no place in the hereafter, that we are raised into new bodies which are as real as the ones we had before, but not physically continuous with them. That would be 'into body' but not 'from body'. With the help of this distinction, I will summarize the argument: *Jesus was raised from body and into body. We shall be raised from body and into body. But the 'from body' in his case is significantly different but importantly related to the 'from body' in ours; and the 'into body' in his case is significantly different but importantly related to the 'into body' in ours.*

I have revealed the conclusion in advance to remove all unnecessary suspense from this paper; the remainder should be pretty well self-evident.

RESURRECTION FROM BODY IN THE CASE OF JESUS: THE EMPTY TOMB

What happened to Jesus' body after it was taken down from the cross? It might have been disposed of by the Romans in some common, unmarked grave, or thrown into a lime-pit; but the gospel record is so surprising at this point as to command assent, namely that a wealthy member of the Jewish Sanhedrin called Joseph of Arimathea asked for it to be released into his custody, and buried it in the tomb he had reserved for himself. This is surprising because, according to the Synoptic accounts the Sanhedrin had, only the day before, unanimously condemned him to death for blasphemy.[4] So Jesus' body was buried in a known location. But in what manner precisely, we cannot be sure; whether hastily in a shroud without anointing (Mark 15.46); or with great care and one hundred pounds of spices and long strips of linen wrapped tightly round his body (John 19.40).

The next point in the story is also surprising; certain women who were his followers arrived at the tomb on the day after Sabbath, either to anoint the body or to weep and pray; but they found the grave empty – and here again the accounts begin to diverge; they describe different witnesses with different motives in different topographies. Mark's tomb, for instance, is a large cave with a heavy stone that three women are incapable of rolling away (Mark 16.3). John's tomb is a more confined space, and the stone had been 'lifted off' (John 20.1, cf. v. 5). They agree roughly on the timing, Sunday morning, whether just before or after sunrise, and precisely on just one point: the chief discoverer of the empty tomb was called Mary of Magdala. If we did not know this fact about her, history would not know anything at all about her; for this is her sole contribution to the gospel record.

There have been many attempts – and there still are[5] – to dismiss this story as later fabrication. One can easily understand why those outside the Church might wish to do this; but it is intriguing that quite a number of Christian theologians have offered implicitly Christian reasons for rejecting the empty tomb. Some dislike the idea of a crude interventionist miracle, or the idea of supplying physical evidence to justify a tenet of faith;[6] others seem to be afraid that the great life-transforming belief in resurrection will be trivialized by relating it to anything so freakish as the disappearance of a body; and many feel that since we today do not expect to walk out of our tombs at some point in the future, it is unnecessary and inconvenient if Jesus did so.[7]

Against all such doubts, however, the evidence of the Gospels hardens up and resists easy explanation at the two principal points mentioned above: Jesus' tomb belonged to Joseph of Arimathea and was discovered empty by Mary of Magdala. It is almost impossible to

deny the truth of these two points. For if so, we would have to suppose not just the wish-fulfilment born of devotion, but deliberate
falsification backed up by the invention of two quite fictitious characters.

RESURRECTION INTO BODY IN THE CASE OF JESUS:
THE RESURRECTION APPEARANCES

There are two sorts of resurrection appearances recounted in the New
Testament: those like Paul's or the group appearance at the end of
Matthew's Gospel, in which the glorified Jesus appears as though
from heaven to instruct his followers about their future mission, and
those like the Gospels of Luke and John, in which the element of
physical presence goes beyond 'being seen' to something more
tangible, like movement, eating, facial recognition, and being
touched.[8]

A common view has been to treat the Lucan and Johannine stories
as late accretions designed to emphasize the physicality of Jesus'
resurrection against sceptics, whether Jews or (Christian) docetists.
But this is most unlikely, for the accounts short-circuit themselves
when the physical Jesus proceeds to walk through solid walls (John
20.26) and disappear suddenly at will (Luke 24.31). And we can be
sure that Luke and John did not think of their stories in this way, for
they were not themselves interested in providing physical proof to
refute sceptics. In Luke's editing the stress falls squarely on proof
from Scripture (Luke 24.27, 44) and in John's on the idea of faith
that believes without sight (John 20.29).

Turning to the other type of resurrection appearance, in Paul and
Matthew, there is surprisingly little emphasis on the idea of resurrection 'into body'. The last words of Matthew's Gospel, for instance,
read, 'Lo, I am with you always, to the close of the age' (28.20);
Jesus is a ubiquitous spiritual presence, available still in the
evangelist's own day in the same way that he was for the first witnesses. Similarly, when Paul discusses the resurrection, in chapter 15
of 1 Corinthians, he lists his own visionary experience (v. 8) along
with that of all the others to whom Jesus had appeared, allowing no
distinction, even though he personally had not known Jesus of
Nazareth, we may safely assume, so that the element of personal
recognition would have been lacking in his case. While he admits a
qualified use of the word 'body' to describe resurrection hope (1 Cor.

15.35–44), he categorically rejects the idea that 'flesh and blood' can 'inherit the kingdom of God' (1 Cor. 15.50).

In recent times, the theological debate about the appearances has turned on the question of how much body needs to be present to produce a vision. Not much, is the general conclusion. One set of theologians would argue that a so-called objective vision is required to account for the following facts: first, that group experiences and not just individual ones are attested (the Twelve; five hundred brethren at one time; the apostles (1 Cor. 15.3–8)), and second, that the vision must carry sufficient conviction to form the basis of a reversal of post-crucifixion despair into firm Easter faith; it must therefore have been a different experience from that of seeing in a dream.[9] Another set of theologians believes that it is enough to posit divine inspiration of these experiences in the hearts of individuals or of groups, without any kind of ophthalmic vision at all. One could call this the school of 'veridical hallucination' if that description was not even more obscure than the thing described.[10] A third option argues that the resurrection appearances are expressions of prior theological beliefs, and that no kind of externally triggered vision, whether objective as in the first case or subjective as in the second, needs to be posited.[11] The main difficulty with this third view – that appearance stories are an expression of faith – is of course to explain how the disciples acquired that faith in the first place. Those who support this view might answer the objection by saying that the first Christians simply projected on to Jesus the traditional picture of the resurrection of the dead at the end of the age. But there are two fatal objections to this: first, the resurrection of the dead in Pharisaic eschatology was always general resurrection on the last day; for it to be anticipated in one particular case, without any other features of the end-time scenario being present, would be inexplicable, especially since other, perfectly satisfactory schemas were available to early Christians in their same Jewish tradition, viz. Elijah's transportation to heaven in a fiery chariot, the assumption of Moses, the ascension of Isaiah. Second, if eschatology was the cause, not the effect, of belief in the resurrection of Jesus, we should expect the appearance stories to conform more to type. But there is no loud trumpet-blast; Jesus does not appear wearing a crown or with a sword coming out of his mouth, nor does he boom with a voice from the beyond the grave; in fact, he talks in a normal and friendly tone, often with a personal address and/or a question (e.g., Acts 26.14; John 20.15–16; 21.5, 15; Luke 24.17, 25). Despite the evident continuity and normality, the early Christians nevertheless described this event as 'resurrection from the dead'. They must therefore have started from some experience, whether objective or subjective, and have interpreted it in the light of Jewish apocalyptic and perhaps also Jesus' own teaching about the death and resurrection of the Son of Man, and then in turn started to reinterpret the eschatology in the light of their experience.

What can we say from a historian's viewpoint about the evidence for Jesus' rising 'into body'? I think we can say this: that different people, some of whom were followers of Jesus in his lifetime, some of whom were not, like Paul and James the Lord's brother, sincerely believed that they had seen him, and deduced from some aspect of their vision a belief in his resurrection; and that they told stories about this which reflected the differences in their experiences of glory and light, on the one hand, or of vividness and recognition, on the other, and which reflected also differences in their preconceptions of the life to come, some emphasizing heavenly commission (Paul and Matthew), and others (the traditions underlying Luke and John) emphasizing recognition and reunion.

We could summarize our conclusions so far as follows: that on the evidence of the empty tomb, Jesus rose from the body; but on the evidence of the appearances, it is not so clear that the body into which Jesus was raised was thought of as straightforwardly physical.[12]

FUTURE RESURRECTIONS OF THE BODY

Now I turn to our resurrection from body and into body; and I am going to argue the opposite thesis: *of Jesus, it is clearer that he rose from body than that he rose into body; of ourselves, we may be clearer that we shall rise into body than that we shall rise from body.*

I do not really need to spend long on resurrection from body in our case. Christians used to be buried in marked and consecrated ground, near to a church preferably, so as to be in the right place when they rose from the dead; but many Christians now accept the practice of cremation. If we really expect to be raised 'from body', this does seem more than a little perverse – that we should burn our mortal remains, grind them up and scatter them, and say to the Lord, 'Put that together again if you can!' Even before the modern practice of disposing of corpses, the notion of resurrection 'from body' was recognized as a problem, a problem nicely expressed in the Yorkshire folk-song 'On Ilkley Moor'. No part of our individual bodies, not even the bones, can expect to escape ultimate dissolution. Almost certainly, we all possess some atoms that were once possessed by somebody else. The body is no longer understood to be the means of continuity between earthly and resurrection life. If we are raised 'from the body' in any sense, it will have to be as part of the re-creation of all the interrelated and shared matter of the universe, a corporate and collective resurrection 'from body', not an individual resurrection from body like that of Jesus.

Resurrection 'into body' in some sense, however, does seem to be indispensable to make the notion of life after death philosophically coherent. It is impossible to conceive of human existence without introducing some sort of analogy to body – i.e., a local and limited expression of the individual self – for an unlocalized and unlimited human self is a contradiction in terms.[13] Christian doctrine adds several other reasons peculiar to itself for preferring the language of resurrection into body to that of a surviving immortal soul; among them chiefly, that it emphasizes that it is God and not nature who is the source of hope for a future life; that it takes with full seriousness the discontinuity of physical death; that it portrays eternal life as more, and not less, real than this life, a new beginning and not merely a lingering afterglow of existence; and lastly, that it casts a positive value backwards on to material existence on this side of the grave. These are the specifically religious connotations of bodily resurrection that make it a so much more satisfying doctrine than emaciated talk of the survival of the soul.

All that said, the actual form of resurrection life remains a mystery, a subject for speculation or reverent silence rather than for doctrinal definition. As an illustration of this, if I may cite a personal anecdote, a few years ago I took my children to visit their maternal great uncle who had lost his arm at the age of sixteen, an under-age recruit in the Great War. Before the visit, they were informed of his disability, and warned not to stare. As it happened, they were not shocked at all by his stump, but fascinated by the way he ate his food with the sharpened edge of his fork serving as a knife, and the way he demonstrated for us his skill in tying his shoe-laces with one hand – for these were the very things that children of their age have most difficulty mastering, even using both hands. It was clear from con-versation with the old man that he was still conscious of the invisible arm; he knew where it would have been in space, and he could feel cold and heat in it, as in the rest of his body. On the one hand, if you will excuse the gruesome joke, his character – his resilience, courage, and self-possession – had been crucially formed by his disability; on the other, he was still psychologically in possession of the arm he had lost. If I may ask a foolish question, bearing St Paul's rebuke always in mind (1 Cor. 15.36), 'In the resurrection, how many arms will he have?'

I have argued that resurrection 'into body' in our case is a philosophical and doctrinal necessity. But in two respects we may have to say that our resurrected bodies are bound to be different from that of Jesus. First, presumably, we will need resurrection bodies in order to be ourselves, in order to re-enter relationship with those we have known and to grow in relationship with others. For this there needs to be a clear boundary between what is me and what is not me, which boundary we may call 'body'. We will also need some way of remaining distinct from God the Creator, if the prime activity of heaven is to be the love and worship of God. In New Testament eschatology, the notion of an undifferentiated absorption into the divine is always resisted, because God must remain God, whatever else happens in the future.

However, these broad considerations do not apply in the case of Jesus; he does not have to preserve his individuality in order to improve his relationships, nor does he need to remain distinct as a creature from the Creator. He was raised 'to the right hand of the Father', there to be immediately related but at the same time qualitatively different from all other beings. So my argument can be summed up finally like this: *Jesus was raised from an individual body into a corporate body, and we will be raised from a corporate body, (the transformation of all matter in the universe) into individual bodies.* The empty tomb and the resurrection appearances, then, are not patterns for the destiny of the individual after death, as though Christians were especially privileged to look into something that remains hidden in God's future. They are rather symbols, actualized in history, of the corporate hope for a new world. That is why Paul can say, 'As in Adam all die, so in Christ shall all be made alive' (1 Cor. 15.22); and that is why he calls the risen Christ the first-fruits of those who sleep (1 Cor. 15.23), the representative of the offering of the whole harvest to God. Jesus is the last Adam, not merely in the sense of being the first to be raised, but as being 'the life-giving Spirit' (1 Cor. 15.45) who gives resurrection and eternal life to others. This idea is surely at the root of Paul's language about 'being in Christ' and of the Church as the body of Christ.

It is possible, then, to believe in the empty tomb and the resurrection of Jesus and to relate that event coherently in a significantly analogical way, but not by direct one-to-one correspondence, with our still future and as yet unknown hope for life after death. In other words, we can be reasonably orthodox as regards the Easter event and still be appropriately modest about our claims to know anything about the future.

The requirement of the historian's art is that one should, eventually, be willing to say something about history. This is not so obviously a requirement laid upon the theologian, who may properly decide ultimately to say nothing. To be both a historian and a theologian is to walk, as Leslie Houlden has himself once described it, 'backward into light'[14] in a double sense: both to return to source and recover initial vision, and also, more awkwardly, to move backwards into God's future, glimpsing only from the corner of one's eye the lure of the life to come.

Notes

[1] J. L. Houlden, *Connections: The Integration of Theology and Faith* (London: SCM Press, 1986), and esp. ch. 9, 'The Resurrection'.

[2] 'Sleep is the little mystery of death' according to the ancient Greek proverb.

[3] And cf., in close proximity, vv. 14 and 16 of 1 Thess. 4.

[4] John's account in the passion narrative differs slightly, in that it was not the whole Sanhedrin but only Annas and Caiaphas (18.13, 24) and a few others who interrogated him. There is however a relevant meeting of the full Sanhedrin placed some days earlier (11.47).

[5] From H. S. Reimarus, *Fragments* (1774–8), to more recently P. M. Casey, *From Jewish Prophet to Gentile God* (Cambridge: Cambridge University Press, 1991) and the novelist A. N. Wilson *Jesus* (London: Sinclair-Stevenson, 1992).

[6] e.g., David Jenkins, *God, Miracle and the Church of England* (London: SCM Press, 1987).

[7] See G. W. H. Lampe and D. M. MacKinnon, *The Resurrection* (London: Mowbray, 1966).

[8] The distinction partly but not entirely follows the geographical distinction between appearances in Galilee and Jerusalem.

[9] See C. F. D. Moule (ed.), *The Significance of the Message of the Resurrection for Faith in Jesus Christ* (London: SCM Press, 1968), Introduction.

[10] See Don Cupitt, *Christ and the Hiddenness of God* (London: SCM Press, 1971).

[11] See the debate between Moule and Cupitt in, Don Cupitt, *Explorations in Theology 6* (London: SCM Press, 1979), ch. 4.

[12] It is perhaps worth noting that, since in the resurrection appearances Jesus is appearing to people who are not yet risen themselves, a certain degree of 'accommodation' is involved in any narrative presentation; i.e., the degree of bodily presence is dictated by the requirements of bodiliness of the spectators; so we could not legitimately use the gospel stories as evidence for the nature of postmortem bodily existence, even if we wanted to. Cf. M. J. Harris, *Raised Immortal* (Grand Rapids, MI: Eerdmans, 1985).

[13] See further, e.g., J. Hick, *Death and Eternal Life* (London: Collins, 1979).

[14] See J. L. Houlden, *Backward into Light: The Passion and Resurrection of Jesus According to Matthew and Mark* (London: SCM Press, 1987).

13
The Mark of the Nails

Frances Young

They were afraid
with heart-bumping, palm-sweating, hair-tingling fright
as they gazed
at that dark-ghosting, spine-shivering, mouth-gaping cave
empty!

Weak and gullible women they'd seem.
They'd come to the tomb . . .
and they were afraid,
afraid of a future of unknown fears.
No more gentle tears!
Where – where have they laid him?
What – what more – done to abuse his body?
They were afraid
with death-whitening, jaw-dropping, stomach-caving dread.

Is faith born of fear?
Is Resurrection here?

The End of the Gospel[1]

It is Mark, of course, who notoriously ends his Gospel with fear:
'*oudeni ouden eipon ephobounto gar* – they said nothing to anyone
for they were afraid' (16.8).[2] Yet in Matthew, while there is also joy
(28.8), the fear associated with the event is, by comparison with
Mark, heightened. The guards quake with fear (28.4). The women
need immediate reassurance: 'Don't be afraid'. Rushing away to tell
the news, they meet with Jesus: 'Don't be afraid' – the words are
repeated (28.5, 10). Luke, too, speaks of the women being frightened
and bowing their faces to the ground when the two figures appear at
the empty tomb (Luke 24.5).

The fear associated with the event of resurrection in the gospel narratives is not a feature that tends to be appropriated by believers

meditating on the stories, and in a way that has ever been so. Already in Matthew's version, a definite message about resurrection, obeisance and worship, as well as 'great joy', are features that have the effect of turning the empty fear of Mark into awe. In Luke, fright is linked with the seeing of apparitions and is soon turned to joy when the real Jesus is revealed (Luke 24.36–43). John speaks only of 'fear of the Jews' (John 20.19). Believers have always found it hard to associate anything other than gladness and relief with the return of the Lord. John alone emphasizes the mark of the nails and the wound in the side, and in that Gospel's narrative this seems at first sight but a guarantee, a sign that this is authentically Jesus . . .

Characteristically, Leslie Houlden, in whose honour this volume is written, protested at 'the common tendency to see Jesus' resurrection as somehow cancelling out his death and ensuring that the story has a happy ending'. His solution to the triumphalist focus on 'the Risen Christ' was to take account of the whole story: 'The career of Jesus-as-a-whole forbids such easy slipping into the mood of spring . . . On the basis of Jesus, it is an ultimate hope held to in the very teeth of suffering and diminution.'[3]

To the ever-lively contribution of Leslie Houlden I am delighted to pay tribute, especially as we have shared an interest in pursuing New Testament study that is rooted in scholarly exegesis but prepared to break out of the confines of its accepted parameters and engage with systematic theology. Two problems *vis-à-vis* the resurrection have preoccupied this age of uncertainty, and Leslie's discussion bears witness to them both: (1) the question of historicity, factuality, what happened, the nature of the event; and (2) this business of triumphalism. The first problem is not the principal concern of this essay, though it may prove to bear on the debate about physical and spiritual. What is proposed is an approach to the second which is different but complementary to that proposed by Leslie Houlden.

The starting-point of this reflection is the notion that literary texts, or indeed oral narratives, shape world-vision.[4] We understand the world, indeed 'create' our own story, through entering the stories we are told as children, the narratives we read as adolescents. Despite the style and genre of much analytical writing, whether in newspapers or scientific journals, we live a story-shaped existence and have a story-shaped identity. We conceive of our selves, and of others and our relationship with them, through the *mimesis* (not so much 'imitation' as 'representation') of human existence in narrative, and then we experience 'reality' through these narrative conceptions. The appropriation of the resurrection stories works at the level of narrative-shaping, and the tendency to encourage triumphalism that so concerns Leslie Houlden bears that out.

So the perception that a particular story has the potential to shape our world immediately raises questions about the kind of 'vision' incarnated in the narrative. Roughly speaking, one can observe in the structure of stories two fundamental views of life, the 'tragic' and the 'comic'. Both words may, of course, be used in a sensationalizing or trivializing popular sense, but we are concerned here not with everyday usage or with *kitsch*. The issue is this: does the resurrection mean, as some have suggested, that there can be no genuinely tragic vision within Christianity? Does it provide the 'happy ending' that simply turns the Christian story into comedy? What I suggest is that inherent even in the New Testament resurrection stories is a deeply tragic element, captured in the response of fear, embodied in the mark of the nails. For in tragedy, as Nietzsche put it,[5] one 'stares at the inexplicable'.

TRAGIC VISION

What constitutes the essence of tragedy is a much-discussed topic.[6] Tragic narrative has a variety of characteristics, many peculiar to the insight of particular dramatists or narrators within particular cultural traditions: there are 'tragic visions' of human existence, rather than a single tragic view.[7] It is easier, then, to identify actual narratives as tragic than to come up with any generally applicable formula. Wisely, Cheryl Exum eschews offering 'a theory of tragedy or an investigation of the genre as such',[8] and we will do likewise, instead tracing key elements in a 'bridge' example.

T. S. Eliot's *Murder in the Cathedral* is a modern tragedy written from within a Christian world-view yet modelled on classic Greek tragedy. The play opens with the Chorus full of foreboding and articulating one notion common to much tragic drama:

Destiny waits in the hand of God, shaping the still unshapen:
I have seen these things in a shaft of sunlight.
Destiny waits in the hand of God, not in the hand of statesmen
Who do, some well, some ill, planning and guessing,
Having their aims which turn in their hands in the pattern of time.

The Chorus are 'the poor' for whom 'there is no action, / But only to wait and to witness'; though women, they are representatives of 'the common man', the 'human kind' which 'cannot bear very much reality', immersed in the trivialities of the domestic process of keeping alive, 'living and partly living'. They want to be left in peace. But by the end of the play they are praying for forgiveness – for they too are exposed as implicated. If we say that we have no sin, there is no health in us.

The Knights who perpetrate the deed are full of self-justification, excuses, whitewashes, making out there were effectively no alternatives, as in all arguments for a just war, all acts of oppression, even little dishonesties . . . In matter-of-fact prose that contrasts with the poetry of the rest of the play, they reveal their blindness to their own responsibility. An exposure, a judgement, is going on.

But then there is the tragic hero, Thomas. Fully conscious of the possibilities, he faces up to the temptations of his position. Three temptations are obvious – the predictable ways of getting out of his vocation and responsibilities. The fourth is more interesting: it highlights the possibility that acceptance of vocation may itself be corrupt and self-seeking – to be the glorious martyr! How marvellous! Until purged of that tainted pride, Thomas cannot be the true martyr, whatever happens. What you are is more important than what you do:

> The last temptation is the greatest treason:
> To do the right deed for the wrong reason . . .
> Sin grows with doing good . . .

The terrible truth emerges that our worst faults may be the inescapable obverse of our greatest virtues – more exposure of the ambiguities of human action and moral choice.

Eliot offers in this presentation of Thomas à Beckett a challenge to the importance of historical fact. Truth is found rather in the mysterious depths that have to be explored through rituals acknowledging pollution and shame, and opening up the possibility of purgation.

Cheryl Exum suggests that attention to examples of tragic narrative or drama shows time and again that 'fate and flaw present an essential combination in tragedy'.[9] The themes of doom or destiny recur, implying a 'hostile transcendence', a sense that the protagonist is caught up in things beyond his or her control, as does the exploration of faults in the great hero's character, deeds that have a strange inevitability, and yet are the hero's responsibility. Essential to the tragic, she thinks, is a noble struggle against catastrophe. 'Tragedy is made possible when human freedom comes into conflict with the demands of the cosmic order.' So there is an issue about the possibility of tragedy without God.

Martha Nussbaum's book title *The Fragility of Goodness* shows that she would agree that the subject-matter of tragedy is the vulnerability of human greatness, the contingencies and dilemmas of human existence. Her analysis, however, illuminates the 'everydayness' of the dilemmas faced in Greek tragedy. With or without God, there is the interplay of luck and choice that we all recognize – and the paradox that in practice we hold people responsible for what they do even when the cards are stacked against them. A feature of some Greek tragedy is the sensitive exploration of impossible choices, where deeply held moral principles are in conflict and there is no right decision. Whatever choice is made, there will be guilt. Nussbaum, it would seem, does not require God for there to be tragedy.[10] The effect of seeing tragedy in a theological frame, however, is that what Nussbaum would call 'luck' becomes a sense of destiny.[11]

The interplay of 'fate' and 'flaw' and the heroic struggle against fate seem central, but the feature that Exum particularly highlights as the tragic sense of life is the acknowledgement of 'the ultimate disharmony of existence', a phrase she borrows from Jaspers:

> What distinguishes this vision from its opposite, the comic or classic vision, is that it lacks comedy's restorative and palliative capacity. Comedy gives voice to a fundamental trust in life . . . [It] may also embrace questions, doubts and ambiguities, but . . . it removes their terror. The tragic vision isolates the hero over against an arbitrary and capricious world, a world in which – to get to the crux of the matter – the problem of evil is irreducible and unresolvable into some larger, harmonious whole.[12]

Exum's insistence on the tragic being irrational and inexplicable is in tension with her recognition that the very act of presenting it invests the unintelligible with some kind of meaning. 'The representation, *mimesis*, of this vision in a particular literary work becomes an attempt to tame it by giving it aesthetic form.'[13] It is precisely here that I would want to go beyond Exum and insist that tragedy is a creative, and therefore inherently redemptive, engagement with the mystery of the ambiguities and darkness of human existence. The drama or narrative is both revelatory of the hidden depths we prefer to keep veiled, and a performative act of resolution and reconciliation.

In classical Athens, tragedy arose in a ritual context. The action, originally presenting the story in song and dance as part of a religious festival, gradually evolved into the classic dramatic shape. The presentation was a liturgy performed before and on behalf of the whole community. When this is recognized as the context, Aristotle's classic statement takes on new dimensions:

> Tragedy, then, is a representation of an action which is serious, complete and of a certain magnitude – in language which is garnished in various forms in its different parts – in the mode of dramatic enactment, not narrative – and through the arousal of pity and fear effecting the *katharsis* of such emotions . . .[14]

The post-Romantic era has tended to understand this in terms of a great 'emotional steam-bath', as the great director Peter Brook once put it,[15] and its supposed effect has then become problematic.[16] But if *katharsis* is taken seriously in its religious context, it will be seen to have a rather different implication.

As the anthropologist Mary Douglas explains in her book *Purity and Danger*,[17] primitive peoples took things that were taboo, things like blood and death, and, by putting these fearful things into a ritual context, 'sacralized' them, transformed them from being life-denying to life-affirming: 'The special kind of treatment which some religions accord to anomalies and abominations to make them powerful for good, is like turning weeds and lawn cuttings into compost.' That is what sacrifice was all about: it took the taboo substance blood and turned it into a means of purification. What was involved was a shift in perspective as the taboo subject was handled and faced and put into another context. That too, I have previously suggested,[18] is how tragedy works: it makes it possible for human beings to avoid escapism, to confront things they dare not face. Normally we cannot stand too much reality, but here we can. In great tragic drama we are enabled to face up to those things about the human condition we would rather forget or deny.

Martha Nussbaum draws our attention to the theory of Burkert that tragedy originated from sacrifice.[19] 'The ceremony of animal sacrifice . . . expressed the awe and fear felt by this human community towards its own murderous possibilities.' By ritually killing an animal and surrounding this killing 'with a ceremony indicative of the killers' innocence and their respect for life', the sacrificers both acknowledged and distanced themselves from their potential for violence. 'It is the work of tragedy, song of the goat-sacrifice, to continue and deepen this function of ritual by bringing the hidden threat to light . . .'

So Peter Brook suggests that there is 'Holy Theatre'.[20] 'We are all aware that most of life escapes our senses. We know that the world of appearance is a crust – under the crust is the boiling matter we see if we peer into a volcano.' In theatre, the 'invisible becomes visible', we find liberation from our ordinary everyday selves. This is what makes 'the theatre a holy place in which a greater reality could be found', often in the paradox of a loss that is also gain. Great tragedy probes for the meaning behind it all. It exposes the truth about the human condition so that it may be faced and ritually dealt with. Is this not what we saw embodied in Eliot's play?

Nietzsche suggested that the tragic perception 'in order even to be endured, requires art as a safeguard and remedy'.[21] He speaks of 'the enormous power of tragedy, exciting, purifying, and disburdening the entire life of a people',[22] and of the transformative effect of tragedy as the spectator '. . . shudders at the sufferings which will befall the hero, and yet anticipates therein a higher and much more overpowering joy. He sees more extensively and profoundly than ever, and yet wishes to be blind.'[23] This 'curious internal dissension' Nietzsche likens to the 'wonderful significance of *musical dissonance*'. 'The joyful sensation of dissonance in music' explains the origin of 'the joy that the tragic myth excites'.[24] So the shaping in artform provides a context in which the dissonant chord is resolved into a harmonious cadence, and, as Raymond Williams put it, 'the tragic action, in its deepest sense, is not the confirmation of disorder, but its experience, its comprehension and its resolution'.[25]

THE PASSION NARRATIVE AS TRAGEDY

No one who has had the privilege of sitting at the feet of Donald MacKinnon, as I have, could escape his persuasive insistence that the Christian story is more profound than the 'historical failure of the traditional doctrines of atonement',[26] and that great tragic drama explores the depths of the problem of evil in a way that throws light on the cross. The victory of Jesus is ambiguous:

increasingly one sees that the reality of Christ's humanity resides precisely in the fact that as he lived he was confronted with real choices, fraught, in consequence of the way in which he chose, with disaster as well as achievement in their train.

The 'actuality of irretrievable disaster' is presented in the Gospels. The victory 'remains mysteriously and inescapably tragic'.[27]

If there were no resurrection in the aftermath, such a reading would be entirely persuasive. Mark's Gospel, though its language is the crude rough Greek of a Palestinian, is written with unconscious literary art. The central figure of the drama foresees the destiny he has to face, struggles with it in Gethsemane, and then is progressively isolated, misunderstood, betrayed by a friend, denied by his right-hand man, despised, mocked, rejected, finally forsaken even by the God whose will he strove to perform. As the tragedies of the ancient world found meaning in the interplay of necessity and choice, so Mark makes it clear that this is the playing out of a destiny long fore-shadowed – in ancient prophecies, in terrible tales like the sacrifice of Isaac – yet freely chosen. As in Eliot's tragedy, all participants are exposed as implicated in the deed.

The Epistle to the Hebrews, though reflecting on the event rather than narrating it, draws out other features classic in tragedy: the paradox of one innocent yet guilty, as the sacrificial victim is without blemish yet ritually bears the sin of the people; the *pathei mathos* – the learning through suffering that Greek tragedy explored; the great-ness yet vulnerability of one who struggles with the contingencies of the human condition, sharing in human flesh and blood, praying with loud cries and tears, yet able to 'sanctify' those who share his human nature.

So the cross of Christ functions like tragedy. The hero is caught up in events over which he has no control, yet chooses to engage in the struggle. The ensuing drama exposes the reality of human sin, the insoluble conflicts that so often lead to the suffering of the innocent, the banishment and destruction of what is good, the mobilization of the political and religious structures to eliminate change or challenge. Christ is thrust 'outside the camp', banished like the scapegoat, destroyed so that purity could be maintained. All humanity is involved in the shame of it. Yet the story of the cross (without reference to the resurrection) is redemptive. For the things we fear, the taboos of blood and death, the curse of the most cruel and despicable punishment devised by humanity, these are 'sacralized', put in a positive context in which they can be faced and not merely neutralized but overcome. Not for nothing did the medieval hymn sing '*O felix culpa*' – O fortunate fault – as the terror of guilt and sin was transfigured in the terror of the cross.

The drama effects an exposure of the truth. It becomes a universal narrative, a story told by an inspired poet, not a mere chronicler or historian. As Aristotle put it, 'poetry is both more philosophical and more serious than history, since poetry speaks more of universals, history of particulars'.[28] The terrible truth of human complicity in evil, of goodness snuffed out, of God's abandonment, is exposed and faced; faced as in a ritual context the thing that is taboo is turned into something holy, the sin we cannot bear to face is redeemed, the pollution we usually fail to observe is revealed, and *katharsis*, in the sense of purification or atonement, is effected.

THE RESURRECTION IN THE LIGHT OF THE PASSION

Does the resurrection undermine the force of the passion? Is it true that Christian hope renders Christian tragedy impossible?

Of course, quite apart from the triumphalism of *Christus Victor*, the resurrection may be presented as a dramatic reversal: a *deus ex machina*, an intervening deity, miraculously sorts it all out, and a 'comic' happy ending is appended to the passion. It may be suggested that, unlike the realistic 'ordinariness' and ambiguity of the stories in the Hebrew Bible, which turn out to be as perplexing as real life, the New Testament provides closure, gives meaning and conclusion to things,[29] and the resurrection is the chief purveyor of this sense of 'rounding off'. None of this encourages the attributive 'tragic'.

Yet might it not be suggested that the Christian story is strangely capable of being read both as tragedy and as comedy? The 'classic' resolution restores harmony, order, vision, and hope, after the reversal of the fall, failure, and fatality. The 'recapitulation' of fall and redemption in early Christian theology would bear out the force of the classic or comic reading. The problem then is whether the tragic reading can hold. Somehow, despite *The Marriage of Figaro*, a tragi-comedy does full justice to neither form. So what I want to propose is the distinction yet coinherence of tragic and comic visions; one cannot 'see' both at once, but they are genuine alternatives – like the famous duck-rabbit sketch. Each reading offers its own kind of resolution, and yet subverts the other.[30]

How, then, would the resurrection function in a tragic reading? Despite the tendency to 'closure' in the New Testament, Josipovici notes how the gospel writers adopt different strategies 'to avoid the trap into which the apocryphal gospels fall, of returning us to the world of fairy-tale from which the Passion had freed us'.[31] He explores the Marcan ambiguities with which we began this essay. We might add that in the New Testament as a whole, so far from providing unambiguous resolution, the resurrection reopens the ambiguities and questions and tensions: those who triumphantly imagine the resurrection has happened already are apparently Paul's opponents, while Paul himself speaks of being conformed to the sufferings of Christ, and struggles with the 'now' and the 'not yet' of new creation in Christ. There is a new beginning in the apparent ending, and for all the 'fulfilments' of the New Testament, 'closure' is not reached in the narrative: in the Book of Revelation, it remains a vision for the future.

Nor is the resurrection a simple reversal, a restoration that puts things back as if nothing had happened. The tedious debate about whether it was physical or spiritual introduces an irrelevant dichotomy. No Christian believer would simply want to speak of resuscitation; every Christian believer would want to affirm transfiguration, metamorphosis of some kind. And it is this mystery that narrative and testimony struggles to convey. The marks of the nails remain and are somehow 'transvalued'. It is perhaps John's Gospel that most effectively holds together cross and resurrection, as the passion becomes the 'hour of glory', the pain, suffering, sin, guilt, destiny, darkness, vulnerability to death and the powers of evil, indeed the frighteningly inexplicable, becomes even more inexplicably the theophany, the blinding dazzling light of exposure, judgement, revelation. It is in tragedy rather than comedy that one expects to confront the *mysterium tremendum et fascinans*, the Holy One, to be moved with pity and terror, with awe and fear of the Lord.

Which brings us back to the fact that these stories are not tales of joyful recognition and the restoration of normality. Jesus does not go off to Egypt, marry Mary Magdalene and live happily ever after! Mary is cruelly brushed off as she tries to make contact with the Jesus she knew: 'Do not cling to me, for I have not yet ascended to the Father' (John 20.17). His presence with her and with the disciples is fraught with ambiguity, with an open and terrifying future, with insecurity. There is a hiddenness and awefulness that belies any sense of triumph. Pilate and the powers of oppression remain untouched, and whatever resolution there is, is like the mystery of tragic drama. Those who witness this passionate action are enabled to gaze on the reality of death and the reality of God, the taboo and terrifying reality of which humanity cannot bear too much.

To develop Nietzsche's image, the resurrection contains the tumult and dissonance of the passion in a kind of harmonic resolution, but the climax has a disturbing intensity, and the cadence a questioning quality – a note of awesome expectation, sending shivers down the spine.

Notes

[1] The poem is my own.

[2] There is, of course, debate about whether the original ending is lost, and that may be so. But it is conceivable that Mark wanted to end in mystery, given the 'secrecy' motif and other features of the narrative; see also Robert Hamilton, 'The Gospel of Mark: Parable of God Incarnate', *Theology* 86 (1983), pp. 438–41, where he argues that the Gospel of Mark has the overall character of parable in that it subverts its own good news, ending with this note of fear. In any case, for the purposes of this essay, it is assumed that a reading of the Gospel as ending at 16.8 is viable, and it is not necessary to establish authorial intention. The addition of the ending (16.9–20) at an early stage of textual transmission confirms the need to bring the story to closure and resolution, reducing the 'fear' motif: cf. next paragraph of this essay.

[3] Houlden 1986, pp. 150–1.

[4] A useful discussion of this is found in Booth 1988, esp. chs 8–11. The emergence of the so-called 'narrative theology' movement necessarily presupposes the same kind of stance.

[5] Nietzsche 1909, p. 119.

[6] The classic delineation of Greek tragedy is found in Aristotle's *Poetics*, but it soon becomes evident that his analysis is not

universally applicable, not even to the classical tragedies of his own time and culture (see Kitto 1950), let alone modern tragedy. Cheryl Exum (1992; see opening chapter *passim*) argues that despite the fact that Aristotelian categories do not apply to biblical material, the 'tragic vision' nevertheless appears 'in various biblical guises'.

[7] Williams 1979 draws out the historical and cultural diversity of tragedy.

[8] Exum 1992, p. 2.

[9] ibid., p. 10.

[10] In practice, of course, it is the gods who in Greek tragedy place conflicting obligations on human beings, but this simply heightens the helplessness of humans caught in the cross-fire.

[11] Whether tragedy is possible where a God of justice produces a vision so ordered and rational that retribution and reward is guaranteed is a serious issue beyond the scope of this essay. See discussion in Exum 1992.

[12] ibid., p. 5.

[13] ibid., p. 5.

[14] Halliwell 1987, ch. 6, p. 37; cf. commentary on the passage, p. 88.

[15] Brook 1968.

[16] See, e.g., Norwood 1948, and Halliwell 1987.

[17] Douglas 1966. Every society, according to Mary Douglas, has purity regulations. Dirt implies 'a set of ordered relations and contravention of that order . . . Dirt is the by product of a systematic ordering and classification of matter, in so far as ordering involves rejecting inappropriate elements' (p. 35). Culture provides the ordered categories within which members of a given society order ideas and values. But inevitably this gives rise to 'anomalies'. The question is how does a society deal with anomalies and ambiguities. The desire for purity may lead to expulsion, but that kind of purity

proves to be 'hard and dead'; 'purity is the enemy of change' (p. 162). Ambiguity may produce laughter, revulsion or shock at different points and intensities, but it is also creative: the richness of poetry depends on ambiguity (p. 37). There is power in the margins, the things that don't fit. So in primitive religions, it is not uncommon to find that one or other of the anomalies, a thing that is taboo, becomes in religious ritual the very thing that can produce cleansing and new life (pp. 163ff.).

[18] Young 1990b, p. 177; 1990a, p. 188.

[19] Nussbaum 1986, p. 37.

[20] Brook 1968, ch. 2; quotes from pp. 42, 52, 54.

[21] Nietzsche 1909, p. 119.

[22] ibid., p. 159.

[23] ibid., p. 168.

[24] ibid., p. 183.

[25] Williams 1979, p. 83.

[26] MacKinnon 1968, p. 100.

[27] MacKinnon 1979, p. 194.

[28] Halliwell 1987, ch. 9, p. 41.

[29] Josipovici 1988, p. 47: 'The Christian order [of the canonical books] is one we find perfectly natural and easy to understand . . . partly because it corresponds to a profound need in each of us for closure and for a universe shaped according to a clearly comprehensible story.'

[30] Josipovici 1988, p. 307: '. . . the peculiarity of the Bible is that it keeps calling into question our ability to make sense of our past, and of stories to explain ourselves or describe the world. There is, it is true, a strong tendency in Christianity, already evident in the New Testament, to search for the single story that will give shape to the

world; but that tendency exists in tension with the sense, present in the Gospels as well as in much of the Hebrew Bible, that if there is such a story it is not one we will ever be able to know or tell.' Reading the Bible 'will never be able to attain a universal perspective or come to an end'.

[31] Josipovici 1988, p. 230.

BIBLIOGRAPHY

Booth, Wayne C. 1988. *The Company We Keep: An Ethics of Fiction*. Berkeley and London: University of California Press.

Brook, Peter. 1968. *The Empty Space*. London: MacGibbon & Kee.

Douglas, Mary. 1966. *Purity and Danger*. London: Routledge & Kegan Paul.

Eliot, T. S. 1935. *Murder in the Cathedral*. London: Faber & Faber.

Exum, J. Cheryl. 1992. *Tragedy and Biblical Narrative*. Cambridge: Cambridge University Press.

Halliwell, Stephen. 1987. *The Poetics of Aristotle: Translation and Commentary*. London: Duckworth.

Houlden, Leslie. 1986. *Connections: The Integration of Theology and Faith*. London: SCM Press.

Josipovici, Gabriel. 1988. *The Book of God: A Response to the Bible*. New Haven and London: Yale University Press.

Kitto, H. D. F. 1950. *Greek Tragedy: A Literary Study*. 2nd edn. London: Methuen.

MacKinnon, Donald. 1968. *Borderlands of Theology and Other Essays*. London: Lutterworth Press. Especially chapter 5, 'Atonement and Tragedy'.

MacKinnon, Donald. 1979. *Explorations in Theology 5*. London: SCM Press. Especially chapter 13, 'Ethics and Tragedy' (1971).

Nietzsche, F. 1909. *The Birth of Tragedy*. Trans. W. A. Haussmann. London: Allen & Unwin.

Norwood, Gilbert. 1948. *Greek Tragedy*. 4th edn. London: Methuen.

Nussbaum, Martha. 1986. *The Fragility of Goodness*. Cambridge: Cambridge University Press.

Williams, Raymond. 1979. *Modern Tragedy*. Revd edn. London: Verso.

Young, Frances. 1990a. *The Art of Performance*. London: Darton, Longman & Todd.

Young, Frances. 1990b. *Face to Face: A Narrative Essay in the Theology of Suffering*. 2nd edn. Edinburgh: T. & T. Clark.

14

The Descent into Hell:
Hans Urs von Balthasar and Pastoral Theology

Gordon Mursell

Descendit ad inferna. Until recently, English liturgical texts translated this article of the Apostles' Creed as 'he descended into hell'. Modern revisers, however, have exhibited some uncertainty: the Church of England's Series 2 rite kept 'he descended into hell' but added a coyly explanatory footnote: 'Hell = the place of the departed.' And the Alternative Service Book of 1980 has 'he descended to the dead'.

The confusion over the translation reflects, of course, changing views about what is meant by 'hell'. But it may also mask a deeper uncertainty about exactly what, if anything, *'descendit ad inferna'* means – an uncertainty which in turn may help to explain the relative lack of interest in this subject among contemporary theologians.[1] To be fair, the uncertainty is almost as old as the doctrine itself; and it is clear that, long before its definitive inclusion in the creeds in the sixth century, the belief that Christ had descended into hell had already given rise to many and various interpretations.[2] Broadly speaking, these can be divided into four.

The first line of approach affirms the fact that Christ did, really, die, thereby underlining (though not significantly adding to) the previous article in the creeds describing his crucifixion and burial.[3] On this view, adopted by various patristic writers such as Hilary of Poitiers, Christ's descent was part of what it meant to be human – i.e., to submit to the law of death.[4] The second follows 1 Peter 3.19 in maintaining that Christ descended into hell in order to preach to 'the spirits in prison', though the exegesis of this text is much controverted.[5] The third affirms that Jesus did battle with Satan in order to liberate these departed spirits: this interpretation, which came to be known as the 'Harrowing of Hell', became enormously popular in the Middle Ages, but can be traced back to second-century texts such as the Gospel of Nicodemus.[6] The fourth line of interpretation sees the descent into hell as simply describing in general terms Jesus' presence with the departed (cf. Luke 23.43; Rom. 10.6–7).[7]

In view of this uncertainty, together with the modest biblical material relating to the idea, and the highly mythological language in which it is generally articulated, it is perhaps not surprising that most modern theologians have observed Hans Küng's theological health warning[8] and steered clear altogether of Christ's descent into hell. But one recent theologian has given this half-forgotten myth exceptional prominence: Hans Urs von Balthasar. It is the purpose of this article to consider the implications of Balthasar's approach for contemporary pastoral theology.

Balthasar's interest in the descent into hell seems to have originated in the intense mystical experiences of his soul-friend and confidante Adrienne von Speyer.[9] It is a subject to which he returns frequently in his vast *oeuvre*, particularly in the seventh and last volume of his theological aesthetics *Herrlichkeit* (translated into English as *The Glory of the Lord*), and in *Mysterium Paschale*. There have been several recent analyses of Balthasar's theology of Holy Saturday:[10] here our concern is more with its implications. In effect, Balthasar reduces the four interpretative approaches to the descent into hell outlined above to two: solidarity and deliverance. Both of these need briefly to be delineated.

On the first view, what is stressed is not action but presence: it is Christ's solidarity with the dead, not his rescue of them, which is emphasized. This approach is common in patristic texts,[11] and finds its most powerful classical expression in Irenaeus – commenting on Jesus in Gethsemane, he writes:

> When he found the disciples asleep the first time, he left them; the second time, he roused them, showing that his Passion was the awakening of the sleeping disciples, for whom he also descended into the lower parts of the earth to behold with his own eyes the unfinished part of creation (*descendit ad inferiora terrae, id quod erat inoperatum conditionis visurus oculis*).[12]

This vivid evocation of hell as all that is incomplete or inchoate in the created order is taken up by Balthasar in *Mysterium Paschale*, where he writes that on Holy Saturday Jesus has to 'take in with his own eyes what in the realm of creation is imperfect, unformed, chaotic, so as to make it pass over into his own domain as the Redeemer'.[13]

Christ enters into the raw primeval chaos of Genesis 1.2, into the formlessness that represents for Balthasar the greatest possible antithesis to the *Gestalt Christi*, one of the principal components of his entire theological system.[14] In his view hell is dis-order, the furthermost extremity and consequence of sin. Irenaeus' text thus becomes for Balthasar a description of Christ undergoing the ultimate contemplative experience: the unfiltered encounter with the most extreme manifestations of all that is wasted, unfinished, rejected, and lost. In *The Glory of the Lord* Balthasar writes:

> This act of seizing fate and destiny, and wrenching them out of their axes, takes place in the deepest silence of death. The Word of God has become unheard, and no message forces its way upwards to speak of its journey through the darkness: for it can do this only as not-word, as not-form, through a not-land, behind a sealed stone. And this 'doing' itself is no longer active, but is only something that is done. So all the traces that the living Word of God left behind on earth are as it were wiped out; the soul that comes back from the untraceable land, the body that rises from the sealed grave, is 'no longer Christ according to the flesh', but 'a new creature'. 'The old is past: behold, the new has come!' (2 Cor. 5.16f).[15]

Christ, then, encounters and experiences what von Speyer described as 'the sin of the world become anonymous':[16] the structure of sin itself, rather than simply individual sinners. Balthasar, citing another German author, describes hell as the final 'residue and phlegm which it is absolutely impossible to restore to life', where the 'hate which belongs to enemies is absolutely objectified'.[17] Elsewhere he says that 'the fact of being with the unredeemed dead, in the Sheol of the Old Testament, signifies a solidarity in whose absence the condition of standing for sinful man before God would not be complete'.[18] The descent into hell, on this view, is no triumphant affair but a passive 'being removed' similar to the experience of Jonah:[19] unlike the heroes of classical antiquity – Odysseus, Orpheus, Aeneas – on their journeys to the underworld, Christ descends as a dead man, not a living conqueror. And, because he did this, our own dying is a 'being dead with the dead God',[20] so that not just the act of dying but the objective fact of being dead becomes known and shared by Jesus. Why? Balthasar's response is the assertion of Irenaeus that only what has been endured is healed and saved.[21] Indeed, this interpretation of the descent into hell fits perfectly into Irenaeus' doctrine of *recapitulatio*: if Christ is to redeem humanity, he must embrace and undergo every aspect of human experience – even death. Thus Balthasar can declare that 'the golden gleam of Irenaean glory shines even into the dark powers of the world, for the world is *capax gloriae Patris* (*Adv. Haer.* 2), this world in its finitude, out of which God has still been able to make his work of art and his image'.[22]

The second interpretative approach to the descent into hell adumbrated by Balthasar is that of deliverance. This too has strong patristic precedent, and is vividly expressed in an anonymous patristic homily for Holy Saturday – Christ goes in to the prisoners in Hades, holding his cross, and says:

> Awake, sleeper, I have not made you to be held a prisoner in the underworld. Arise from the dead; I am the life of the dead. Arise, O man, work of my hands, arise, you who were fashioned in my image. Rise, let us go hence; for you in me and I in you, together we are one undivided person.[23]

Here solidarity is not replaced by, but actually becomes, deliverance. The *Gospel of Nicodemus* records what happened next ('And he took them and leaped out of hell') in language that has evoked countless medieval and Eastern Christian representations of the harrowing of hell.[24] As Balthasar points out, behind the story of deliverance is the idea of a struggle between the divinity and the hostile power that guards its prey.[25] Patristic writers had understood this story in the light of Jesus' reference to the binding of the strong man (Mark 3.27),[26] and Balthasar does the same: for him, this story 'shows clearly that the total depotentiation of the enemy coincides with a forcible entry into the innermost terrain of his power'.[27] With the forces of evil defeated (symbolically represented in the *Gospel of Nicodemus* by Christ setting up his cross in the midst of hell[28]), the dead can be delivered, and are: one icon represents the victorious Christ rising from hell while holding Adam's and Eve's wrists and reuniting them with each other. This approach is in one respect the mirror-opposite of the other: Christ becomes a new Orpheus returning from the underworld (though without making the mistake of looking back at the wrong moment). And the power of this interpretation, especially for early and medieval Christian generations whose *mentalité* was clouded with demons and darkness, is incontrovertible; although (as Balthasar points out), without the complementary stress on solidarity, it could all too easily become a mere anticipation of Easter on the part of a Christ whose power would be too effortlessly demonstrated, and whose victory would then show little signs of the depth of suffering he has undergone.[29]

So much, then, for the two principal interpretative approaches of Hans Urs von Balthasar to the ancient Christian myth of Jesus' descent into hell. What Balthasar in effect suggests, through his treatment of the descent into hell, is that without it Christian belief in the cross and resurrection of Jesus all too easily becomes narrowed, privatized, with both the cost and the consequence of what Christ did significantly restricted. It remains to be considered what implications this story, and Balthasar's interpretations of it, may have for contemporary Christians, and in particular for pastoral theology. (For *pastoral* theology? the reader may ask. That question too will merit our attention.)

The significance of presence, rather than action, as one of the defining ingredients of Christian pastoral work is crucial, though it is of course not dependent on the descent into hell for its biblical legitimation: for example, the image of the women at the foot of the cross (John 19.25), silently but courageously sharing his suffering, is an equally evocative metaphor for all priestly and pastoral ministry. None the less, the view of Christ's descent into hell as representing his solidarity with the dead, and with death itself, underlines a further, no less crucial point: that no part of human experience is cut off from Christ's concern, or unreached by his love. The two events that frame our lives – birth and death – represent solitude in its most extreme form. The descent into hell is Christ being solitary with the dead, with the fact of death itself: where Good Friday represents an active solidarity, a suffering-with, Holy Saturday stands for a passive one – 'Christ', says Balthasar, 'belongs now with the *refa'im*, with those "deprived of strength".'[30] And if, as 1 Peter 3.19 appears to suggest, even the wicked generation of Noah's day (and the fallen angels whom Noah's contemporaries may have been intended to represent for the first readers of 1 Peter) are not beyond the reach of the proclamation of Christ's love and victory, then the same is true of the least amenable or seemingly redeemable parts of ourselves and our world.

And the implications of this are surely as much pastoral as soteriological. In a world in which pastoral work (and the theology that underlies it) is often conceived in terms of human potential and personal fulfilment, the encounter of Christ with the reality of death and chaos is a prophetic reminder of the obligation laid upon Christians to ensure that such work takes account of – perhaps even begins with – the furthermost extremities of human and creaturely experience. A pastoral theology predicated primarily on the development of human gifts and strengths will be silent in the face of (say) irreversible dementia or the sheer destructive uselessness of so much suffering. And in a society where the problem of what to do with waste – whether of finite resources, poisonous nuclear leftovers, human potential, or misspent time – remains both unsolved and urgent, the story of the descent into hell may have a contribution to make. For it is precisely those aspects of our lives which Irenaeus' *id quod inoperatum conditionis* represents; and the true contemplative is the one who is able unflinchingly to comprehend it.

The second view of the descent into hell offers an approach to pastoral theology which may be said to form an essential corollary to the first. Behind the mythical descriptions of the harrowing of hell is a world-view which, however different from our own, remains enduringly relevant: for it is one in which evil is treated with the utmost seriousness – and not just as the potential for wickedness which exists within individuals, but also as a reality in its own right, capable of acquiring, in structural form, a power that is more than the sum of its parts. The story of the descent into hell expresses the conviction that Christ entered into the most extreme manifestations of evil that it is possible to imagine; and entered them, not simply in order to *share* them, but in order to *fight* them. The response of Christians to some terrible event is invariably to affirm that Christ was in (say) the gas chambers, or the ruins of Sarajevo. But the harrowing of hell is the proclamation that Christ is fighting, and bleeding, in the gas chambers and the ruins of Sarajevo; and that he is there, not just to hold people's hands, but to drag people out. This directive approach to pastoral work is less fashionable today, and with some reason: it can clearly create a state of helpless or inappropriate dependence which is not only undesirable in itself but is palpably contrary to the Jesus of the Gospels, who is presented as discouraging precisely that. Yet solidarity alone cannot be enough, even if sometimes it must suffice: the binding of the strong man, and the harrowing of hell, offer something more. And in as much as the latter story conveys, in innumerable artistic representations as well as in theological analyses such as that of Balthasar, the sense of Christ's act of deliverance as restoring life and hope where hitherto there had been neither, it remains a powerful metaphor for all pastoral activity conducted in his name.

We can go further still. The two interpretations of the descent into hell need not be taken simply as referring to something that happens 'out there'. If the reality of evil is manifested above all in structures of oppression or apathy or waste, it is manifested first inside us. Life is, after all, irreversible. The pastoral and spiritual question is: what do we do with what is done to us? So the story of Holy Saturday also speaks of a descent deep within ourselves: of a God who enters into the darkest, most useless, most unredeemable parts of our lives, and draws them out, like the dead from Hell, 'so that nothing may be lost'. Milton wrote:

> O goodness infinite, goodness immense!
> That all this good of evil shall produce,
> And evil turn to good; more wonderful
> Than that which by creation first brought forth
> Light out of darkness![31]

The essence of Christian pastoral work, then, must be both a being-with and a wresting-from, if the full extremity of both human evil and divine love are to be taken seriously. However, a final question remains to be considered. How appropriate is it to apply ancient Christian myths of this kind, however imaginatively they are resurrected by theologians like Balthasar, to contemporary belief, let alone to *pastoral* strategy and practice? Any such application is clearly fraught with hazard if pressed too far: thus (to take only the most obvious example), the inference that all pastoral ministry is in some sense a descent into hell is one that only the gloomiest or most cynical of pastors would wish to make. But to the general question, two responses are worth making.

First, some early Christian texts describing the descent into hell speak not only of Christ descending there, but of the apostles doing so too; and it is clear that they (as perhaps also does the author of 1 Peter) view the deliverance from hell as a metaphor for baptism. From earliest times, then, the story of Holy Saturday was seen not just as an unrepeatable part of the paschal mystery, but as a model for pastoral and evangelistic work: Christ in and through us, entering the ultimate recesses of life and death, and drawing up from them the chaotic matter of evil and incompletion to share in his resurrection.

Second, the question of how we may legitimately appropriate the truths of ancient stories has been answered by a British theologian of a very different school from Balthasar, but with whom the great Swiss scholar would surely agree. Leslie Houlden was writing about the resurrection, but what he says is no less true of the event believed by so many early Christians to have preceded it:

> We recognize in that conviction of the first Christians an act of audacious and total hope in the very midst of life's unintelligible ambiguities of pain and joy. To be given the chance to make that hope our own, even unto death, is one of the most significant legacies of earliest Christianity to its successors, with their multiplicity of idioms and circumstances. It is a hope that has often not been grasped, partly because literal adherence to the terms of the first days has obscured the spirit within. Modern New Testament study, by way of painful realism about history and about beliefs, leads us to do better.[32]

Notes

[1] So far as the present writer is aware, the last major study of Christ's descent into hell in English was that of McCulloch 1930.

[2] On the history of the doctrine in relation to the creeds, see Kelly 1950, pp. 378–83.

[3] See the sensitive comments on this interpretation in *A New Catechism* 1967, pp. 176–7.

[4] Hilary, *Enarrationes in Psalmos 53 and 138*, quoted in McCulloch 1930, p. 241.

[5] For a detailed study of this text and of 1 Pet. 4:5–6, see Reicke 1946; Kelly 1969, pp. 152–8 and 172–6; and Reicke 1964, pp. 109–12. See also St Augustine, *Epist.* 164:14–17.

[6] For which see James 1924.

[7] See McCulloch 1930, p. 240.

[8] Küng 1977, p. 366: 'There is perhaps no other statement in the creed which shows so clearly the uselessness of invoking isolated articles and the caution required when interpreting traditional teachings.' Küng offers a succinct history of interpretative approaches to the descent into hell (pp. 366–70).

[9] For her exploration of the descent into hell, see von Speyer 1966, and Saward 1990, p. 108.

[10] See especially Saward 1990, ch. 8, and O'Donnell 1992, ch. 8.

[11] McCulloch 1930, p. 230.

[12] Irenaeus, *Adversus Haereses* IV,22:1, PG 7:1047 (my translation).

[13] Balthasar 1990, p. 175.

[14] See Balthasar 1984–90, vol. 1: *Seeing the Form*.

[15] ibid., vol. 7, pp. 234–5.

[16] von Speyer 1970, p. 295; Saward 1990, p. 121.

[17] Balthasar 1990, p. 174, citing A. Gügler.

[18] ibid., p. 161.

[19] Balthasar 1984–90, vol. 7, p. 230.

[20] Balthasar 1990, p. 181.

[21] ibid., p. 165; Irenaeus, *Adversus Haereses* III:23,2, PG 7:961.

[22] Balthasar 1984–90, vol. 2, pp. 75–6.

[23] From the translation used in *The Divine Office* 1974, p. 321.

[24] Translation in James 1924, p. 139. Mâle 1961, p. 224, says the descent into hell was the most important subject in medieval religious art.

[25] Balthasar 1990, p. 151.

[26] So Origen, *Comm. in Rom.* 5; PG 4:1019, 1051.

[27] Balthasar 1990, p. 155.

[28] James 1924, p. 139.

[29] Balthasar 1990, p. 181.

[30] ibid., p. 172.

[31] *Paradise Lost* XII.469-73.

[32] Houlden 1986, p. 152.

BIBLIOGRAPHY

Balthasar, Hans Urs von, 1985-90. *The Glory of the Lord* (ET of *Herrlichkeit*). 7 vols., Edinburgh: T. & T. Clark.

Balthasar, Hans Urs von, 1990. *Mysterium Paschale* (ET of *Mysterium Salutis Grundriss heilsgeschichtlicher Dogmatik*, vol. III, part 2). Edinburgh: T. & T. Clark.

Daniélou, Jean. 1964. *The Theology of Jewish Christianity* (*The Development of Christian Doctrine before the Council of Nicaea*, vol. 1). London: Darton, Longman & Todd.

The Divine Office: The Liturgy of the Hours According to the Roman Rite. 1974. Vol. II. London: Collins.

Houlden, J. L. 1986. *Connections*. London: SCM Press.

James, M. R. (ed.). 1924 (repr. 1953). *The Apocryphal Gospels*. Oxford University Press.

Kelly, J. N. D. 1950. *Early Christian Creeds*. London: Longmans.

Kelly, J. N. D. 1969. *A Commentary on the Epistles of Peter and of Jude*. London: A. & C. Black.

Küng, Hans. 1977. *On Being a Christian*. Trans. E. Quinn. London: Collins.

Mâle, Emile. 1961. *The Gothic Image*. London: Fontana.

McCulloch, J. A. 1930. *The Harrowing of Hell. A Comparative Study of an Early Christian Doctrine*. Edinburgh: T. & T. Clark.

A New Catechism. 1967. ET of the Roman Catholic Dutch Catechism. London: Burns & Oates.

O'Donnell, John. 1992. *Hans Urs von Balthasar*. London: Geoffrey Chapman.

Reicke, B. I. 1946. *The Disobedient Spirits and Christian Baptism: A Study of 1 Peter 3:19 and its Context*. Copenhagen: Munksgaard.

Reicke, B. I. 1964. *The Epistles of James, Peter, and Jude*. The Anchor Bible. New York: Doubleday.

Saward, John. 1990. *The Mysteries of March*. London: Collins.

von Speyer, Adrienne. 1966. *Kreuz und Hölle* (part 1): *Die Passionen*. Einsiedeln.

von Speyer, Adrienne. 1970. *Das Wort und die Mystik*. Vol. II. Einsiedeln.

15
'The Body of Christ has AIDS':
Resurrection and Pastoral Theology

Anthony Dyson

He has been, it is plain, at great pains to destroy the conventional form of the novel.[1]

INTRODUCTION

This essay, which is essentially about whether, and, if so, how, the doctrine of resurrection might address HIV/AIDS, and how HIV/AIDS might address the doctrine of resurrection, is divided into four sections.

The first section examines the concept of 'pastoral theology', drawing attention to major transformations in the method and content of pastoral theology over recent years. I reach the conclusion, which may seem unusual to some and heterodox to others, that pastoral theology has now to be placed centrally in the pattern of theological disciplines, thus ousting dogmatic theology and biblical theology, which have held that central position, off and on, for many periods. The 'doctrine of resurrection' is caught up in this process of 'decentralization' of dogmatic and biblical theology, with striking consequences.

'Resurrection' has inherited, and attracts, many meanings. It can refer to the resurrection of Christ. That meaning may be developed from the tradition of the empty tomb, and/or of appearances of Jesus. There is discussion about the nature of the resurrection body of Christ. For the theologian Bultmann, following a totally different track, the resurrection of Jesus is the same thing as the rise of the Easter faith among the followers of Jesus. But resurrection is also applied to human beings, sometimes to believers and sometimes to all, and also to the 'events' at the 'end of history' and of the 'cosmic order'. In this connection, there is resurrection of the dead and other outcomes. Again, there is dispute about the nature of the resurrection body. There is difference of opinion about the contrast between resurrection of the body and the immortality of the soul. But resurrection is treated, by many modern scholars, as intimately bound up with the cross of Christ. Some see all or most of the above material as mythological or metaphorical. Be that as it may, countless believers consider resurrection as in some sense the key to the world's destiny and the objective guarantee of their own future. But in fact there seems no way of rescuing a convincing account of 'objective resurrection' from this heterogeneity of improbably historical, dogmatic, and speculative interpretation in order to give confidence about living positively in the vulnerable movements of contingent nature and history.

In the second part of this essay, I bring the method and commitments of pastoral theology to bear upon the actuality of HIV/AIDS. This cannot be achieved by the traditional dogmatic and biblical modes of interpretation. I explore one of the approaches that is appropriate, namely cultural analysis. In the third part, I continue to follow the method of pastoral theology, already outlined above, but this time by drawing on evidence of the experience of some people afflicted by HIV/AIDS. In the final part of the essay I bring together a revised theological perspective on resurrection which, I argue, necessarily calls for a revised understanding and practice relating to HIV/AIDS on the part of the Church and of the wider community.

The interpretation of the first part of the title, borrowed from an American source, is left in suspension throughout the essay. This is deliberate. Is it a metaphor asserting that in some sense the Church has lost its spiritual immune system? Does the Church 'have' AIDS in the sense that it shares in the socio-political construction to which I refer in the third section? Is the body of Christ, as distinct from the visible Church, characterized as such by suffering, as in liberation theology the true Church is characterized by poverty? Is it that the empirical Church, having conspired from a distance against 'the black community', 'the gay community', and 'the drug-addicted community', is now obliged to acknowledge HIV/AIDS within its own ranks? Is it that the Church is dying a slow and painful death for which it is responsible or not responsible? Or is the Church some or all of these in various permutations?

PASTORAL THEOLOGY

Until recently, two genres of pastoral theology have been normative. The first, which has its origins in the ancient Christian writers and which focused on the work of the priest, consolidated itself in the Counter-Reformation and beyond. This genre of pastoral theology has been closely involved with the practice of the sacrament of penance. Its closest disciplinary links have been with moral theology and with canon law; its links with dogmatic theology have been tenuous. It is directed at the individual.

The origins of the second genre of pastoral theology can be located in late nineteenth- and early twentieth-century Protestant America. Many ministers expressed dissatisfaction with the prevailing pastoral theology books, which did not begin to help them to cope with the increasing demands that were thrust upon them, especially in the middle-class cultures of the new and burgeoning cities in the Progressive Era. The seminaries sought to respond by introducing a pastoral curriculum. But ministers were bidding for a professional status. After some decades there emerged the movement of clinical pastoral education, with its many centres and schools of thought.

In the 1970s and beyond, both these tendencies were subjected to criticism. Rahner's writings on pastoral theology contain a strongly worded appeal for treating it as an independent and primary theological discipline.[2] As such, it is not a matter of the 'application' of truths that have first been determined somewhere else. The discipline of pastoral theology is concerned with the 'church's self-actualisation here and now'. This form of theology is not confined to the work of the clergy. Everything is its subject-matter: e.g., homiletics, catechetics, missiology, welfare work. Pastoral theology, according to Rahner, is not a formal science alongside other sciences,

> but a quite unique one, a testing of the spirits with a view to the act of committal [which] . . . implies a prophetic element – which one may be permitted to call 'political' – since it must be aware of the impulse of the church's Spirit, which is not simply identical with the perpetually valid truth in the church, but translates the latter into the concrete challenge valid at the particular hour.[3]

Rahner goes on to say that pastoral theology is 'critical' towards the Church. He continues: 'It attempts to be of service in continually overcoming the church's given deficient self-realisation and transcending it in the next new form to which the church is being called.'[4]

Schuster's article on pastoral theology[5] repeats some of Rahner's points, and in some cases does so even more emphatically. A particular target for Schuster is the clericalism mentioned above – 'this obstinate misunderstanding' by which 'the individual Christians and the church congregation stood before [the individual clergyman] . . . passively, as something "directed", "led" and indeed "sanctified" by him'.[6] Instead, Schuster describes pastoral theology as 'the practical theological discipline which deals by the methods of scientific theology with all that constitutes, conditions and makes possible the action incumbent on the Church from day to day'. He goes on to explore more precisely the distinctive nature of this pastoral theology by referring to its dealings 'with the church as a reality with a social and historical structure, and therefore concerned with empirical data'.[7] So this pastoral theology has to fulfil all the fundamental functions deriving from the Church's essential mission; but the way in which they must be carried out 'is *not simply known all along*'.[8] A sharp contrast is then depicted between the way in which, on the old view, 'the contemporary scene with its actual social and cultural structures was to a large extent regarded merely as external, resistant material, or simply as "the world" against which spiritual pastoral activity had to work' and, on the other hand, 'the contemporary situation at any given time as *the inescapable summons of God to the church, reminding it of its ever new task of formulating and announcing the gospel of Jesus for – not against – human society as it exists here and now*'.[9] Rahner and Schuster are clear examples of an approach that challenges the clerical scheme of pastoral theology with its dedicative dependence on dogmatic theology and church law. Does the Protestant tradition of pastoral theology, firmly fixed on counselling as its normative expression, also attract criticism today?

To answer this question I will turn to three writers, one of whom, Lapsley, is a transitional figure, the other two, Campbell and Pattison, belonging more to the 'new school'. Lapsley's essay occurs under the title 'Pastoral Theology Past and Present'.[10] Lapsley, at the beginning, emphasizes Hiltner's view that 'pastoral theology is a definite "branch" of theology – albeit an "operation-centred" branch as distinguished from the "logic-centred" branches of the traditional disciplines. Hence it proceeds by the asking of theological questions of the pastoral "data" and moving toward theological conclusions regarding these.'[11] But, although Lapsley begins his definition of pastoral theology as 'the study of all aspects of the care of persons',[12] he strongly adumbrates the 'need for increased attention to the communal aspects of life in church and society alike'.[13] Again, he states that 'we must learn to relate to communal man [sic] or find that we have by degrees become completely irrelevant'.[14]

Campbell's tentative essay 'Is Practical Theology Possible?' is none the less significant.[15] I will summarize his five principles to which a redefinition of pastoral theology must conform. First, pastoral theology is concerned with the 'study of specific structures in which God's continuing work in the world may be manifest. *These may occur either inside or outside the life of the church.*'[16] Second, pastoral theology can no longer draw upon the functions of the ordained ministry as normative for its subject-matter and scope. Third, the relationship between pastoral theology and the other theological disciplines is 'neither inductive nor deductive. The relationship is to be seen as a "lateral" . . . one.'[17] Fourth, given the 'situations-based' method that it uses, pastoral theology can expect to be fragmentary, rather than systematized and comprehensive. Fifth, the 'findings' of pastoral theology will be mostly 'concrete proposals' for the 'restructuring of the church's life . . . *for the style of life of individual Christians within the "secular" structures of society, and for the renewal and reforming of the secular structures themselves*'.[18]

In his *A Critique of Pastoral Care*,[19] Pattison observes that 'the socio-political dimension is a central concern of British writing on pastoral care today'. What factors does this commitment reflect? Pattison lists five such factors. First, human beings are constituted in a number of dimensions: 'mind, body, intimate relationships, relationships with nature and the biosphere, relationships with significant institutions, and relationships with God'.[20] Second, although pastors or churches might lay claim to political neutrality, the ideas and practices of pastoral care always belong to a specific social and political context. Third, pastoral care is obliged to promote the values that the Church proclaims. These include justice and peace, which are, in part at least, socio-political in character. Fourth, the actual experience of giving and receiving pastoral care forms people to take responsibility for themselves and for their world. Fifth, the Bible – although this often passes unobserved – is a fertile source of insights into the socio-political dimension of pastoral care. Sixth, there are a good many socio-political elements in the Christian pastoral care tradition.

At a number of points in the 'new' pastoral theology literature, the question of an appropriate methodology was raised. In particular, a deductive derivation of pastoral principles from theological norms has been widely regarded as inadequate. But nothing much more specific emerged. Later, important steps were taken by some American theologians to spell out, even though still not in great detail, an appropriate hermeneutic. Particularly influential in this connection has been the development of David Tracy's theological concept of 'mutually critical correlation' into the pastoral context:

> [Pastoral] theology is thereby appropriately a generalist discipline that draws freely upon the specialised knowledge of many different, more narrowly structured perspectives and ways of accumulating knowledge about the world. That appropriation of specialised knowledge must, however, be a disciplined appropriation that is itself shaped by the process of mutually critical correlation which tests the perspectives of other narratives by their abrasion against the Christian narrative, even as that narrative is itself tested and reinterpreted.[21]

AIDS: DISEASE AND SOCIAL FANTASY

In this section I turn to secular analyses of HIV/AIDS in a form that lends itself to mutually critical correlation. There is a mountain of relevant material, so that I confine myself to looking at one representative piece which is also important in its own right. The essay is 'AIDS: The Intellectual Agenda', by Jeffrey Weeks.[22] This essay is a cultural analysis directed at the HIV/AIDS phenomenon and disclosing a number of significant self-interests, including religious and ethical ones.

Weeks begins by drawing attention to the way in which all diseases have social, ethical, and political dimensions. What makes diseases, then, culturally and historically important is the way in which meanings and interpretations are attached to illness and death, refracted through a host of differing, and often conflicting and contradictory, social possibilities. So, illness becomes a metaphor in which the specifics of the illness are lost in a welter of social fantasy. As well as social meanings, there are also many moral meanings that become attached to illness or disease – an attachment which is particularly common in periods of heightened social anxiety. This follows the pattern of nineteenth-century epidemics – e.g., cholera and typhoid – which gained a massive symbolic significance and became bearers of a heavy burden of moral anxiety because they have been linked with individual sexual failings, social marginality, and moral inadequacy.

These false assumptions then infiltrate medical theories and mould popular attitudes.

Weeks therefore argues that HIV/AIDS is a recent example of many such processes of specious moral inflation. But two aspects are distinctive in the case of HIV/AIDS. First, though we live in, and have in many respects made our own, a powerful technological society, a radical loss of faith is experienced as HIV/AIDS confounds technology. Second, the meanings that are generated and complex- ified by HIV/AIDS in our culture, covering social composition, racial boundaries, and social marginality represent a host of fears, anxieties, and problems. So there is the not infrequent phenomenon of moral panics occurring in complex societies when deep-rooted and difficult to resolve social anxieties become focused on symbolic agents that can be easily targeted. Promiscuity, drug-taking, and other political, social, and moral anxieties were condensed into a crisis over HIV/AIDS. HIV/AIDS, as a symbolic phenomenon, grew out of, and fed into, potent bearers of homophobia and racism. Deeply rooted fears about the unprecedented rate of change in sexual behaviour (including fluidity of sexual identities) and in social mores have marked the last two generations and have led to the emergence of new sexual communities in the 1960s. Thus there was 'an immanent prob- lem awaiting a symbolic resolution'; 'AIDS was a crisis waiting to happen'.[23] 'AIDS manages to combine in one word sex, homosexuality, death, communicable disease, disfigurement, young people, drugs and addiction – all our taboos.'[24]

LIVING WITH HIV/AIDS

I present this section of my essay in an *impressionistic* manner. My purpose is to collect comments, by those living with HIV/AIDS and by those who are close to them, which reveal insights and emotions about HIV/AIDS, Christianity, and the Church.[25]

'[Having been diagnosed positive], it was the sudden emotional need that shocked him. He had never felt helpless before.' Suddenly 'they were very isolated and very alone'. 'One of the things that makes the church extremely unattractive for me is its attitude to sexual sin: as if flesh should be whacked into submission or it will overpower us and we will descend into utter chaos.' 'I am a victim of circumstances over which I have no control. I am victim to a virus that has robbed me of the chance to have children . . . I resent it and

I am filled with a persistent sense of the utter futility and horror of it all. It hurts.' 'All I know in my own life is that I need to face the fact of this virus in all its negativity and life-denying threats. There is nothing hopeful about it. There is nothing good about it. There is nothing positive about it. It is painful, degrading, and fearful.' 'I am filled with anger and remorse and, at moments, real despair.' After AIDS appeared 'gay men were a threat again, not simply to "family life" but now to life itself: and those who declared themselves our opponents did not hesitate to use this new "plague" to feed the fires of hatred'. 'I had hoped that, in the face of disease and oppression from "outside", the church would stand up and support us . . . But no. In the face of cries of "the wrath of God" the church not only did sweet f.a. but in many cases actually sided with those who were out to destroy us.' 'I think that [church groups] . . . would have been much happier if I had been in a hospital bed, if I had gone away to die . . . This is an evasion, a running away from their own fears about disease, sexuality and death.' 'Facing the ever-present reality of death, of the loss of the other, of the letting-go which does not signify rejection.' 'There is no denying the pain and tragedy of L's dying. Though at the end L came to a sense of unity and purpose in life and death.'

'For many who pronounce themselves "religious" and "moral", the whole AIDS disaster is a display of God's masterfulness: the punishment of sin, the condemnation of sexuality, divine horror at the satisfaction of desire. More terrible is what goes on inside some of those who are wrestling with what it means to be living and dying with HIV.' 'We have come to symbolise every confusion about sexuality in modern history, and thus, we are objects of fascination and abhorrence.' 'Mostly we talk about what it feels like to be treated like lepers who are treated as if they are morally, if not literally, contagious.' 'I feel grateful that through my journey into my despair and anger and hopelessness I have become aware, I have been released into a sense of the massive potential of life.' 'Only a handful of dentists in London are prepared to treat HIV +ve patients. Many GPs have crossed them off their lists.' '[A] vengeful and incompetent God who, in his fundamentalist desire to wipe out homosexuals and drug addicts, seems clumsily to kill haemophiliacs, Africans and faithful wives at the same time.' 'What, though, I was not prepared for was how AIDS affected children.' 'Her husband had died four weeks earlier. It was he who had contracted AIDS in the first place and unknowingly had passed it on to her. He had contracted it from contaminated blood in the US. I tell you this because I want to try and describe real anger: her eyes were wide, her mouth moving excitedly, her words full of venom and hate. What had I to say?' '[I]t is still true that many people who are HIV positive face a great deal of discrimination and even violence. There is still a lot of ignorance and fear. But I think things have changed to some extent.' 'World-wide the burden of AIDS will be borne by women, women as daughters, sisters, mothers, grandmothers, wives, sexual partners, as carers, educators, wage earners and workers. I am deeply concerned about the silence of women in relation to AIDS.'

RESURRECTION AND AIDS

Following the model of pastoral theology discussed above, it becomes clear that the primary expression of resurrection arises out of a mutual critical correlation between *our discernment* of the false and the true in HIV/AIDS, in the kind of perspectives described in the two preceding sections of this essay, and *the sense of call* to us out of those situations to strain ourselves to prophetic responsibility. It is this to and fro that constitutes the basic dialectic of resurrection. Clericalism, on the other hand, patrols the borders of supposed sacral resurrection, distracting us from recognizing resurrection as, primarily, bound up with the critical knowledge that we acquire from and in 'secular' settings.

But we must not underestimate the profound difficulty of entering upon this dialectic of resurrection in the experience of, or closeness to, HIV/AIDS. For in the approach to HIV/AIDS we come upon factors that thoroughly mislead us, such as distortions of male sexuality, racism, and gender discrimination which give rise to and exacerbate feelings of isolation, inferiority, and contagion which we in fact encounter in ourselves, in others, and in our society. Along with all this, there is much implicit and some explicit reinforcement of these distortions from within the churches. That is at least one of the meanings of 'the body of Christ has AIDS', which is in turn an expression of what has been called 'co-operative sin', which constitutes the Church as an anti-community. Faced both by what HIV/AIDS is and by what we have constructed it to be, our first response should not be to offer 'ultimate' consolation, which has regrettably become the greater part of the Church's construction. Instead, we are to live out the dialectic of the Christian narrative and the narrative of HIV/AIDS in mutual abrasion and reinterpretation. This, we may subsequently conclude, was and is the stuff of resurrection.

So, instead of pastoral theology being derivative from dogmatic and biblical theology, and so being for the most part shaped by past-centred norms, we may explore the thought-experiment and the experience-experiment of pastoral theology being the *constitutive* theological discipline, governed mainly by present-centred norms. The acute problem about resurrection as a dogmatic-biblical theme is how we deal with the theological sediment that accumulates in and around it through the centuries and in succeeding cultural milieux. It seems clear, as this essay has tried to show in relation to HIV/AIDS, that we must envisage ways of dispensing with that sediment in ways which open up contemporary, and often bitter, experience which proffers none or very little of that 'consolation' of resurrection that we have been led to believe is our portion and privilege.

HIV/AIDS, in calling forth new methods and resources on the part of theologians, seems to require something like a commitment to destroy the conventional form of resurrection as, according to Woolf, Meredith purposed to destroy the conventional form of the novel. The motive behind the first of these apparently barbarous acts is somewhat clarified by what Woolf goes on to say about the second:

> He [Meredith] makes no attempt to preserve the sober reality of Trollope and Jane Austen; he has destroyed all the usual staircases by which we have learnt to climb. And what is done so deliberately is done with a purpose. This defiance of the ordinary . . . [is] there to create an atmosphere that is unlike that of daily life, *to prepare the way for a new and an original sense of the human scene.*[26]

Notes

[1] Virginia Woolf on George Meredith, in *The Common Reader: Second Series*, new edn (London: Hogarth Press, 1935).

[2] Karl Rahner, 'Practical Theology within the Totality of Theological Disciplines', *Theological Investigations, IX* (London: Darton, Longman & Todd), pp. 101–14.

[3] ibid., pp. 103f.

[4] ibid., p. 104.

[5] H. Schuster, 'Pastoral Theology', in Karl Rahner et al. (eds), *Sacramentum Mundi* (London: Burns & Oates, 1969), vol. 4, pp. 365-8.

[6] ibid., p. 365.

[7] ibid.

[8] ibid., p. 366, my italics.

[9] ibid., my italics.

[10] James Lapsley, 'Pastoral Theology Past and Present', in William B. Oglesby, Jr (ed.), *The New Shape of Pastoral Theology* (Nashville, TN: Abingdon Press, 1969), pp. 31-48.

[11] ibid., p. 32.

[12] ibid., p. 43.

[13] ibid., p. 44.

[14] ibid., p. 45.

[15] Alistair Campbell, 'Is Practical Theology Possible?', *Scottish Journal of Theology* 25 (1972), pp. 217-27.

[16] ibid., pp. 224f.

[17] ibid., p. 225.

[18] ibid., p. 226, my italics.

[19] Stephen Pattison, *A Critique of Pastoral Care* (London: SCM Press, 1988).

[20] ibid., p. 89.

[21] Charles V. Gerkin, *Widening the Horizons: Pastoral Responses to a Fragmented Society* (Philadelphia: Westminster Press, 1986), p. 54; see further, Anthony Dyson, 'Pastoral Theology: Towards a New Discipline', *Contact* 78 (1983), pp. 2-8, and 'Pastoral Theology', in

Alastair Campbell (ed.), *A Dictionary of Pastoral Care* (London: SPCK, 1987), pp. 201–3.

[22] Jeffrey Weeks, 'AIDS: The Intellectual Agenda', in Peter Aggleton, Graham Hart, and Peter Davies (eds), *AIDS: Social Representations, Social Practices* (London: Falmer Press, 1989), pp. 1–20.

[23] ibid., p. 10.

[24] Gordon Macphail, 'AIDS, Sin and the Society of Friends', *Friends' Quarterly* 26 (1990), pp. 126–32; quote at p. 127.

[25] Margaret Morris, 'Women, AIDS and Religion', *Modern Churchman* 32.4 (1990), pp. 19–26; James Woodward (ed.), *Embracing the Chaos: Theological Responses to AIDS* (London: SPCK, 1990), *passim*; Christopher Webb, 'People with AIDS', *New Blackfriars* 71 (1990), pp. 320–4; Simon Robson, 'Through the Eye of a Needle', *New Blackfriars* 71 (1990), pp. 354–7; Stuart Mason, 'AIDS and All Saints', *New Blackfriars* 67 (1986), pp. 510–15.

[26] Woolf, *The Common Reader*, p. 229, my italics.

16
Global Threats and Global Hope
in Multi-religious Perspective

Alan Race

In a perceptive essay on the resurrection, Leslie Houlden made the following observation: 'The history relating to the resurrection is obscure, its interpretation is manifold.'[1] Such candid assessment of the twin aspects of the language of resurrection in Christian debate ought to put a brake on many of the confusing arguments about it that periodically come to public prominence. If the lesson of scholarship is that (at the historical level) we assume we know more than is possible to know, and that (at the theological level) we infer too much belief from such a slender base, then we may benefit by holding our silence for a time.

Yet the arguments about the resurrection conceal a genuine anxiety that should not be overlooked. Whatever else it has been taken to mean, there is no avoiding the recognition that the language of resurrection has been intimately bound up with the Christian virtue of hope. The content of that hope may have varied through history, but the link with 'the resurrection' has always been assumed. However, given the opacity of the language of resurrection, the question presents itself of how best to provide the appropriate theological grounding for the enterprise of Christian hope today.

Leslie Houlden offers the hint of an alternative way forward when he suggests that we ought not to detach 'the resurrection' from its rightful setting in the apocalyptic expectations of the first-century churches and force it to do a theological job that it is incapable of doing outside that cultural setting. Therefore, he suggests, it is better to consider the whole impact of Jesus' life and death as generating a focus of hope in relation to God's presence in the world. '"The resurrection"', he says, 'may then take its place as an icon of the fact, inescapably involved in faith, that Jesus is the focus of hope and life.'[2] Theologians of a more conservative hue may think that this 'demythologized' formulation of the resurrection hope is too inexact.

But it has at least the merit of rescuing the enterprise of hope from a rigid dependency on the outcome of sterile debates about, for example, what really happened at 'the resurrection'. It also has the advantage of opening up alternative possibilities for engaging in fresh explorations of the meaning of hope for today, given a radically different cultural world from that of first-century Christianity.

In the remainder of this essay, I wish to explore these possibilities of hope in the new context of global consciousness. By global consciousness I mean the recognition that all cultural life is interconnected. Global travel, global trade, global economics, and global politics, bind the nations together in one world community. Our experience may feel local, but it is ineradicably shaped by the global. The destiny of my community is bound up with the destiny of all other communities, and with the destiny of the planet.

If hope is the human capacity to entertain a vision of fulfilled life in the face of threats to its sustainability, many experience those threats at the end of the twentieth century as overwhelmingly destructive. And there is good reason for this: we have only to think of ecological degradation, growing militarism, the rapid spread of diseases such as HIV and AIDS, increasing poverty through economic inequalities, and the world-wide increase in refugees, to name just a few of the problems. It is easy to be alarmist about the nature of the threats confronting the globe, but it is easier still to block them out of consciousness because of the scale of the potential destruction that they pose. By way of illustration, let me briefly indicate what is at stake from the two areas of ecology and militarism.

While we are becoming aware of the ecological ramifications of human activity, we have scarcely begun to absorb the scale of the ecological crisis confronting the globe. 'Today's destruction of the environment', say Ulrich Duchrow and Gerhard Liedke, 'differs from all earlier destruction of the environment because it is systematic, faster than the natural regulating mechanisms and is of worldwide dimensions.'[3] Already, as these authors point out, a staggering 72% of the tropical rain forests of East and West Africa have been destroyed, and 42% of the world's total rain forests have disappeared. Global warming, caused mainly by the greenhouse gas, carbon dioxide, has irrevocably been set in train, but by how much and by when estimates differ.[4] Nevertheless, the seas are likely to rise in the next fifty years. And so on: the catalogue of potential irreversible ecological disasters is lengthening every day. One writer has interpreted the extent of human interference in the processes of nature as the 'end of nature'. There is no place that is unaffected: 'We have deprived nature of its independence,' avers Bill McKibben, 'and that is fatal to its meaning. Nature's independence *is* its meaning; without it there is nothing but us.'[5] This is more than a romantic yearning for a lost good. It is not only plant and animal life that suffers through the destruction of the ecological basis of life. Loneliness is inimical to the human spirit: symbolically it undermines hope.

In relation to the threat from militarism, Western perceptions have been dominated, since the end of the Second World War, by the East–West conflict. With the end of the Cold War, many consider that the threat from militarism, or at least from a war of indescribable destruction carried out by weapons of mass destruction, has all but disappeared. The real global picture is inevitably more complex, and probably more dangerous. Nuclear weapons have not been outlawed (in Britain, acceptance of the Trident nuclear weapons system represents a sixteenfold *increase* in destructive capability!); and the development of biological weapons seems set to escalate. A recent study has concluded that 'the military momentum of the Cold War years has given us a legacy of global militarisation which will long outlast that era'; and that 'the very arms races of the 1970s and 1980s have spawned new types of weapons, and these are now proliferating across the world'.[6] With the shift in the axis of world tension from East–West to North–South, and with the rich North targeting places in the poor South where access to dwindling natural resources may be blocked (as in the Gulf War of 1990/91), the scope for devastating conflict remains considerable. Hope that the international community may find alternative ways of settling its disputes seems as far off as ever.

Confronted with such daunting threats on a global scale, the images of hope that human beings are summoned to embrace most readily are those which promote the imperative for survival. 'The energy for creating the future depends on the possibility of survival,' says Richard Falk, a long-standing advocate of introducing social values and law into foreign policy and world-order studies.[7] Survival may seem like a minimal focus for hope. Yet if the powerlessness engendered in individuals by the pressure of global threats is not to cut the quick of human hope, survival may be more of a positive notion than we have usually thought. Clearly, more is involved in the process of survival than searching simply for alternative political and economic policies that will bring us back from global disaster. Fundamentally, survival refers to resources in the imagination for envisaging alternative futures over against ones that project present circumstances into an indefinite future.

In response to the global crises of the late twentieth century, and in the light of our being 'thrown together' as a global community, it has been suggested that what the world needs is something approaching a new world ethic in order to sustain future hope. One example of this kind of proposal was the *Declaration Toward a Global Ethic*, which was launched by religious leaders at the 1993 World's Parliament of Religions, held in Chicago. In a multi-faith world, the religious and ethical basis for participation in such a project was necessarily a shared basis, and was set out as follows:

> We affirm that a common set of core values is found in the teachings of the religions, and that these form the basis of a global ethic.
>
> We affirm that this truth is already known, but yet to be lived in heart and action.
>
> We affirm that there is an irrevocable, unconditional norm for all areas of life, for families and communities, for races, nations, and religions. There already exist ancient guidelines for human behavior which are found in the teachings of the religions of the world and which are the condition for a sustainable world order.[8]

The *Declaration* proceeded to outline an ethic of interdependence and truthfulness in relationships, basic compassion for all people, partnership between age groups and the sexes, non-violence in the settling of disputes, and social and economic justice in an ecologically sustainable world order. Underpinning it all was the Golden Rule, evident in all religious traditions, that we do to others what we would have them do to us.

If all people and institutions acted in accordance with the ideals of love and compassion at the heart of a global ethic, then clearly the hope of sustaining a global future in the face of the many threats working against that future would in principle be realizable. Such dreams are utopian; but not romantically so, we may trust. The truth of the ancient saying that where there is no vision the people perish holds good. But exactly how the shared ideals of love and compassion can be embodied in human behaviour is a matter for the dialogue between the religions (together with all other groups and ideologies concerned with a global ethic) to work out. This is bound to be a complex process, and it probably should begin with the religions themselves making amends for the failure of their own relationships in the past. Even so, there are at least two major difficulties in the proposal of a global ethic. The first stems from the ambivalence of religious commitment in the modern age. As believers search their traditions for the theological and ethical resources which will contribute towards a global ethic, this does not entail that these resources can be applied prescriptively. Ancient traditions will need also to be open to change, particularly in the light of new challenges that have arisen partly from criticism and partly from global consciousness itself. The second difficulty is the epistemological problem of providing a philosophical/theological basis for co-operation between the religions. For if it is true that the ethical outlook of a religion coheres with its philosophical/theological belief system in fundamental ways, then without some grounding in epistemology, the notion of a common set of core values found within the religions will be no more than a will-o'-the-wisp.

I wish now to discuss both of these difficulties in turn, in order to show that they are not insurmountable obstacles on the road towards developing a global ethic for the sake of future hope.

At the foundational level, the religions do not appear to be ambivalent in their beliefs and normative values. This is because images of future well-being spring from the heart of a religion in what we might call its salvific dimension. All religions present a matrix for transcendent vision and human transformation. Whether it is through the experience of *satori* as in Mahayana Buddhism, *salvation* as in Christianity, *chosenness* as in Judaism, *liberation* as in Hinduism, *surrender* as in Islam, and so on, all religions recommend a pathway of change that issues in ethical ideals and norms for human behaviour. At the theological/philosophical level, the 'better way' proclaimed by the religions is conceptualized in different forms. But at the ethical level there is often a great deal of overlap: all the great religious traditions promote the ideals of compassion, goodness, forgiveness, and love. Admittedly, these ideals easily cohere at this generalized level, while in practice they have been expressed in radically different ways. But there is worth in drawing the religions together at this point, for the principles of love and compassion can act as common criteria by which the religions are judged. More than that, these ideals affect our basic humanity, suggesting the possibility, therefore, of a global ethic with a shared religious basis.

However, the ambivalence of the religious traditions appears when we note how human well-being has been both enhanced and also demeaned by religious practices. As examples of the latter, one could cite Christianity's support for slavery; Hinduism's encouragement of *suttee*, the burning of widows at the funeral pyre of their husbands; Islam's disproportionate punitive legislation for the amputation of a thief's hand; or the resistance to the notion of human rights by many of the religions in the modern period. The challenge which modern consciousness puts to the religions, therefore, is whether they are capable of absorbing the heightened sense of human dignity and autonomy that has arisen over the last two hundred years.

In response to these challenges, it may be that different traditions will need to undergo reconstruction in different ways, depending on the manner by which they have hindered human development. For example, in spite of the high priority the prophetic traditions (dominant in the West) have given to the freedom of the human will, the strong notions of divine sovereignty within these traditions have often functioned to undermine a proper sense of responsibility that human beings now need to feel for the future. This sense of responsibility can no longer be deflected by subsuming it under belief in the triumph of the divine plan for the world. Probably it is Judaism, through the experience of the Holocaust, that has had to face this challenge in the profoundest manner. But Christianity, with its strong stress on *belief* as the right mode of relationship with God, has also had to experiment with alternative conceptions of God's relation to the world. Whatever metaphors have been employed to envisage the God–world relationship in order to take account of radical human freedom, the general trend has been towards searching for a sense of God's presence *in* and *through* the world. In terms of ethical activity, if the world is viewed as the locus of the divine presence, the social and political implications of religious hope are likely to assume a more prominent place in the scheme of things.

For the so-called mystical religions dominant in the East, the challenge of modernity has been to what many commentators have seen as their innate quietism. There are of course caricatures that have to be guarded against in this characterization of the Eastern traditions. We must avoid the polarity that Christianity has been the bearer of a positive view of history while Hinduism and Buddhism have been fatalistic about history, for this disregards the major role that modern science and the democratic ideal has played in awakening Christianity to its full historical and social vocation. Nevertheless, it is noticeable that Buddhism, at least in some manifestations, is developing a 'social face' in order to dispel accusations of quietism;[9] and in the nineteenth and twentieth centuries it is interesting that the desire of a figure such as Swami Vivekananda (1863–1902), disciple of Sri Ramakrishna (1834–86), to 'modernize' Hinduism included teachings on social reform, education, and social service.[10]

The Swiss Catholic theologian Hans Küng has expressed the ambivalence of the religious task as I have outlined it by pointing out the dialectical relationship between religion and human well-being that underlies that task. On the one hand, 'True humanity is the presupposition for true religion. That means that the *humanum* (respect for human dignity and basic values) is a minimal requirement of any religion'; and on the other hand, 'True religion is the fulfilment of true humanity. That means that religion (as the expression of all-embracing meaning, supreme values, unconditional obligation) is an optimal presupposition for the realization of the *humanum.*'[11] Küng may have drawn the net too narrowly in the *humanum*, given the dawning of ecological awareness in recent years. However, with that caveat, Küng has here neatly summarized the religious vocation in its role as broker for a global ethic.

In practical terms, the utopian ideal behind the notion of a global ethic will be heavily qualified both by the possibilities and limitations within the opportunities for co-operation between the religions afforded by global consciousness, and also by the challenges that this consciousness itself presents to traditional patterns of thinking and behaviour. For these reasons, proposals for a global ethic are bound to remain precarious. Nevertheless, there does seem to be some family resemblance between the religions at the level of ethical aspiration, providing at least a *prima facie* case for a global ethic.

Given, therefore, a world picture of rapid change, disorientation, and apocalyptic scenarios, the religions face a crossroads: whether to co-operate for the sake of providing the world with a shared hope, or to continue along separate trajectories as rival world-views. For those who wish to respond to the new circumstances, the dual task of grounding human hope in shared religious values, and of allowing the religions themselves to be challenged by modern global conscious-ness, represents a turning-point for the religions themselves. The model of dialogue and co-operation that they will need for this dual task will inevitably be complex. It will combine commitment to one's own tradition with maximum openness to other traditions. Above all, it will be orientated towards alleviating and reversing the great threats to the future as manifest, for example, in mass poverty, the arms trade, and ecological destructiveness.

We now come to the second area of difficulty, which I alluded to earlier, in the project to construct a global ethic. This is the epistemological problem of the relationship between the world religions, a problem that has begun to trouble many philosophical and theological minds. In one sense, of course, there is no need to solve this problem prior to any practical co-operation between the religions. But the problem cannot be shelved indefinitely. For there is a paradox that hovers over all attempts at mutual co-operation: at the practical level, the traditions are attracted by the possibilities of working together for justice and peace in the world; and yet, at the theoretical level, the theological and philosophical distinctiveness of the traditions pulls them apart again. Without attending to this paradox, the air of suspicion hovering over interreligious encounter will not be dispelled.

Keith Ward has made one helpful suggestion as to how this paradox might be approached. 'It might be better', he writes, 'to see the different faiths, not as in radical opposition but as having a range of agreed values, but varying ways of interpreting them in the light of a developing understanding of the world.'[12] Nevertheless, creative as this possibility may seem, a greater degree of self-criticism on the part of all the traditions is going to be required if the mutual suspicions between the religions are to be overcome. One strand within the roots of these suspicions has been the absoluteness inherent, it seems, within religious commitment itself, whereby one tradition either thinks of itself as wholly superior or considers its own message as somehow more complete or more profound than that of others. These versions of absoluteness have, in turn, fostered antagonism and war between the religions, though the degree of that antagonism has been shaped inevitably by historical and political circumstances. If the religions are to contribute towards global hope, then the condition for their co-operation is that they will have to find ways of reinterpreting their traditional claims to absoluteness, so as to render them more provisional. The basis for making this move already exists in the distinction, found within all the traditions, between the Ultimate Reality that in essence cannot be conceptualized, and the knowledge of Ultimate Reality that is imaged in different cultural and material, and therefore provisional, forms.

At the very least what seems required is a commitment on behalf of the traditions to a process of their mutual transformation in the light of dialogue and co-operation. This will bind the traditions to one another, such that their future developments will be the result of their mutual interaction. Distinctiveness of tradition will be preserved, yet with maximum openness to change in the light of new information and challenge that come from the dialogical encounter itself.

Commitment to mutual transformation in dialogue may be sufficient for the foreseeable future as a loose epistemological backing of sorts for practical co-operation between the traditions. However, it does seem to me that this commitment harbours an expectation that something of Ultimate Reality will be encountered through the dialogue. And this naturally leads us to ask whether it is possible for the religions to come to view one another as reflections of the same Ultimate Reality, yet glimpsed under different forms. Suggestions of how this is conceivable have been made, even if they have not as yet received the general approval of the theologians and philosophers of the traditions.[13] But those who resist the attempt have to ask themselves whether by refusing to grant an equal validity to the religions, both as responses to the Ultimate Reality and as matrices of transcendent vision and human transformation, they are perpetuating, albeit by default, the mutual suspicion between the traditions.

In this essay, I have tried to sketch an outline of how a future global ethic might draw on the religions of the world in order to explore the possibilities of shared values. It is a project of co-operation and dialogue in which the religions will make their distinctive contributions, each being prepared to offer and receive criticism, in the light of self-criticism. The Christian contribution will stem from the traditions of Jesus, who, through the application of the apocalyptic language of resurrection, has become a 'focus of hope and life'. In this respect, Leslie Houlden's recasting of the language of resurrection enables us to interpret its impact in terms applicable to the modern world. But it is an interpretation that is also, in principle, not exclusive of other perspectives on 'hope and life'.[14] By adopting a multi-religious perspective, therefore, it becomes both possible and attractive for Christians to collaborate with other religious traditions in a new kind of venture – one that has the interests of the globe at heart because it has the interests of *shared* hope and life at heart.

Notes

[1] J. L. Houlden, *Connections: The Integration of Theology and Faith* (London: SCM Press, 1986), p. 150.

[2] ibid.

[3] Ulrich Duchrow and Gerhard Liedke, *Shalom: Biblical Perspectives on Creation, Justice and Peace* (Geneva: WCC, 1987), pp. 16f.

[4] See Stephen H. Schneider, *Global Warming: Are We Entering the Greenhouse Century?* (Cambridge: Lutterworth Press, 1989).

[5] Bill McKibben, *The End of Nature* (Harmondsworth: Penguin, 1990), p. 54.

[6] Paul Rogers and Malcolm Dando, *A Violent Peace: Global Security after the Cold War* (Brassey's, 1992), pp. 49, 64.

[7] 'The Role of Imagination in Overcoming Indefensible Weapons' (a conversation between international lawyer Richard Falk, feminist theologian Catherine Keller, and peace researcher Roger Williamson) in R. Williamson (ed.), *The End In Sight?: Images of the End and Threats to Survival* (Uppsala: Life and Peace Institute, 1993), p. 106.

[8] 'Declaration Toward a Global Ethic', in Hans Küng and Karl-Josef Kuschel (eds), *A Global Ethic: The Declaration of the Parliament of the World's Religions* (London: SCM Press, 1993).

[9] Examples include: Ken Jones, *The Social Face of Buddhism: An Approach to Social and Political Activism* (Wisdom Publications, 1989), in the UK; and the many writings of the Vietnamese Thich Nhat Hanh, especially originally in *The Lotus in a Sea of Fire* (London: SCM Press, 1967).

[10] As Ninian Smart observes: 'With Vivekananda, Indian national self-consciousness came of age', *The World's Religions* (Cambridge: Cambridge University Press, 1989), pp. 392–8.

[11] Hans Küng, *Global Responsibility: In Search of a New World Ethic* (London: SCM Press, 1991), p. 91. Küng was also a prime mover behind the 'Declaration Toward a Global Ethic' launched at the 1993 Parliament of the World's Religions, see n. 8.

[12] Keith Ward, *A Vision to Pursue* (London: SCM Press, 1991), p. 190.

[13] See the bases for the pluralist option in John Hick and Paul F. Knitter (eds), *The Myth of Christian Uniqueness* (London: SCM Press, 1987); and also Gavin D'Costa (ed.), *Christian Uniqueness Reconsidered* (Maryknoll, NY: Orbis, 1990) for criticisms. See my *Christians and Religious Pluralism*, 2nd edn (London: SCM Press, 1993) for a defence of the pluralist option in the light of the last ten years of debate.

[14] If the glorification after death of a religious founder is one expressive mark of being a 'focus of hope and life', archetypal figures from other traditions could equally qualify alongside Jesus. One could cite, for example, how the Mahayana belief in the 'glorified body' (*sambhogakaya*) of the Buddha is the means by which he is present as a 'focus of hope and life' to those who believe in him.

17
Resurrection in Music

John Bowden

When it comes to describing resurrection, words and images break; so if there is any medium that might hope to go further here, it would be music, which needs neither words nor images to communicate, and, when joined to them, gives them an extra dimension. So an exploration of the expression of the theme of resurrection in music has its own fascination. As far as I can see, this particular exploration – which is precisely that, no less and no more – is a first one; I have been unable to discover any article or book on the subject. It is offered to Leslie Houlden, a wise friend and helper of many years, with the hope that he will enjoy reading it as much as I have enjoyed researching and writing it.

The beginning of the quest is not an encouraging one. 'Resurrection' is not a theme that appears in any of the great dictionaries of music in any language. And if one looks merely for works entitled 'Resurrection', the results are meagre in the extreme: the evidence leads into the remotest by-ways of music. It seems to take a truly second-rate composer to embark on a great subject.

The new Grove and the catalogue of the BBC music library produce five works entitled *Resurrection*, but none of them is in the mainstream of classical music. First comes an early oratorio, Schutz's *Historie der Auferstehung Jesus Christi*, written in 1623, which, like several other similar works, is a setting of a compilation of biblical texts. Then there are two very late nineteenth-century oratorios, the style and content of which I have been unable to ascertain. One is by Georges Hué (1858–1948), who succeeded Saint-Saëns at the Académie des Beaux-Arts; the other is by Lorenzo Perosi (1872–1956), at one time a highly popular musical director of the Sistine Chapel, who wrote oratorios on both the resurrection of Christ and the resurrection of Lazarus: he had a spiritual crisis and a mental breakdown, and spent much of his long life in mental hospitals.

Though equally abstruse, a third *Resurrection* can actually be heard by anyone who feels inclined to listen, since it has just been recorded (1992). This is by Franco Alfano (1875–1954), whose chief claim to fame is to have finished Puccini's *Turandot*[1] (badly) after its composer's death. Unfortunately, it is no more than an opera based on Tolstoy's novel, which is turned into a drama of personal relationships set, successively, in a railway station, a prison for prostitutes, and a Siberian labour camp – all in Italian verismo style with a harmonic language derived from Debussy and Ravel. Local colour and the resurrection reference are provided by bells and a Russian-style Easter chant.

That leaves Handel and his very early oratorio *La Risurrezione*, written in Rome in 1707, when he was twenty-two. It is in two parts: in the first, set on the night before Easter Day, Lucifer exults over the death of Christ and St John cheers lamenting women with the hope of resurrection; in the second, set in the garden of Joseph of Arimathea, Mary Magdalene narrates the appearance of the risen Christ. Modern critics have little praise for anything in the work except Lucifer's aria '*O voi dell'Erebo*'; here the devil really does have the best tune. 'St John has an unfortunate and undeniable tendency to exhibitionism and his superfluous semiquavers have the flavour of ineptitude'; the work has just two choruses, and it is 'difficult to decide which is the worse'.[2] That the music is hardly distinctive in its treatment of resurrection is indicated by the fact that Handel later transferred it to his opera *Agrippina*, giving a good deal of Mary Magdalene's music, unaltered, to the triumphant mother of Nero.

And that is that. Bach, so famous for his *Passions*, surprisingly seems to have written very little relating to Easter and resurrection: of his more than two hundred cantatas, only two, no. 4, '*Christ lag in Todes Banden*', and no. 31, '*Der Himmel lacht*', were written for performance on Easter Day; and in addition to them there is just the *Easter Oratorio* (BWV 249). This last has no biblical quotations or narratives: it depicts the discovery of the empty sepulchre on Easter morning, by Mary, mother of James, Mary Magdalene, Peter and John, in recitative, da capo arias and chorus, and contains a particularly fine aria (known as the 'sleep' aria) for tenor, recorders and muted strings, '*Sanfte soll mein Todeskummer*'. Remarkably, the work was first performed as a 'birthday entertainment', for Duke Christian of Weissenfels in February 1725.

But Bach also wrote music about resurrection in another context, a context that is far more promising for my theme. Settings of the Latin mass run right through the history of Western music from an early stage, and in the *Credo* the composer is given the dramatic contrast between '*Crucifixus etiam pro nobis sub Pontio Pilate*' and '*Et resurrexit tertia die*' as what virtually amounts to a centrepiece for his work. Here a contrast between Bach and some of his successors is illuminating, and shows vividly the difference between those great composers whose personal faith expressed itself easily in the music and those whose relationship to the Christian tradition was rather more problematical.

First comes Bach himself, in his B Minor Mass. The '*Crucifixus*' here is an archetypal lament. A deeply passionate, chromatic chorus in E minor, with obbligato parts for flutes, violins, violas, and continuo, in form it is a passacaglia set over an ostinato, which, as Wilfred Mellers has pointed out, recurs in other great musical laments: Dido's 'When I am laid in earth' in Purcell's *Dido and Aeneas*; Melisande's death scene in Debussy's opera; the 'Thebes is dying' chorus from Stravinsky's *Oedipus Rex*, and Elgar's threnody on Gerontius' death.[3] But by a remarkable series of enharmonic changes, the pain is transformed into peace, and in the last two bars the E minor becomes its relative G major, and the chorus dies peacefully away into silence, with the singers all at the bottom of their register. 'There is no more remarkable example of the physiological and psychological impact of tonality, whether we consider it in relation to this magical moment or in the context of the mass as a whole.'[4] Silence. And then comes D major, trumpets and drums, soon to be joined by bubbling flutes in a movement of lightness and sheer joy. Few other pieces of music convey such unalloyed rejoicing.

With Mozart, of course, things are not so simple. As Hans Küng has well reminded us, Mozart's settings of the mass are more than just commissions dutifully undertaken for an ecclesiastical master. His Catholic faith is by no means to be dismissed.[5] Words written to his mortally-ill father in 1787, four years before his own death, convey something of Mozart's profoundly religious attitude to life:

> I never lie down at night without reflecting that – young as I am –
> I may not live to see another day. Yet not one of all my acquaint-
> ances could say that in company I am morose and disgruntled. For

this blessing I daily thank my Creator and wish with all my heart that each one of my fellow-creatures could enjoy it.[6]

These words could be set over Mozart's Coronation Mass (K 317), a jewel among his masses, written on the eve of the French Revolution. Since Mozart was fully aware of the social and cultural changes taking place at the time, and had by no means an unquestioning faith, one would not expect anything like Bach's joyful assurance. Moreover, in a work that lasts only twenty-five minutes, as compared to the just under two hours of a modern performance of Bach's B Minor Mass, everything goes by much more quickly. The drama and its resolution is none the less clearly present, albeit in a different way. Here again the '*Crucifixus*' is in the minor, a slow chorus following the one point of repose in the *Credo*, the '*Et incarnatus*' with its solo chorus. Despite the pace, more than with Bach, one is immediately aware of the words because of Mozart's thoughtful treatment of them: '*passus*' is repeated three times, and '*sepultus est*' is spelled out syllable by syllable for a second time, before a resurrection which, with its rising quavers, leads directly into ascension and sends the risen Lord to heaven with a burst of joyful C major. And the energy thus generated carries right through to the end of the *Credo*, spurred on by the soloists who make their appearance with the coming of the Holy Spirit.

With Beethoven, the solemnity and the shadows deepen. Of all the settings of the '*Crucifixus*' which precedes the resurrection, Beethoven's in his *Missa Solemnis* is the most anguished. We know from a letter he wrote to his publishers in 1810 that he admired the '*Crucifixus*' of Bach's B Minor Mass, but whereas – as we saw – Bach is depicting a universalized suffering, Beethoven's is personalized; it is as though in his body and mind he knew what crucifixion felt like. 'The short notes, tied to the long, effect metrical dislocations emphasized by the sforzandi, and scrunch onto dissonant suspensions and diminished sevenths, reinforced by shuddering repeated notes and tremolandi.'[7] But if the '*Crucifixus*' is so deeply personal, the '*Et resurrexit*' comes as a great surprise to the listener: no outburst from the orchestra; no sudden unleashing of rapid motion; no triumphant C major as the preceding cadence might have suggested, but six ambiguous bars of modal music, sung by unaccompanied chorus in archaic Mixolydian harmony. This is not personal music at all. One might not want to go so far as Martin Cooper, who comments that 'subjective feelings are no longer relevant here; for after the tenors' "prick of light" at "*et*", the risen Christ is an objective presence as real and incontrovertible as the sun';[8] perhaps Wilfred Mellers' 'undemonstrative' and 'childish' are nearer the mark.[9] But here, in the almost silence, we are faced with mystery. The perceptive (or tutored) listener may recall that modal music similarly accompanied the '*Et incarnatus est*', and that there, as here, the repeated *et* almost gives the impression of stammering:

> It is as though in the stammered repetitions and silences, he is *waiting* for the divine light. This may imply doubt as to whether it will come . . . It also and more significantly suggests that the light Beethoven is waiting for is far beyond that implicit in rational Enlightenment, and even that in the Nicene or any other Creed. Momentarily, dubiety and inapprehensibility stifle the flame of inspiration: so there is a catch in the breath, a faltering of the pulse.[10]

There is no such faltering with Anton Bruckner, writing later in the century. His F Minor Mass, finished in 1868, was written not least as a mark of gratitude for his recovery from a serious nervous ailment that had afflicted him the previous year. It is perhaps the last great classical setting of the mass written from a deep and serene Christian faith, comparable to that of Bach.

Here the '*Crucifixus*', an E-flat slow movement, is a chorale accompanied by rising and falling string passages, and punctuated by a bass soloist, repeating '*etiam pro nobis*' three times and '*passus*' five times. The movement conveys above all an air of gentle resignation and finality, ending as it does with a closing cadence of four bars of unaccompanied chorus echoed in four more bars of brass chorus (horns and trombones). Silence follows, the key underlined further by two pianissimo pizzicato E-flats on cellos and double bass. And then it happens. The pizzicatos go up a semitone to E and are joined first by a drum-roll from the tympani and then by a driving string figure that is to go on for one hundred bars; the composer also used it in his setting of Psalm 150 and his *Te Deum*. Woodwinds join in the great crescendo, first clarinets and bassoons almost inaudibly, then oboes and flutes, and finally the full orchestra thunders out '*Et resurrexit*': sopranos up on E rising to G-sharp, and tenors on G-sharp from the start in a blaze of glory. The end of a tradition, perhaps, but what a way to go!

In musical language, the French composer Olivier Messiaen (1908–92) is worlds apart from Anton Bruckner, but he shared with Bruckner a deep Catholic faith, and was one of the rare modern composers of stature to devote his work to praising God in art. The theme of resurrection into glory appears in many of his works, particularly his great organ cycle *Les corps glorieux*, a contemplation of resurrected bodies and the resurrected environment, with its great centrepiece on resurrection, '*Combat de la mort et de la vie*', and the orchestral *L'Ascension*, both from the 1930s. However, perhaps his best-known work on the resurrection theme is *Et Expecto Resurrectionem Mortuorum*, written in 1964. With its orchestra of thirty-four players supplemented with percussion including bells and gongs, it has all Messiaen's characteristically dramatic colouration, but the cencerros, tam-tams, and brass and woodwind choirs are at the service of music that is above all liturgical, deriving its power from the symmetry and repetition of its structure. In the preface, Messiaen speaks of Grünewald's risen Christ 'who seems to be flying in a rainbow generated by his own light'; over the second movement are inscribed Paul's words about Christ's dominion over death, 'Christ, being risen from the dead, dies no more', and the fourth movement looks to that time in heaven 'when the morning stars sang together and all the sons of God shouted for joy'.

The musical language of the work draws on two resources that Messiaen uses elsewhere, birdsong and plainchant; thus in the first movement Christ calls his people to resurrection with the sound of an Amazonian bird, and the fourth movement alternates an Easter antiphon with the call of the Calandra lark. In this work, too, Messiaen sees his music in terms of colour, as in its immediate, shorter, predecessor, *Couleurs de la cité céleste*. Again in the preface to the score, he recalls the first performance in the Ste Chapelle in Paris, where 'the blues, the reds, the golds, the violets resounded in each window with the music . . . It was eleven in the morning and the sun also played its part, bringing here and there new touches of colour with the rebounding of the sounds.'[11]

Colour and light also go with a modern British work, Robert Saxton's *Music to Celebrate the Resurrection of Christ*, an orchestral piece lasting some ten minutes. This was written in conjunction with a BBC2 television film centred on Coventry Cathedral, itself a symbol of resurrection from destruction. As in the *Credo* from the Latin mass, the music begins with echoes of the crucifixion before reaching a state of peace. The composer remarks that it was inspired by memories of beauty and calm in Jerusalem in the early evening, especially on the Mount of Olives. Eventually a point of illumination is reached, representing the first moment of light on emerging from a sepulchre. The music quickly increases in speed and becomes a wild dance of joy, exploding into octave Es for the whole orchestra (shades of Bruckner!) which illustrate intense blinding light, before building to a radiant conclusion of affirmation and hope in E major.

Like Messiaen's, Saxton's work, too, might be said to stand in a liturgical, iconic tradition rather than representing an attempt to respond to the existential questions of death and resurrection. And should current fashion be any pointer to the future, the popularity of the music of John Tavener suggests that if the resurrection becomes a theme again in the future, the inspiration is as likely as not to come from the tradition of the Orthodox Church, inspired by its imagery.

Which leaves Mahler's Second, 'Resurrection', Symphony as being the one work, as far as I can see, that takes on the gigantic task of responding to the theme of death and resurrection in music in all its existential force.[12] Gustav Mahler was one of those composers who have felt that composition is a response to a mysterious, unknown force from outside oneself. Nowhere does this seem to have been more the case than in the composition of his Second Symphony. He had written the earlier movements, but was having problems with the finale when the conductor Hans von Bülow died. On a March morning in 1894, a great funeral ceremony took place in Hamburg, the climax of which was a performance of Klopstock's chorale '*Auferstehn*' by the women and children of the cathedral choir. This, and the tolling of the bells, made a deep impression on Mahler, for whom the emotional atmosphere had deepened still further when he conducted the funeral march from Wagner's *Götterdammerung* outside the opera house as the cortège moved to the cemetery.

That afternoon a friend found Mahler seated at his desk, his head bent over manuscript paper. 'I have it,' he exclaimed. One of his rare autobiographical texts explains just what had happened:

The atmosphere in which I found myself and the thoughts I dedicated to the dead man were very much in the spirit of the work I was then carrying within me. All of a sudden, the choir, accompanied by the organ, intoned Klopstock's chorale '*Auferstehn*'. It was as if I had been struck by lightning; everything suddenly rose before me clearly. Such is the flash for which the creator waits, such is sacred inspiration.[13]

Mahler did not, however, set all of the Klopstock chorale he heard at the funeral. The original, in three stanzas, is a heartfelt cry of confidence in resurrection from the grave, with Hallelujahs at the end of the first two verses. Mahler omits the Hallelujahs and the third verse, and adds lines of his own: 'Believe, my heart, that nothing has been lost to you. You were not born in vain, did not live and suffer in vain. What has come into being must pass away; what passes away must rise again. Yes, you will rise again.'

Those who know the music to which these words are set will be aware of the power of the great chorale which, after the terrifying march that precedes it, when all hell is literally let loose, rises in a whisper out of silence broken only by the gentle bird calls of flute and piccolo. It is one of the great moments in all music, certainly one of the greatest attempts ever made to respond to the message of resurrection.

I love Mahler's Second Symphony, but if I had to choose one piece to represent resurrection in music today, it would be something rather different. It is Easter Day in a Sicilian village, a day that will end with bloodshed and tragedy, but for the moment the sun is shining and the villagers are gathering in the square. Led by a peasant girl, Santuzza, they begin to sing an Easter hymn, '*Inneggiamo, il Signor non è morto; ei fulgente ha dischiuso l'avel*' ('Let us rejoice that the Lord is not dead, and in glory has opened the tomb'). When listening to Mascagni's *Cavalleria Rusticana* in the opera house or on radio or record, we are at two removes from the hymn: first, it is being sung by others; and second, they in turn are at this stage essentially serving as a background to the drama of love and jealousy that is being enacted. But what a background! This may just be a rather hackneyed piece of operatic drama, but I listen to it at least every Easter Day, and as I hear it I can echo to the words as an expression of what I believe, even more naturally than with Mahler's hard-won affirmation. A message comes over; something is being said. But what? I wouldn't venture to say, just listen. Resurrection and music: both are strange and mysterious, and sometimes I wonder which is more so.

Notes

[1] Since biblical exegetes can get a theological message out of virtually anything if they really try, I would love to see a detailed treatment of 'Nessun Dorma' from this opera which would bring out its resurrection message: after all, the name that none shall know is clearly a reference to Revelation 19.11, and the conquering at dawn is a clear pointer to Mark 16 par.

[2] Percy M. Young, *The Oratorios of Handel* (London: Dennis Dobson, 1949), p. 41.

[3] Wilfred Mellers, *Bach and the Dance of God* (London: Faber & Faber, 1980), p. 221.

[4] ibid.

[5] Hans Küng, *Mozart: Traces of Transcendence* (London: SCM Press 1992).

[6] *Letters of Mozart and His Family*, ed. and trans. Emily Anderson, third revised edition by Stanley Sadie and Fiona Smart (London: Macmillan, 1989), p. 907.

[7] Wilfred Mellers, *Beethoven and the Voice of God* (London: Faber & Faber, 1983), p. 325.

[8] Martin Cooper, *Beethoven: The Last Decade, 1817–1827* (London: Oxford University Press, 1970), p. 249.

[9] Mellers, *Beethoven and the Voice of God*, pp. 328, 329.

[10] ibid., p. 321.

[11] For more on this work and Messiaen's resurrection music, see Paul Griffiths, *Olivier Messiaen and the Music of Time* (London: Faber & Faber, 1985), pp. 207–10.

[12] Here I am deliberately keeping to the theme of *resurrection* from death with some Christian inspiration; if one extended it to, say, life and death or death and transfiguration, as in C. H. H. Parry's *From Death to Life* or Richard Strauss's *Tod und Verklärung*, the amount of material to cover would be impossibly large.

[13] Henry-Louis de la Grange, *Mahler*, vol. 1 (London: Gollancz, 1974), p. 294.

18
According to Poetry

John Drury

Most biblical critics have done their utmost to discover facts in the New Testament, and have been backward and timid in asserting its spectacularly imaginative character – above all when it comes to the crucial point of the first Good Friday and Easter Sunday. They have had strong reasons for doing so. It has kept them in good rapport with the modern world's great intellectual project: the discovery of facts, historical and natural, through experiments conducted counter-intuitively or against the grain of the prejudices of imagination. This Enlightenment project has had enormous success. By joining it, critics have provided the Bible with an alternative base to mere ecclesiastical authority – and a better one too, because more open-minded, precise and debatable. And there was always the hope, formative of much criticism, that scholarship would confirm as factual what was already believed *de fide*.

As so often in human affairs, the positive side of this great exercise was beneficial and its negative side was harmful. The insistence on well-tested fact gives biblical criticism a charter of liberty, a properly tough discipline and a decent place in the republic of science and letters. But the shying away from imagination is a big fault. It is untrue to history in general. Imagination is a determinative force, both in what happens historically and in the writing and teaching of it. It was inadequate to the Bible, where imaginative forces – realistic or fantastic, practical or speculative – mark every page, and not least those that tell of resurrection. In Ezekiel's vision of the valley of dry bones, the poetic imagination is strong and shameless in the physicality with which it describes a mass resurrection into *this world*. In Paul's 1 Corinthians 15 the poetic imagination is ethereal and in full myth-borne flight as it describes resurrection into heaven and *the next world*. In Luke's walk to Emmaus it is realistic, back in this world again, touchingly pedestrian and delicately interested in inward human emotion. They are all different, except that in them all imagination is in command. Which means that the usual, fact-oriented, kind of biblical criticism will never get the measure of resurrection in the Bible – and least of all when it tortures legends for direct historical evidence.

There is another kind. In 'A Memorable Fancy' from William Blake's *The Marriage of Heaven and Hell* (1790), we can see it at its most striking and exuberant – qualities in which it is much more like the Bible itself. Blake entertained the prophets Isaiah and Ezekiel. Over the dinner-table he asked Isaiah a fundamental question about the power of imagination: 'Does a firm persuasion that a thing is so, make it so?' It was an obstreperous question, set dead against the fact-oriented thinking of the scientific Enlightenment and its kind of biblical criticism, which Blake distrusted. Isaiah replied: 'All poets believe that it does, and in ages of imagination the firm persuasion removed mountains; but many are not capable of a firm persuasion of anything.' Indeed, with Ezekiel 'firm persuasion' of the power of *ruach* (wind, breath and spirit combined into inspiration with lively physical effects) raised the dead to life. Ezekiel is there to explain it: 'We of Israel taught that the Poetic Genius (as you now call it) was the first principle, and all the others merely derivative.' In other words it was divine: 'our God' he calls it – and under the Christian designation of the Holy Spirit this is orthodox enough, considering that Blake never went out of his way to be orthodox.

The historical distance and the cool concern for objective fact – the alienation, to put it sharply – which we are used to in biblical criticism are so completely absent here that it looks as if Blake's 'Fancy' has nothing to do with biblical criticism at all. In fact it has everything to do with it. Blake is very close to the Bible, and is exerting a definite critical view upon it. There is no alienation and no historical distance, because the three people round the table, Blake and the ancient prophets, are colleagues. They are chatting about their shared work: how they do it and what they believe about it. It is criticism from within, the criticism of inspired authors by an inspired author. The Hebrew prophets were poets like Blake. This is a major truth of biblical criticism, and it was famous at the time when Blake wrote *The Marriage of Heaven and Hell*. Only three years before, Robert Lowth's *Lectures of the Sacred Poetry of the Hebrews* had been translated into English from the Latin in which they had been delivered to the University of Oxford thirty years before. Their disclosure, both of the expressive poetic forms of the Psalms and of their source in the firm persuasions and urgent emotions of their sacred author, had already persuaded one poet to become a modern David. In *Jubilate Agno* Christopher Smart had written a great psalm of his own, inspired by his own feelings of despair and praise (he had been hospitalized as a manic depressive), and packed with the minute details of his own circumstances and acquaintances – his cat, his friends, his warders. Poets had often put the psalms into the metrics of their day before. To use David's metrics, as revealed by Lowth, to psalmodize in such a forthrightly personal way was something new. The critic's work had discovered the ancient poetry that was the archetype and progenitor of all poetry. And this had made it available to the literary world, without resort to the Church, as a model and inspiration. Lowth became Bishop of London and went on to give similar treatment to the prophecy of Isaiah. And Blake took up that hint, becoming a prophet as Smart had become a psalmist, and writing his great neo-biblical prophetic books as tracts for the times.

This eighteenth-century alliance of criticism and poetry carried on into the next century. Coleridge, in *Confessions of an Inquiring Spirit* (1825, published 1840 and reprinted in 1971 by the Scolar Press), mustered all his experience as poet, critic and devout believer to oppose the doctrine that 'the [biblical] writers, each and all, were divinely informed as well as inspired' (p. 13). This insistence on total factual accuracy 'plants the vineyard of the Word with thorns for me' (p. 15) because there is so much in the Bible that is metaphor, image, and parable. It

> petrifies at once the whole body of Holy Writ with all its harmonies and symmetric gradations – the flexile and the rigid – the supporting hard and the clothing soft – the blood *which is the life* . . . This breathing organism, the Doctrine in question turns into a colossal Memnon's head [an ancient Egyptian sculpture that emitted sounds, miraculously or because of the wind], a hollow passage for a voice. (pp. 31–2)

Coleridge opposed the rigidity of religious dogma in the name of the vital flux of religious life. The doctrine's 'ventriloquism' was a stiff parody of the liquid inspiration that he had known and craved. Above all he found in the Bible, as Lowth had, the vivid comfort of 'heart-awakening utterances of human hearts – of men of like passions with myself, mourning, rejoicing, suffering' (p. 35). For a man so splendidly and agonizingly errant, inerrancy was no salvation, no religious use or good. He wanted comfort and company, and found them in the Bible, which, read as a human book and as poetry, spoke of God's love.

The same cause was taken up again some fifty years later. Matthew Arnold was spurred to write *Literature and Dogma* (1873) by hearing Lord Salisbury appeal for funds for the completion of Keble College by insisting on the inseparability of religion from dogma. Like Coleridge, Arnold believed this to be a category mistake that could only be fatal to religion. Religion was feeling, poetry, and conduct. To mistake it for science was to condemn it to misunderstanding and, ultimately, falsity. A theological utterance is 'by no means a term of science or exact knowledge, but a term of poetry and eloquence, a term *thrown out*, so to speak, at a not fully grasped object of the speaker's consciousness' (Souter's edition, p. 171). It is the 'poetry of life', imagination taking short cuts to what is ardently desired and dimly glimpsed, embodying it in fairy tales meant to improve conduct rather than inform curiosity.

Until quite recently, this kind of biblical criticism has been marginalized, or more commonly ignored, in the churches and the theological faculties and colleges. Church leaders had begun to stop their ears to it well before Matthew Arnold wrote. Aghast at the publication of George Eliot's translation of Strauss's *The Life of Jesus Critically Examined* in 1846, and the relentlessly cumulative power of its argument that one wonderful incident in the Gospels after another was formed by Christian imagination actualizing Old Testament prophecies, battered by the terror generated by conservatives high and low over *Essays and Reviews* in 1860, reflective churchmen had to reckon that they were taking their ecclesiastical lives in their hands if they said anything to further such a cause. It was a pity, since the great men who had developed it were Christians of one kind and another, all deeply concerned to discover the springs of their religion and let them irrigate the life of their times. But it was simply too much. After the Second World War a book called *The Bible Designed to be Read as Literature* appeared. In Oxford, where Lowth had begun it all two centuries before, Austin Farrer began to trace the creative imaginative strategies of New Testament writers while sedulously avoiding saying that he was dealing with myths or legends – as his contemporary Rudolf Bultmann was doing in Germany, to orthodox dismay and denunciation. More recently some of the best literary critics have been taking up where Matthew Arnold left off and have achieved biblical insights of unusual (in the stale context of more conventional studies) penetration and scope. So there are signs of revival. But the main encouragement must come from the intrinsic merits of the literary criticism of the Bible, its freedom from fear and religious prejudice, the sympathy and delicacy with which it handles its texts, and, above all, its vivacity.

The vivacity is both promising and problematic. Fact-oriented, historical criticism has given religion a lot of trouble with its suspicion and its probing, but it has achieved an uneasy accommodation with it. After all, it comes from outside with the attitude of an open-minded visitor. It does not claim to be strongly religious or to have to do with the inspiration on which religion depends for its life. It is not so much threatening as just looking. It might turn out to be supportive. But the kind of literary-critical work that we have been looking at claims the sacred territory of inspiration for its own – particularly when it turns to its own practical psalmody and prophecy. This ties the poet and the sacred Scriptures so fast together as to invite glossing the clause about Christ in the Nicene Creed, 'he rose again according to the Scriptures', as 'he rose again according to poetry'.

The invitation is worth considering, and the best way to do so is to scrutinize two poems of resurrection. The imagination working any-old-how, which is how die-hard fact-oriented criticism suspects it of working, is not capable of producing any poetry worth reading. The two poems proposed are well known because they are fine, so they are particularly promising for finding out how the imagination works in the field of Christian resurrection. The sort of criticism to be deployed will be religious as well as literary. This means two things. The first is quite formal and simple. Their Christian credentials can be tested by discovering the sources in Christian tradition that each poem uses. How the poet uses them, with what insight and sensitivity, is an important question that shades into the second focus of inquiry. We ought to expect imagination that is at least as disciplined, acute, and patient of reality – particularly when the reality is unwelcome – as the most exacting kind of critical analysis. Poets may be prophets. If so, they must be critics too. This way we should get some grip and Christian evaluation of slippery and volatile imagination.

That Nature is a Heraclitean Fire
and of the Comfort of the Resurrection

by G. M. Hopkins

Cloud-puffball, torn tufts, tossed pillows | flaunt forth, then
    chevy on an air-
built thoroughfare: heaven roysterers, in gay-gangs | they throng;
    they glitter in marches.
Down roughcast, down dazzling whitewash, | wherever an elm
    arches,
Shivelights and shadowtackle in long | lashes lance, lance, and
    pair.
Delightfully the bright wind boisterous | ropes, wrestles, beats
    earth bare
Of yestertempest's creases; | in pool and rut peel parches
Squandering ooze to squeezed | dough, crust, dust; stanches,
    starches
Squadroned masks and manmarks | treadmire toil there
Footfretted in it. Million-fuelèd, | nature's bonfire burns on.
But quench her bonniest, dearest | to her, her clearest-selvèd
    spark
Man, how fast his firedint, | his mark on mind, is gone!
Both are in an unfathomable, all is in an enormous dark
Drowned. O pity and indig | nation! Manshape, that shone
Sheer off, disseveral, a star, | death blots black out, nor mark
        Is any of him at all so stark
But vastness blurs and time | beats level. Enough! the Resurrection,
A heart's clarion! Away grief's gasping, | joyless days, dejection.
        Across my foundering deck shone
A beacon, an eternal beam. | Flesh fade, and mortal trash
Fall to the residuary worm; | world's wildfire, leave but ash:
        In a flash, at a trumpet crash,
I am all at once what Christ is, | since he was what I am, and
This Jack, joke, poor potsherd, | patch, matchwood, immortal
    diamond,
        Is immortal diamond.

The title is cumbersome, but interesting and important because it serves as a programme for the poem, a note of what it is going to take on. It announces that two ways of seeing and describing the world are to be put together. One is pagan and the other is Christian. In the title

they are joined simply by 'and'. How that 'and' is going to work out
in the poem itself, what part it will play in its structure and movement, and just how the two world-pictures will go together, is a major
question to which the title alerts the reader.

Before there was philosophy in ancient Greece, there was religious
ritual and the poetry of Homer and Hesiod – a fact familiar and congenial to Lowth. Heraclitus belonged to a group of writers, now
called the Pre-Socratics, whose work survives only in fragments.
They turned from looking to the festivals of the gods and the legends
of their dealings with humanity, to looking at the cosmos, the unified
structure of all that is. Consequently, their theology turned away from
Homer's polytheistic anthropomorphism. Hopkins, who had been
interested in them for a long time, described it in an early notebook as
'an undetermined Pantheist idealism'.[1] Anaximandros, for example,
saw a world in which 'moisture dries out, fire causes melting, moved
air turns into wind, which forms the clouds into clusters and breaks
them up in lightning'. There is no place for Homer's thunderbolt-
throwing Zeus. The flux of nature is balanced and checked by a more
remote and impersonal, though pervasive and eternal, divinity.
Anaximenes was even more strongly on the side of matter in flux and
even more suspicious about personal divinities. Air or vapour was the
beginning of everything, and from its condensation and rarefaction
arises 'what was, what is and what will be, gods and the divine ones'.
Heraclitus himself believed similarly of fire. The world order is 'an
everlasting fire, kindling in measures and going out in measures'.
Parmenides had what Hopkins called 'his great text, which he repeats
with religious conviction, that Being [more exactly, 'what is'] is, and
Not-being is not'. And he noted at the end of his paper about
Parmenides, 'Men, he thought, had sprung from slime.'

All this is obviously relevant to the first part of the poem as its
source and theme: the clouds, the drying wind on the slimey lane with
its human footprint and nature's bonfire. Parmenides had something
else that interested Hopkins. He believed in a tight cohesion between
the business of comprehending things by thought, the utterance, and
the things themselves. Hopkins called this chain of communication
'instress'. By this he meant the inrush of revelation when anything of
God or nature was impressed upon him and driven inwardly home to
him. He was exhilarated to find that he and Parmenides shared a way
of looking at the world and speaking it. 'I have been in this mood and
felt the depth of an instress . . . that nothing is so pregnant and

straightforward to the truth as simple *yes* and *is*.' Such notions are meat and drink to the closely-observing nature poet, concentrating his mind and stimulating his eye. But they carry within them a lurking challenge to the Christian priest.

Hopkins is getting into danger. His imagination is in deep sympathy with these ancient Greeks, their insistence on the one world of what is and its eternal changefulness. He, on the other hand, was bound, both heart and soul, and by priestly allegiance, to Christianity, which is a religion deeply marked and structured by two split-world traditions: Platonism and Jewish apocalyptic. The second of these pervades the formative source of the second part of his poem: 1 Corinthians 15. 'The Resurrection, | A heart's clarion!', the writing off of flesh and matter as 'mortal trash', the sudden change 'In a flash, at a trumpet crash' when 'I am all at once what Christ is, | since he was what I am', and the final triumphant achievement of immortality – all these come from this chapter of Paul. There Paul spoke of resurrection as the transformation whereby our physical bodies, made of dust like Adam 'the man of dust', are changed into spiritual or heavenly bodies like that of Christ, the 'man from heaven' who became as we are that we might become as he is. Paul is in outright apocalyptic vein at the end of the chapter, in a passage that Hopkins condenses but follows closely. It depends entirely upon there being two worlds, the heavenly being the stronger, and reveals resurrection as the sudden change from one to the other by heavenly intervention.

> Behold, I shew you a mystery; We shall not all sleep, but we shall all be changed, in a moment, in the twinkling of an eye, at the last trump: for the trumpet shall sound, and the dead shall be raised incorruptible, and we shall be changed. For this corruptible must put on incorruption, and this mortal must put on immortality. So when this corruptible shall have put on incorruption, and this mortal shall have put on immortality, then shall be brought to pass the saying that is written, Death is swallowed up in victory. (1 Cor. 15.51–4)

Reviewing Hopkins' sources results in admiration for the power of his imagination to assume the point of view of other writers. The Pre-Socratics could not speak better for themselves than Hopkins does for them up to the climax of 'nature's bonfire'. Indeed they usually spoke worse, as far as their fragmentariness lets us judge, and were often awkward and obscure. Paul's description of the resurrection is not without a prolixity that weighs it down a little. Hopkins makes it airborne and realizes its momentariness in whip-crack diction where Paul obtrudes lugubrious abstraction – though the reverent precision and sheer actuality of the Heraclitean part of the poem are missing from this Christian part. Which is an ominous unevenness. So does Hopkins get the two together? What, in other words, is the strength or weakness of that 'and' in the title?

Spirited and sensual at once, the first nine lines have the integration of happy seeing. The movement and transformations of clouds, the shifting scatter of light through branches and on to whitewashed walls, the action of drying wind on mud – all these are clear and delightful. The mood changes as Hopkins ponders the implications of the vanishing footprint. Man is nature's 'bonniest, dearest | to her, her clearest-selvèd spark', but he is as transient as this trace of him. The unity of the poem is starting to come apart with this assertively anthropocentric privileging of man. Hopkins has come back anxiously to himself after the healthy ecstasy of going out of himself to the world. This is the first fracture of the poem's fabric, marked by a change from the perception intent on nature's minute particulars to larger and vaguer vision. It is only a step to dissociate man from nature altogether. The 'pity and indignation' – reserved for man, while the dissolution of clouds was delightful – make Hopkins take that step. But how? Can man jump out of nature? It sounds like a question from the Book of Job, but unfortunately Hopkins' eye is on other biblical material. His answer is an abrupt switch, the generalized contemplation of death abandoned for a leap into apocalyptic: 'Enough! The Resurrection, a heart's clarion!' And the poem is fractured again, its integrity now shattered.

Shouting 'Enough!' and bringing in a completely different way of seeing the world, or rather, abandoning seeing the world because the dissolution of self is an intolerable thought: this is not the strong imagination that it aspires to be. It has the petulance of impatience, brittle and disruptive. Imagination breaks bounds well and creatively when it goes out to bring the previously unregarded or unwelcome into the fold of literature or religion. So Christ did. That is real strength, because it deals with what is there. Hopkins does not deal with the anxious realism that came to him from what he sees in his path: the vanishing footprints of humanity. He thinks about it, but the thought is too bleak. Feeling supravenes and allows him to stage an orthodox *coup de théâtre* instead.

He did not always do this. In his more famous 'The Windhover' the hawk's buckling and crash to earth were, like the 'blue-bleak embers' that 'fall, gall themselves' from the firegrate, precious emblems of life and Christ's life-giving sacrifice. They were not 'trash' or 'but ash', like matter in this poem. And in 'The Lantern out of Doors' he could ponder the lantern, moving in the outer darkness and held by someone he could not see, as the disappearance of man followed by Christ's love and care. Pastoral modesty and trusting patience make the poem sound.

We have to conclude that the Heraclitean resurrection poem is not, in the end, one of his best. And this means that there are ways of treating the resurrection, ways of imagining it, which are not good, and that one of them is to resort to it as an orthodox exit from anxiety. In more consciously Christian terms, there was no resurrection for Christ before he had drained the cup of suffering to the dregs. In this poem it is more as if Christ in Gethsemane had availed himself of the twelve legions of angels that his Father had ready. For a Christian resurrection poem, this is a fatal evasion. The next poem resists its temptation.

The Flower

by George Herbert

How fresh, O Lord, how sweet and clean
Are thy returns! ev'n as the flowers in spring;
　　To which, besides their own demean,
The late-past frosts tributes of pleasure bring.
　　　　　Grief melts away
　　　　　Like snow in May
　　As if there were no such cold thing.

　Who would have thought my shrivel'd heart
Could have recovered greennesse? It was gone
　　Quite under-ground; as flowers depart
To see their mother-root, when they have blown;
　　　　　Where they together
　　　　　All the hard weather
Dead to the world, keep house unknown.

These are thy wonders, Lord of power,
Killing and quickning, bringing down to hell
    And up to heaven in an houre;
Making a chiming of a passing-bell.
                    We say amisse,
                    This or that is:
Thy word is all, if we could spell.

O that I once past changing were
Fast in thy Paradise, where no flower can wither!
    Many a spring I shoot up fair,
Offring at heav'n, growing and groning thither:
                    Nor doth my flower
                    Want a spring showre,
My sinnes and I joining together.

But while I grow in a straight line,
Still upwards bent, as if heav'n were mine own,
    Thy anger comes, and I decline:
What frost to that? what pole is not the zone,
                    Where all things burn,
                    When thou dost turn,
And the least frown of thine is shown?

And now in age I bud again,
After so many deaths I live and write;
    I once more smell the dew and rain
And relish versing: O my onely light,
                    It cannot be
                    That I am he
On whom thy tempests fell all night.

These are thy wonders, Lord of love
To make us see we are but flowers that glide:
    Which when we once can find and prove,
Thou hast a garden for us, where to bide.
                    Who would be more,
                    Swelling through store,
Forfeit their Paradise by their pride.

A little explanation of some of its knottier parts is needed before getting into literary-religious evaluation of this poem.

Verse 1: The spring flowers are lords of the manor receiving their dues: from their own 'demean' (= 'demesne') or local environment, and from the hostile 'late-past frosts', which make them all the more welcome.

Verse 3: There is play with the bells and clocks that measure time. The 'passing bell' is the death knell that happens only once – or so we suppose – for everyone. But we die more often than that: daily according to St Paul, and hourly according to Herbert. God's power, which Hopkins called 'stress', changes the single knell into the hourly chimes of the church clock. 'Spell' at the end of this verse means considering things contemplatively and acutely, sizing them up and taking them in, as in Hopkins' 'instress'.

Verse 5: The depression caused by the least of God's frowns is a frost that would make the North and South poles seem hot by comparison.

Verse 7: 'Glide' stands for transience, and means to pass unstably from one place to another, to slip and slide away. 'Prove', by contrast, means to get some stable understanding, some intellectual mastery, of all this flux, so that experience becomes order. As St Paul said 'Prove all things. Hold fast to that which is good' (1 Thess. 5.21).

We have just noticed two important points of agreement between the two Christian poets: the stress or power of divine presence upon them, and the proving or instress whereby they take it in. Hopkins had, of course, read Herbert. He shared with him a divinity and a way of apprehending divinity: a God who acted upon him, and whose pressure was to be passively absorbed and candidly answered. Hopkins had the same tender sensuality, with its attendant and constant risk of cruelly felt pain. Herbert's sensuality is evident straight away in his first line, so utterly pure and simple. It flourishes in the sixth verse, where Coleridge found 'a simplicity, a reality' that amazed him:

> I once more smell the dew and rain
> And relish versing

is unforgettable in its emotional-cum-physical unity and actuality. That combination gives the whole poem its strength.

The strength comes from religious discipline – which is what the whole thing is about, and its drama. The last verse declares it. The 'Lord of power' of the third verse is now disclosed as 'Lord of love', and all the ups and downs, deaths and resurrections, winters and springs are revealed as his disciplinary work. A lesson was being taught, and it was transience: 'To make us see we are but flowers that glide.' The drama was the inculcation of the reality of death. If that is not learned, Paradise is forfeited. As a result Herbert's poem has a religious virtue that is quite absent from Hopkins': wisdom. 'He teaches us, through pain, to understand who and what we are.'[2] Indeed Herbert's last verse is a damningly sober critique of Hopkins' rhetorical rejection of this lesson. Hopkins 'would be more' than mortal, and it was an ambition that spoiled his poem. It rejects pain and prefers being overwhelmed to understanding.

Herbert succeeds where Hopkins failed. There are two main reasons for this. The first is that Herbert made a choice, and its benefit is unity. He was not a nature poet. He did not tell of nature on its own (though the pastoral tradition of the classics and his predecessors and contemporaries made that possible), but in coherent integration with God's dealings with himself. English weather and inner religious autobiography are at one in this sensual-spiritual poem. Neither is a mere allegory of the other, because the one God makes both alike. The world is one and real. Nobody can jump out of it into another, and the whole point of the poem is that even to think of doing so involves the arch-sin of pride and the punishment of damnation. There would have been some excuse for Hopkins if he had been confronting the terrifying new Natural History of Darwin's predecessors in his poem, the Nature that doomed whole species to extinction and 'cared for nothing'. Tennyson did that nobly in *In Memoriam*. Hopkins was confronting the age-old offence of mortality – and rejecting it in the name of resurrection.

Herbert's quite different handling of resurrection is, then, the second and determinative reason for his success. Resurrection and the cross, its obligatory condition and counterpart, happen in this world – and both of them not once, but often. This is quite different from the once-only apocalyptic resurrection seized at by Hopkins as an exit from the fate of nature, but its biblical roots are as strong, if not stronger. Apocalyptic wisdom sprang from despair of this world and concerned itself with the secrets of heaven. An older wisdom, found in psalms, proverbs and narrative, sought to understand this world and its ways as a school of obedience to its Creator, and did not dream of another. Herbert knew it through the Scriptures most familiar to him through daily recitation, the Psalms – whose Christianity he would not have questioned. Psalm 90 is a source for this poem, as quotation will show:

> Thou turnest man to destruction: again thou sayest, Come again, ye children of men.
>
> For a thousand years in thy sight are but as yesterday: seeing that is past as a watch in the night.
>
> As soon as thou scatterest them they are even as a sleep: and fade away suddenly like the grass.
>
> In the morning it is green, and groweth up: but in the evening it is cut down, dried up, and withered.
>
> For we consume away in thy displeasure: and are afraid at thy wrathful indignation . . .
>
> For when thou art angry all our days are gone . . .
>
> So teach us to number our days: that we may apply our hearts unto wisdom.
>
> Turn thee again, O Lord at the last: and be gracious unto thy servants . . .
>
> Comfort us again now after the time that thou hast plagued us . . .

We are back with Lowth's Hebrew Poetry. It gave us a biblical starting-point for our enquiry, and now we have found that poetry can sober up the religious imagination as well as stimulate it. Now we can choose how we treat – which means imagining and practically acting out in discipleship – resurrection. The currently normal way, which raised the wind and noise against David Jenkins in the General Synod, derives from St Paul. It is apocalyptic and authoritarian. It imagines two worlds, earthly and heavenly. Resurrection is the way out of the first and into the second. It is authoritarian in that it asserts its facticity by appeal to witnesses who ought not to be questioned, and severely discourages the idea that we have any choice in the matter if we want to stay Christian. But there is another way, derived from other canonical Scriptures. It is wisdom for the here and now rather than apocalypse of the yet to be. It is a more disciplined and down-to-earth kind of imagining, and so more thoroughly and patiently realistic. It imagines one world, and makes waking up to the reality of it the first step in the ethical path of Christian discipleship. Dietrich Bonhoeffer is its modern theologian. In any case, the choice is between two ways of imagining, two kinds of poetry.

Notes

¹ The entry in Hopkins' early notebook is headed 'Parmenides', and is published in Humphry House and Graham Storey (eds), *The Journals and Papers of Gerard Manley Hopkins* (Oxford: Oxford University Press, 1959), pp. 127–30. For the Pre-Socratic philosophers, I have drawn on, and quoted from, Walter Burkert, *Greek Religion*, trans. John Raffan (Oxford: Blackwell, 1985), pp. 317–21.

² Chana Bloch, *Spelling the Word* (California, 1985), p. 305.

19
Tolstoy's *Resurrection* Revisited

Dennis Nineham

I

No one claims that *Resurrection*[1] is one of Tolstoy's great novels, on a par with *War and Peace* or *Anna Karenina*. In fact it has come in for a good deal of negative criticism, principally on the ground that it is not so much a novel as a moral and religious tract, cast in fictional form. Such criticism is not wholly just: Tolstoy was so great a writer that any book on which he lavished as much care as he did on *Resurrection* is bound to provide a good – indeed a compelling – read. The present writer can remember vividly the deep impression a first reading of the book made upon him.

Nevertheless, *Resurrection* is near enough to being a tract to justify us in trying to discover from it what Tolstoy felt about resurrection. In fact, such an attempt has his explicit approval. In a letter replying to an English correspondent who had written criticizing the book, Tolstoy wrote, 'when I read a book, what chiefly interests me is the *Weltanschauung des Autors*: what he likes and what he hates. And I hope that anyone who reads my book with that view will find out what the author likes and dislikes, and will be influenced by the author's feelings.'[2]

II

The story-line is easily reproduced. A youth from a noble Russian family, on a visit to his aunts in the country, is smitten with calf-love for a girl who acts as their maid companion. Two years later, having been coarsened by experience as an army officer, he visits his aunts again, and this time falls genuinely in love with the girl; but in a moment of passion he violently seduces her and then makes off, ashamed, after pressing a hundred-rouble note into her hand. Once back among his boon companions in the army, he soon puts the incident behind him, but the consequences of it for the girl are devastating. When it becomes clear that she is pregnant, she is dismissed by the aunts, and is then involved in a series of sordid experiences in which she goes from bad to worse until she finds herself a professional prostitute accused – unjustly – of murdering and robbing one of her clients.

By coincidence, her seducer, whose name is Prince Dmitry Ivanich Nekhlyúdov, now a balding man on the verge of middle age, is a member of the jury at her trial. He recognizes her, and as the tale of her life is recounted in court, realizes that his treatment of her is largely responsible for her plight. When the jury retires, he is too preoccupied with his feelings of guilt and penitence to notice that his fellow jurors are returning a verdict which, though intended to vindicate the girl, Máslova by name, in fact convicts her. Various petty personal preoccupations had led to a failure on the judge's part to direct the jury as to the verdict they could, and should, have returned, but their decision, once announced, cannot be overturned, and Máslova is condemned to four years' penal servitude in Siberia.

Nekhlyúdov is jolted by these events into a reappraisal of his previous way of life, and becomes convinced that he must both visit Máslova in prison, in order to admit his responsibility and express his regret for what has happened, and also do everything in his power to get the court's decision reversed by higher authority.

The central section of the book is taken up with a detailed description of these two activities. At first Máslova distrusts his approach, and simply uses him as a source of money with which to buy illicit cigarettes and vodka in prison. Gradually, however, she is impressed by his sincerity, and her feelings for him begin to change.

Meanwhile, although, as a member of the nobility, he has connections through whom he can get introductions and exert influence, his ceaseless and energetic efforts on Máslova's behalf achieve nothing, except to make him suspect, and an object of ridicule, in his own circle. The reasons for his failure are one of the main themes of the book.

In the mean time, Nekhlyúdov has offered to marry Máslova, something that would considerably ease her lot in Siberia; and though she refuses his offer, he insists on following her into exile. The last part of this long novel describes his accompaniment of the journey she has to make in the company of hundreds of other convicts, and what happens when they both arrive. Through his prison visits to Máslova, Nekhlyúdov has his eyes opened to the quite inhuman –

indeed subhuman – way in which prisoners (often in fact innocent) and their families are treated; and the appalling conditions he sees them enduring on the journey, conditions so savage that a number of them fall dead, increase his conviction that the organization of society is rotten through and through.

On arrival in Siberia, Nekhlyúdov hears that an appeal he had eventually made to the Emperor in person had been partly successful, and that Máslova's sentence had been commuted from one of hard labour in the worst part of the region to one of exile in one of the less distant districts. Meanwhile he had persuaded the authorities in charge of the prisoners' journey to move Máslova from the company of common criminals to that of the political prisoners – more the sort of people to whom she had been accustomed, and also, many of them unselfish people with high ideals for which they were content to suffer unjustly. One of them in particular, Vladímir Símonson, is attracted to Máslova and forms a deep, but quite disinterested, attachment to her. The nobility of his character and the pure, completely non-exploitative nature of his attachment to her, deeply affect Máslova and begin to alter her entire outlook, already modified by Nekhlyúdov's constancy and devotion.

Tolstoy considered a number of different ways of ending the novel, and the one he eventually chose is somewhat enigmatic. When Nekhlyúdov gives Máslova news of the commutation of her sentence, and earnestly renews his offer of marriage, she replies simply: 'Where Vladímir Símonson goes [i.e., into the furthest part of Siberia] there I shall follow.' It is not clear whether, and if so, in what sense, she has fallen in love with Símonson, or whether her earlier love for Nekhlyúdov has now revived so strongly that she cannot bear to let him undergo the sacrifice he is prepared to make for her sake, and so makes her relationship with Símonson a means of letting him off the hook.[3] In either case she has come through to a remarkable degree of selflessness. Símonson is a remarkable, even a saintly, man, and to have come to appreciate and share his outlook and values implies a quite radical change of heart.

III

Tolstoy clearly means to suggest that both Máslova and Nekhlyúdov had experienced resurrection. Máslova's character and career are too lightly sketched to allow of any full understanding, but she is pictured as pure and deeply religious as a girl, and the change in her is put down to her bad treatment at the hands of Nekhlyúdov and, later, others. What had happened to her, she says, 'could not be borne without evil effects. Any one who believes in God and man, and believes that men love one another, will cease to believe it after going through all that' (p. 303). As for what Nekhlyúdov had done,

> he whom she loved and who had loved her . . . had thrown her away after having enjoyed her . . . She had believed in God and believed that other people also believed in Him; but after that night she became convinced that no one believed, and that all that was said about God and His laws was deception and untruth.

In fact, 'everybody lived for himself alone . . . and all the talk about God and righteousness was deception' (p. 133). It was because he sensed her feelings that Nekhlyúdov, 'looking at the once sweet face, now defiled and puffy and lit up by an evil glitter in the black, squinting eyes', concluded 'this woman is dead' (p. 151). She was seeking satisfaction almost entirely in the pleasures of tobacco, alcohol and sex – we have seen how she treated Nekhlyúdov, when he first reintroduced himself, simply as a means to that sort of gratification, so far as prison conditions permitted. Her treatment of her fellow prisoners is also portrayed as almost entirely self-regarding.

Yet, just as 'evil communications corrupt good manners', so it was the presence of goodness that altered Máslova's whole attitude. Although Nekhlyúdov's offer of marriage struck her as the outcome of magnanimity and penitence for what he had done, rather than real love for her, it was not without its effect; but it was Símonson who 'through his love for her had a decided influence on Máslova' (p. 382). She felt he 'loved her as she was now, and simply because he loved her'. She could not help recognizing his selflessness and that he was in such company only because of his compassion for, and solidarity with, her and other victims of oppression and injustice. The fact that such a man could love her, and love her without any hint of exploitation, made all the difference to her. It gave her the motive power to share his outlook, 'to awaken in herself all the highest qualities she could conceive and to be as good as possible' (p. 383).

Nekhlyúdov is an intellectual, and the workings of his mind are explored more fully. He too is pictured as (relatively) good in youth – as 'an honest, unselfish lad, ready to sacrifice himself for any good cause' (p. 46), who had given away an inheritance of five hundred acres for conscience' sake. 'He had made a rule of always speaking the truth, and really had been truthful' (p. 102). He 'fell' (the word is Tolstoy's own) because he had

> ceased to believe himself and had taken to believing others. This he had done because it was too difficult to live believing oneself: believing oneself, one had to decide every question, not in favour of one's animal *I*, which is always seeking for easy gratification, but in almost every case against it. Believing others, there was nothing to decide; everything had been decided already, and always in favour of the animal *I* and against the spiritual. (p. 47)

The point at issue is not simply that of animal gratification, as is made clear through the words of a strange old man Nekhlyúdov meets towards the end of the novel and who is clearly Tolstoy's mouthpiece. When asked, in a religious context, 'what is your faith, dad?' the old man replies: 'I have no kind of "faith" because I believe no one – no one but myself.' 'How can you believe yourself?', Nekhlyúdov replies. 'You might make a mistake.' 'Never in my life' is the answer. 'Then why are there different faiths?', Nekhlyúdov asks. 'It's just because men believe others, and do not believe themselves, that there are different "faiths" . . . every "faith" praises itself only and so they all creep about like blind puppies. There are many "faiths", but the spirit is one . . . so that if everyone believes himself, all will be united' (pp. 434–5).

It may seem a somewhat optimistic proposition, but we can flesh it out from Tolstoy's non-fictional religious writings. He was convinced that anyone who knew the Gospels, and took them seriously, could not fail to grasp that 'life is a movement towards divine perfection',[4] specifically towards total love and service of others. 'Thou shalt love the Lord thy God with all thy might, and thy neighbour as thyself.' Admittedly, such perfection is in practice unattainable, and those who seek it will constantly find themselves falling short; but they must as constantly renew the struggle, and never make the unattainability of the ideal an excuse for giving up the effort. Tolstoy was convinced that those who made this gospel perfection the lodestar of their conduct would never find themselves involved in the destructive rivalries and violence that characterized the society in which he lived.

Such a strenuous, existential view of the resurrection-life invites a number of comments. First, it may seem Pelagian, priggish and impossibly hectic to the point of being unsustainable; Tolstoy himself cannot altogether be acquitted of the charge of priggishness, and his falls from grace – for example, in his treatment of his wife – were notable.

Second, it is also true that following his own judgement in this way led him into some untenably extreme positions – for instance, his completely negative view of sexuality, or his almost blanket condemnation of punishment. Yet what religious leader would not welcome such determined effort on the part of each individual to discover what perfection means for him or her, and such single-minded pursuit of it? We may ask: can such following of the individual conscience lead to right results? No doubt Tolstoy would have argued that any (moral) mistakes that might result would be more than outweighed by the fact that those who made them 'had to their own selves been true', and that if they followed the ideal they would learn and improve.[5] It is the only way, he would say. For it is made clear in the novel that the character of the new life is love. As A. V. Knowles puts it, 'Nekhlyúdov loves as soon as he serves. That is the great resounding cry of the book.'[6] His services to Máslova lead him to a proper appreciation of her; at the same time, they also bring him into contact with many of her fellow sufferers, and the innumerable services he renders to them likewise lead to compassion and love. 'Recalling the feeling of regret he had felt . . . at the loss of his property, Nekhlyúdov was surprised how he could have felt it. Now he felt nothing but unceasing joy . . . and a sensation of newness' (p. 239).

Third, the novel makes clear that resurrection life inevitably involves political and social concern. As soon as Nekhlyúdov begins to adopt the true attitude towards his fellow humans, he recognizes that the current organization of society is fundamentally wrong. All this is particularly brought out in the middle section of the book, where Nekhlyúdov constantly makes approaches to various authorities to get justice for Máslova and a number of her fellow sufferers. Although those he approaches often show indirectly that they recognize the justice of the case, they all refuse to help, and in the end it is only by an unholy alliance with the Establishment, and shameless use of its system of influence and patronage, that Nekhlyúdov wins the partial reprieve he gets for Máslova. His constantly frustrated search for some way of helping her is almost Kafkaesque.

Why is this? It is because those in power are unwilling to risk the derision, and the reputation for eccentricity, unsoundness, and even subversiveness, which those who 'believe themselves', including Nekhlyúdov himself (see, e.g., pp. 47–8), inevitably attract. 'Believing others' is the comfortable course. As we have seen, if you 'believe others', 'everything [has] been decided already, and always in favour of the animal *I*'. Quite apart from this consideration, and the loss of power, prestige and perquisites involved, those who begin to 'believe themselves' soon recognize that the system in which they have been sharing is an indefensible one – simply, even if not consciously, calculated to ensure luxury and privilege for a minority at the expense of needless suffering on the part of the majority. Even 'the law . . . is only an instrument for upholding the existing order of things to the advantage of our class', Nekhlyúdov recognizes (p. 331); and according to Tolstoy, the Orthodox Church, inextricably intertwined with the state system, was quite content that things should be so. It strongly discouraged the gospel understanding of Christianity that led to personal renewal and corporate reform (e.g., pp. 27 and 139). What the Russian aristocracy was doing was to brutalize the peasants and then blame and punish them for the characters and conduct that inevitably sprang from their brutalization. It is true that Russian society in the nineteenth century was a quite exceptionally stratified, unjust, and brutal one; but it is impossible for anyone in the modern West to read *Resurrection* without being given to think hard and critically about current political and economic arrangements.

One outstanding feature of Tolstoy's view of resurrection is that it understands the word as referring not only to something which happened to Jesus a long time ago, but also – and indeed primarily – to a 'risen' way of living in the here and now. For Tolstoy, Christianity is something to be *lived*.[7]

IV

Many readers of the novel will undoubtedly feel that Tolstoy's understanding of the risen life is inadequate. How, for example, does resurrection come about? In Máslova's case, apparently, simply as the result of Nekhlyúdov's and Símonson's treatment of her. In Nekhlyúdov's case, it begins with what appears on the surface as the pure coincidence of his being summoned as a juror at Máslova's trial. Certainly Tolstoy did not believe that resurrections such as Nekhlyúdov's and Máslova's are dependent on the resurrection of Christ in the sort of way asserted by orthodox Christian dogma. 'If Christ be not raised . . . ye are yet in your sins' (1 Cor. 15.17). Tolstoy distrusted Paul, and did not believe in the resurrection of Jesus as historical fact. The metaphysics and atonement theology of the tradi-

tional faith appeared to him something impossible for an educated
person in the modern West to accept with integrity. 'Humanity has
grown out of the period of external religious regulations and we no
longer believe in them.' Indeed, he regarded it as one of the signs of
lack of authenticity in his (educated) contemporaries that they refused
to think the matter through and so come to this conclusion.[8] In religion, as in other spheres, 'believing others' was the comfortable line
of least resistance.

Tolstoy was also suspicious of the traditional understanding of
grace and sacraments – the necessity for grace was too often used as
an excuse for giving up strenuous moral endeavour. 'Jesus said,
"Fulfil this commandment" and he never said that it was difficult to
fulfil. He said, "My yoke is easy, my burden is light" – how then
could I say that this was so difficult as to be impossible without
supernatural help?'

Yet the novel must be read with close attention where this matter is
concerned. R. F. Christian writes of Nekhlyúdov's conversion that 'it
is the result of the author's *sic jubeo*', but he adds, 'and perhaps there
is no other way of showing the sudden moment of awakening to
faith'.[9] There is nothing unusual or wrong in seeing providence as
working through mundane and normal human processes, and this is
how Nekhlyúdov himself understands the coincidence of his being
called to jury service: 'he felt the powerful hand of the Master'
(p. 78). In the same way, Nekhlyúdov's and Símonson's treatment of
Máslova are seen as a revelation to her of the truth about human attitudes: 'Nekhlyúdov . . . knew that . . . an important change was
going on in her soul, and this change united him not only to her but
also to Him for whose sake that change was being wrought' (p. 250).
Tolstoy wrote of his own conversion, 'when and how this change
came about I cannot say',[10] but, as the context shows, he had no
shadow of doubt that it was God's doing. He was a robust believer in
God, and he could speak of 'the divine power that lies within us';[11]
and both in *Resurrection* and in his specifically religious writings he
insists on the part played by the Jesus of the Gospels in bringing
men and women to the resurrection life. Tolstoy's autobiographical
writings make clear that Nekhlyúdov is echoing his creator's own
experience when at the end of the novel he finds himself reading
afresh Jesus' teaching in the Sermon on the Mount.

When he had read the Sermon on the Mount, which had always
touched him, he saw in it to-day for the first time not beautiful

abstract thoughts, setting forth for the most part exaggerated and impossible demands, but simple, clear, practical laws, which if carried out in practice . . . would establish perfectly new and surprising conditions of social life.

This is no external and heteronomous law, for

all he read seemed quite familiar, and seemed to bring to consciousness and confirm what he had long known but had never fully realized and never quite believed . . . if men would obey these laws they would attain the highest blessing possible to them . . . in this lies the only reasonable meaning of life . . .

Recalling the monstrous confusion of the life we lead, he distinctly saw what life could be if men were taught to obey these laws; and rapture such as he had long not felt filled his soul. It was as though after long days of weariness and suffering he had suddenly found ease and freedom. (pp. 459–60)

'A perfectly new life dawned that night for Nekhlyúdov': these words occur on the last page of the book (461), and we are to recognize that henceforth the resurrection life was not to be for Nekhlyúdov simply the hectic, strenuous, effortful thing it had appeared earlier in the book. The need for effort would never disappear, but it would now be encompassed by a sense of peace and freedom.

V

Although, as we saw at the beginning, *Resurrection* has something of the character of a moral, political, and religious tract, far more significant is the fact that it is a novel by one of the greatest of all writers of fiction. It is first and foremost as a work of art that it must be read. To read it in that way is to be seized of a lot of what the risen life means, with a force to which no amount of critical analysis can do justice, and which such analysis can in no way diminish. As often as the book is read with care and attention, Tolstoy's declared intention will be found to be fulfilled: readers 'will be influenced – deeply influenced – by the author's feelings' and his understanding of resurrection.

Notes

[1] Both in the text and the notes, page references not further specified are to Leo Tolstoy, *Resurrection*, trans. Louise Maude (The World's

Classics; Oxford: Oxford University Presss, 1916), and subsequent reprints.

[2] pp. vii–viii; cf. his declaration in 1891, just after he had started work on *Resurrection*: 'I begin to think how nice it would be to write a novel *de longue haleine*, illuminating it with my present view of things, and collecting all my ideas together in it' (Jubilee Edition of Tolstoy's *Works*, vol. 52, p. 5).

[3] Some critics have even suggested that we are meant to think she eventually accepted Nekhlyúdov's offer of marriage, as she certainly did in one of Tolstoy's alternative endings.

[4] A. N. Wilson (ed.), *The Lion and the Honeycomb: The Religious Writings of Tolstoy* (London: Collins, 1987), p. 80.

[5] Cf., e.g., ibid. and p. 68.

[6] A. V. Knowles (ed.), *Tolstoy: The Critical Heritage* (London: Routledge & Kegan Paul, 1978), p. 411.

[7] Tolstoy's beliefs about life after death seem to have varied somewhat from time to time. On the whole he was convinced of the fact of it, but confessed ignorance about its character. Cf. L. N. Tolstoy, *Life*, trans. Isabel F. Hapgood (Walter Scott, 1889), cc. XXIXff.; e.g., p. 237: 'What this . . . life is in itself I cannot know – I can guess, if I like guessing, and if I am not afraid of becoming entangled.' Cf. also Leo Tolstoy, *My Religion*, trans. Huntington Smith (Walter Scott, 1885), pp. 137ff., and Wilson, *The Lion and the Honeycomb*, pp. 142–3.

[8] Tolstoy seems even to have felt that the peasants should come to share this outlook. Cf., e.g., p. 305, and Wilson, *The Lion and the Honeycomb*, pp. 75–6.

[9] R. F. Christian, *Tolstoy: A Critical Introduction* (Cambridge: Cambridge University Press, 1969), pp. 221–2.

[10] Cf. Lyof N. Tolstoï, *My Confession* (Walter Scott, n.d.), p. 114.

[11] Wilson, *The Lion and the Honeycomb*, p. 156.

Leslie Houlden:
Curriculum Vitae

Born: 1 March 1929

Education

Altrincham Grammar School	1940–47
The Queen's College, Oxford Modern History and Theology	1949–54
Cuddesdon Theological College	1953–55

Appointments

Assistant curate at St Mary's, Hunslet, Leeds Deacon, 1955; priest, 1956	1955–58
Tutor and Chaplain Chichester Theological College	1958–60
Chaplain Fellow and Tutor Trinity College, Oxford	1960–70
Principal, Cuddesdon Theological College (now Ripon College, Cuddesdon)	1970–77
Lecturer in New Testament Studies King's College London	1977–85
Senior Lecturer in New Testament Studies King's College London	1985–87
Professor of Theology King's College London	1987–94
Emeritus Professor of Theology King's College London	1994–

Leslie Houlden:
Publications

BOOKS

Paul's Letters from Prison, Penguin NT Commentaries (originally Harmondsworth: Penguin, 1970; now London: SCM Press)

Ethics and the New Testament (Harmondsworth: Penguin, 1973; 2nd edn, London: Mowbray, 1975; 3rd edn, Edinburgh: T. & T. Clark, 1993)

The Johannine Epistles, Black's NT Commentaries (London: A. & C. Black, 1973; 2nd edn, 1994)

The Pastoral Epistles, Penguin NT Commentaries (originally Harmondsworth: Penguin, 1976; now London: SCM Press)

Patterns of Faith: A Study of the Relationship Between the New Testament and Christian Doctrine (London: SCM Press, 1978; reissued 1983)

Explorations in Theology 3 (London: SCM Press, 1978)

What Did the First Christians Believe? (London: Lutterworth, 1982)

Study Guide on 1 Corinthians (London: Bible Reading Fellowship, 1985)

Connections: The Integration of Theology and Faith (London: SCM Press, 1986)

Backward into Light: The Passion and Resurrection in Matthew and Mark (London: SCM Press, 1987)

Bible and Belief (London: SPCK, 1991)

Tr...h Untold (London: SPCK, 1991)

Jesus: A Question of Identity (London: SPCK, 1992)

226 *Resurrection*

ARTICLES

'The Forgiveness of Sins', in W. R. F. Browning (ed.), *The Anglican Synthesis* (Derby: Peter Smith, 1964), pp. 103–13

'Paulinism and Johannism: Rapprochement', *Scripture* 17 (1965), pp. 41–52

'New Testament Studies', in L. Bright (ed.), *Theology in Modern Education* (London: Darton, Longman & Todd, 1965), pp. 18–32

'Good Liturgy or even Good Battlefield? "We Offer Unto Thee This Bread and This Cup"', *Theology* 69 (1966), pp. 433–7

'The Doctrine of the Trinity and the Person of Christ', *The Church Quarterly* 169 (1968), pp. 4–18

'Priesthood in the New Testament and the Church Today', *Studia Evangelica* 5 (1968), pp. 81–7

'The Bible and the Faith', in J. Wilkinson (ed.), *Catholic Anglicans Today* (London: Darton, Longman & Todd, 1968), pp. 1–25

'Man: His Nature, Predicament and Hope – (2) The New Testament', in E. W. Kemp (ed.), *Man, Fallen and Free* (London: Hodder & Stoughton, 1969), pp. 120–41

'Priesthood', in A. M. Ramsey (ed.), *Lambeth Essays on Ministry* (London: SPCK, 1969), pp. 39–50

'Sacrifice and the Eucharist', in I. T. Ramsey (ed.), *Thinking about the Eucharist*, C. of E. Doctrine Commission (London: SCM Press, 1972), pp. 87–98

'Christ and the Church in Ephesians', *Studia Evangelica* 6 (1973), pp. 267–73

'Liturgy and her Companions', in R. C. D. Jasper (ed.), *The Eucharist Today* (London: SPCK, 1974), pp. 168–76

'The Place of Jesus', in C. J. A. Hickling and M. D. Hooker (eds), *What About the New Testament?* (London: SCM Press, 1975), pp. 103–15

'The Creed of Experience', in J. Hick (ed.), *The Myth of God Incarnate* (London: SCM Press, 1977), pp. 125–32

'Jesus Christ "The Word of God"', *The Kingsman* 20 (1978)

'A Wider Framework', in M. D. Goulder (ed.), *Incarnation and Myth* (London: SCM Press, 1978), pp. 104–14

'The Development of Meaning', *Theology* 82 (1979), pp. 251–9

Essays on Peter, Paul, Mary, the Brothers of Jesus, for *The Universal Bible* – project abandoned by publisher

'How Many Christs?', *New Fire* 5 (1979), pp. 341–3

'How Far Will the Past Take Us? Bible, Tradition and Homosexual Relationships', *Crucible* (1980), pp. 100–5

'Post-Critical Spirituality', *ACCM Occasional Papers* 9 (1980)

'John 19:5: "And he said to them, behold the man"', *Expository Times*, 92 (1981), pp. 148–9

'The NT Commentary Scene', *King's Theological Review* 4 (1981), pp. 45–53

'Salvation Proclaimed II: I John 1:5–2:6: Belief and Growth', *Expository Times* 93 (1982), pp. 132–6

'The Gospel and the Covenant', *Theology* 85 (1982), pp. 198–202

'A Response to James D. G. Dunn', *Journal for the Study of the New Testament* 18 (1983), pp. 58–67

'Austin Farrer's Biblical Scholarship', *New Fire* 7 (1982), pp. 201–5

'The Purpose of Luke', *Journal for the Study of the New Testament*, 21 (1984), pp. 53–65

'Trying to be a New Testament Theologian', in A. E. Harvey (ed.), *Alternative Approaches to New Testament Study* (London: SPCK, 1985), pp. 122–42

'Theology Sociologized', in J. Butterworth (ed.), *The Reality of God* (London: Severn House, 1986), pp. 51–68

'Daring to Study the Bible', in P. Eaton (ed.), *The Trial of Faith* (Worthing: Churchman Publishing, 1988), pp. 119–36

'Frontiers of Honesty', in E. James (ed.), *God's Truth* (London: SCM Press, 1988), pp. 96–106

'A Future for New Testament Studies', *Expository Times* 100 (1989), pp. 405–9

'The Limits of Theological Freedom', *Theology* 92 (1989), pp. 268–75

'In a Biblical Perspective', in J. W. Woodward (ed.), *Embracing the Chaos* (London: SPCK, 1990), pp. 103–8

'Beyond Belief: Preaching the Ascension', *Theology* 94 (1991), pp. 173–80

'Is the New Testament Trustworthy?', in A. Linzey and P. Wexler (eds), *Fundamentalism and Tolerance* (London: Bellew, 1991), pp. 32–8

'Rethinking on Principle', in D. Cohn-Sherbok (ed.), *Tradition and Unity: Essays in Honour of Robert Runcie* (London: Bellew, 1991), pp. 93–109

'The Bible and Scholarship', in D. Cohn-Sherbok (ed.), *Using the Bible Today* (London: Bellew, 1991), pp. 18–25

'The Resurrection: History, Story and Belief', in P. Avis (ed.), *The Resurrection of Jesus Christ* (London: Darton, Longman & Todd, 1993), pp. 50–67

'The Resurrection and Christianity', forthcoming in *Theology* 97 (1994)

'The Puzzle of Matthew and the Law', in S. E. Porter, P. M. Joyce and D. E. Orton (eds), *Crossing the Boundaries* (Leiden: E. J. Brill, 1994)

DICTIONARY ARTICLES

Articles on 'Biblical Theology', 'Ecumenism', 'Mercy', in A. Richardson and J. Bowden (eds), *A New Dictionary of Christian Theology* (London: SCM Press, 1983)

Article on 'Spirituality of the Bible', in G. S. Wakefield (ed.), *A Dictionary of Christian Spirituality* (London: SCM Press, 1983)

Articles on 'Jesus' ethical teaching', 'Paul's ethical teaching', 'Kingdom of God', 'Johannine ethics', and 'Parenesis', in *A New Dictionary of Christian Ethics* (London: SCM Press, 1986)

Articles on 'Confession', 'Conversion', 'Life', and 'Repentance', in B. Metzger (ed.), *The Oxford Companion to the Bible* (New York: Oxford University Press, 1993)

Article on 'The Lord's Prayer', in *Anchor Bible Dictionary* (Garden City, NY: Doubleday, 1992)

Articles on 'Ethics', 'Hymns', 'John the Baptist', 'John's Gospel', 'Peter', 'Philippians', and a number of other topics in *Dictionary of Biblical Interpretation* (London: SCM Press, 1990)

EDITORSHIPS

A Celebration of Faith, by Austin Farrer (London: Hodder & Stoughton, 1970)

Theology, 1983–91, Co-editor

A Dictionary of Biblical Interpretation (London: SCM Press, 1990), Co-editor with R. J. Coggins

The World's Religions (London: Routledge, 1991), Co-editor, responsible for Christianity and Judaism

Austin Farrer: The Essential Sermons (London: SPCK, 1991)

Words for Life by Austin Farrer (London: SPCK, 1993), Co-editor with Charles Conti

Companion Encyclopedia of Theology (London: Routledge, forthcoming 1995), Co-editor with P. A. Byrne

REVIEWS

Many reviews, chiefly in the following journals: *Journal of Theological Studies, Theology, Expository Times, New Fire, Times Literary Supplement, New York Times Book Review*; notably the following:

R. Page, *The Incarnation of Freedom and Love*, in *Journal of Theological Studies* 43 (1992), pp. 345–8

J. Barton, *People of the Book?* and R. Morgan with J. Barton, *Biblical Interpretation*, in *Times Literary Supplement*, 5 May 1989

M. D. Goulder, *Luke – A New Paradigm*, in *Times Literary Supplement* 9 March 1990

E. P. Sanders, *Paul*, and A. F. Segal, *Paul the Convert*, in *Times Literary Supplement*, 25 January 1991

J. Ashton, *Understanding the Fourth Gospel*, in *Times Literary Supplement*, 16 August 1991

J. P. Meier, *A Marginal Jew*, J. D. Crossan, *The Historical Jesus*, and A. N. Wilson, *Jesus*, in *Times Literary Supplement*, 25 September 1992

J. D. Crossan, *Jesus – A Revolutionary Biography*, in *New York Times Book Review*, 26 December 1993

L. Alexander, *The Preface to Luke's Gospel*, and J. C. Lentz, *Luke's Portrait of Paul*, in *Times Literary Supplement*, 18 February 1994

Suggestions for Further Reading

Allison, D. C., *The End of the Ages Has Come: An Early Interpretation of the Passion and Resurrection of Jesus* (Edinburgh: T. & T. Clark, 1987)

Alsup, J. E., *The Post-Resurrection Appearance Stories of the Gospel Tradition: A History of Tradition Analysis* (Stuttgart: Calwer Verlag; London: SPCK, 1975)

Avis, P. (ed.), *The Resurrection of Jesus Christ* (London: Darton, Longman & Todd, 1993)

Benoit, P., *The Passion and Resurrection of Jesus Christ* (New York: Sheed & Ward, 1969)

Bode, E. L., *The First Easter Morning: The Gospel Accounts of the Women's Visit to the Tomb of Jesus* (Rome: Biblical Institute Press, 1970)

Brown, R. E., *The Virginal Conception and Bodily Resurrection of Jesus* (London: Geoffrey Chapman, 1993)

Carnley, P., *The Structure of Resurrection Belief* (Oxford: Clarendon Press, 1987)

Cavallin, H., *Life after Death* (Lund: Gleerup, 1974)

Cullmann, O., *Immortality of the Soul or Resurrection of the Dead?* (London: Epworth Press, 1958)

Dillon, R. J., *From Eye-Witnesses to Ministers of the Word: Tradition and Composition in Luke 24* (Rome: Biblical Institute, 1978)

Evans, C. F., *Resurrection and the New Testament* (London: SCM Press, 1970)

Fuller, D. P., *Easter Faith and History* (Grand Rapids, MI: Wm B. Eerdmans, 1965)

Fuller, R. H., *The Formation of the Resurrection Narratives* (London: SPCK; New York: Macmillan, 1971)

Harris, M. J., *Raised Immortal: Resurrection and Immortality in the New Testament* (Grand Rapids, MI: Wm B. Eerdmans, 1985)

Hendrickx, H., *The Resurrection Narratives of the Synoptic Gospels*, rev. edn (London: Geoffrey Chapman, 1984)

Hooke, S. H., *The Resurrection of Christ as History and Experience* (London: Darton, Longman & Todd, 1967)

Hoskyns, E. C. and F. N. Davey, *Crucifixion-Resurrection*, ed. G. Wakefield (London: SPCK, 1981)

Houlden, J. L., *Backward into Light. The Passion and Resurrection of Jesus According to Matthew and Mark* (London: SCM Press, 1987)

Künneth, W., *The Theology of the Resurrection* (London: SCM Press, 1965)

Ladd, G. E., *I Believe in the Resurrection of Jesus* (Grand Rapids, MI: Wm B. Eerdmans, 1975)

Lampe, G. W. H. and D. M. MacKinnon, *The Resurrection: A Dialogue Between Two Cambridge Professors in a Secular Age* (London: Mowbray, 1966)

Lapide, P., *The Resurrection of Jesus: A Jewish Perspective* (London: SPCK, 1984)

Lash, N., *Theology on the Way to Emmaus* (London: SCM Press, 1986)

Léon-Dufour, X., *Resurrection and the Message of Easter* (London: Geoffrey Chapman, 1974)

Mahoney, R., *Two Disciples at the Tomb: The Background and Message of John 20.1–10* (Frankfurt: Peter Lang, 1975)

Marxsen, W., *The Resurrection of Jesus of Nazareth* (Philadelphia: Fortress Press; London: SCM Press, 1970)

McDonald, J. I. H., *The Resurrection: Narrative and Belief* (London: SPCK, 1989)

Moltmann, J., *Theology of Hope* (London: SCM Press, 1967)

Moule, C. F. D. (ed.), *The Significance of the Message of the Resurrection for Faith in Jesus Christ* (London: SCM Press, 1968)

Nickelsburg, G. W. E., *Resurrection, Immortality and Eternal Life in Intertestamental Judaism* (Cambridge, MA: Harvard University Press; London: Oxford University Press, 1972)

O'Collins, G., *Jesus Risen* (London: Darton, Longman & Todd, 1987)

O'Collins, G., *Interpreting the Resurrection: Examining the Major Problems in the Stories of Jesus's Resurrection* (New York: Paulist Press, 1988)

O'Donovan, O., *Resurrection and Moral Order* (London: IVP, 1986)

Osborne, G. R., *The Resurrection Narratives: A Redactional Study* (Grand Rapids, MI: Baker, 1984)

Perkins, P., *Resurrection: New Testament Witness and Contemporary Reflection* (London: Geoffrey Chapman, 1984)

Perrin, N., *The Resurrection According to Matthew, Mark and Luke* (Philadelphia: Fortress Press, 1977)

Ramsey, A. M., *The Resurrection of Christ: An Essay in Biblical Theology*, 2nd edn (London: G. Bles, 1946)

Selby, P., *Look for the Living* (London: SCM Press, 1976)

Stendahl, K. (ed.), *Immortality and Resurrection* (New York: Macmillan, 1965)

Torrance, T. F., *Space, Time and Resurrection* (Edinburgh: Handsel Press, 1976)

Wenham, J., *Easter Enigma: Are the Resurrection Accounts in Conflict?* (Grand Rapids, MI: Zondervan, 1984)

Wilckens, U., *Resurrection* (Edinburgh: Saint Andrew Press, 1977)

Williams, R., *Resurrection: Interpreting the Easter Gospel* (London: Darton, Longman & Todd, 1982)